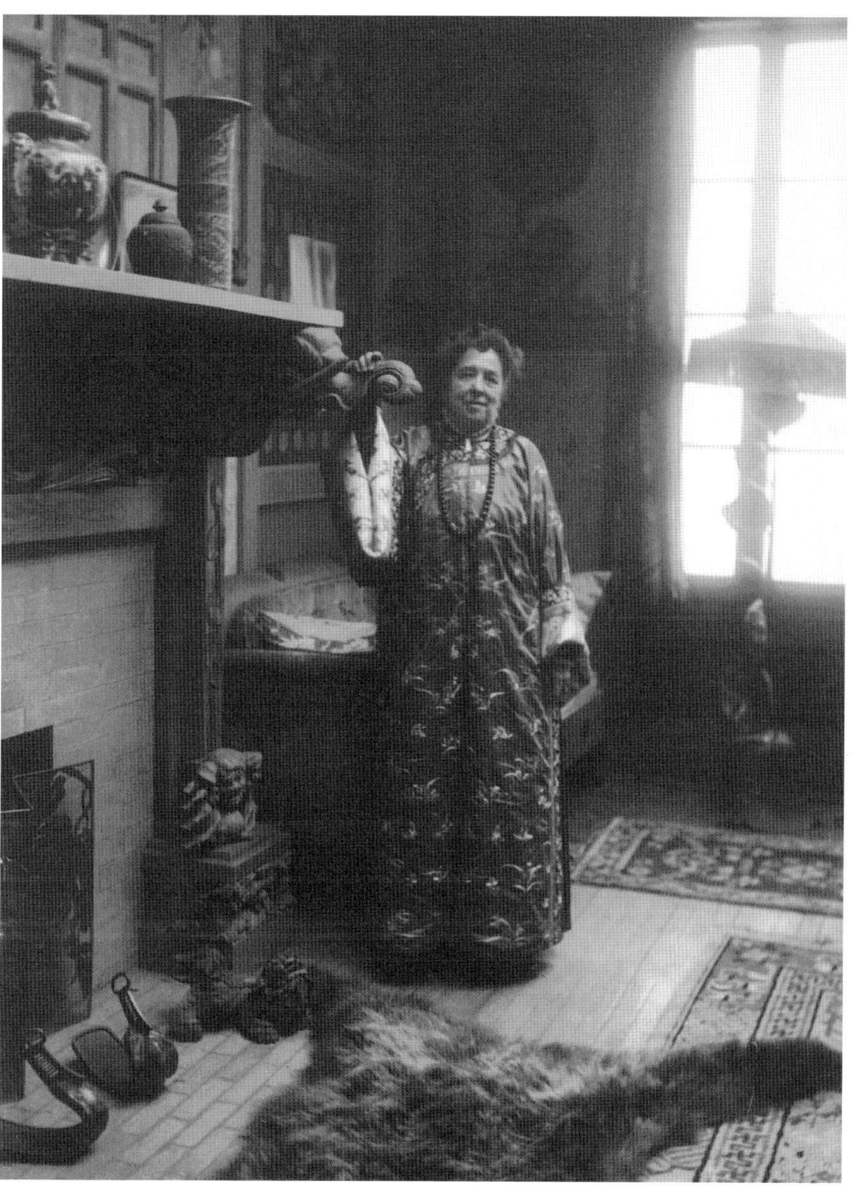

*Emily Noyes Vanderpoel in her New York studio.*
*Courtesy of Litchfield Historical Society.*

Color Problems



ISBN: 978-0-9996099-3-4

Published by The Circadian Press with Sacred Bones Books, 2018.

5 6 7 8 9 10

All requests and correspondence can be addressed to:

Sacred Bones Books
144 N. 7th Street #413
Brooklyn, NY 11249

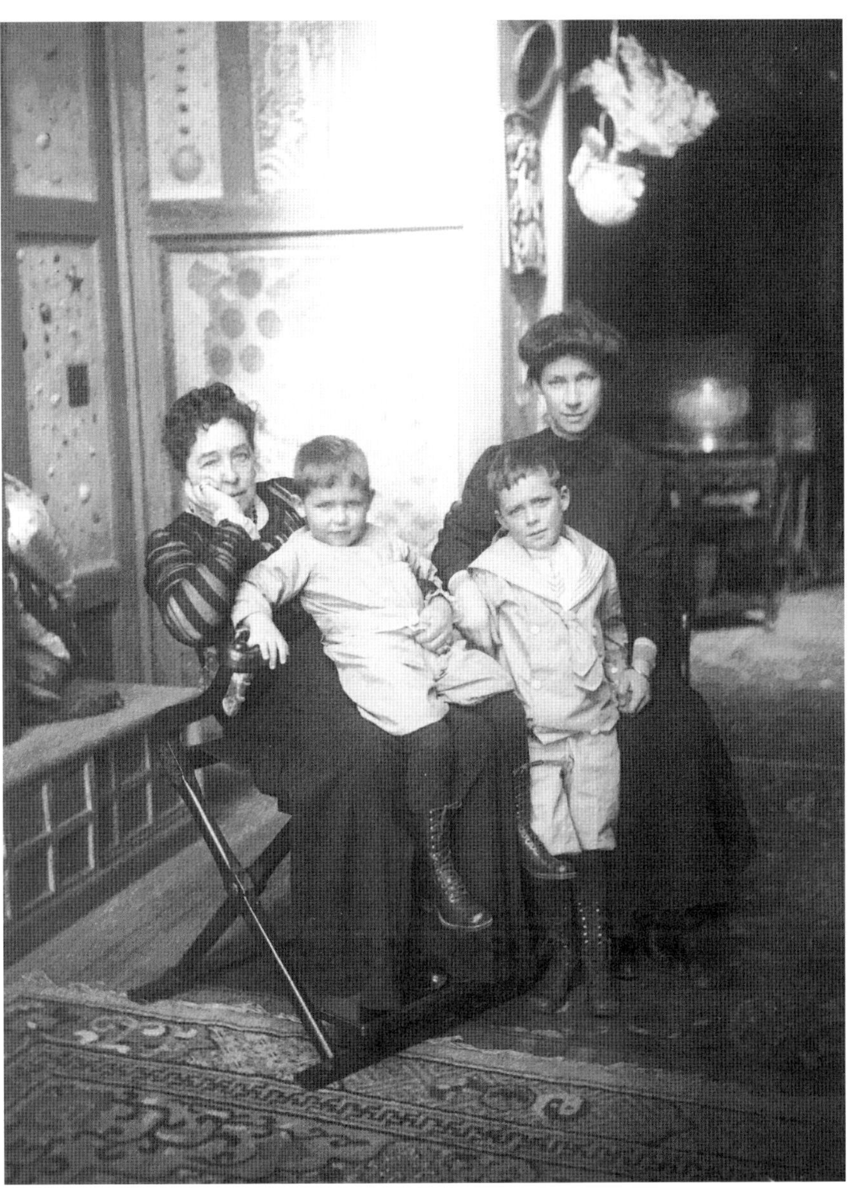

*Emily Noyes Vanderpoel and her Gramercy Park neighbors.*
*Courtesy of Litchfield Historical Society.*

# TO CAPTURE THE MUSIC OF LIGHT

In the Hall of Honor of the Woman's Building at the 1893 Chicago World's Columbian Exposition hung a watercolor painting titled The Spirit of the 19th Century. It was among those awarded the fair's highest jury commendation — a bronze medal designed by Augustus Saint-Gaudens— and was the work of a 51-year-old artist named Emily Noyes Vanderpoel, the author of this fascinating book and creator of the prescient works of art held within. [1] Vanderpoel paints a scene overlooking an urban rail yard of intertwined tracks laid on raw wet earth reflecting a violet grey sky. On the tracks a trio of engines shuttle coal cars beneath a long iron bridge spanning the yard's red brick walls. A single smokestack rises behind and telegraph poles carry wires off into the distance. The engines' trail of swirling white steam fade to pink in the composition's color harmony of red tones. [2]

Accompanied in the Hall by the more conventional portraits, landscapes and allegorical figures painted by her fellow awardees, Vanderpoel's unique expression of the terrible beauty of the industrial infrastructure driving the era yields a sliver of insight into an artist of whom many key traces have since been lost. Lost like traces of a painting titled Ypres which was said to have hung in the "National Art Museum" in Washington D.C. [3] Lost like a cache of her personal papers thought to be discarded by her grandson's wife. [4] Scion of a prominent colonial family, and of a stern and industrious stock that was part of her character [5], Vanderpoel divided her time between New York City and Litchfield, Connecticut. A connoisseur and collector of a wide range of cultural artifacts, Vanderpoel was a proud Daughter of the American Revolution, and a generous local philanthropist. She was a champion of girls' education, women's means for advancement, and society's knowledge and cultivation of traditional craft. [6]

Widowed before the birth of her only son [7], Vanderpoel as an artist and author was active in New York's creative community, centered around the American Fine Arts Building on West 57th Street. The building nurtured an interdisciplinary mix of organizations including the American Watercolor Society, and the break-off New York Watercolor Club — the first such co-ed association of its time, where she served as president. It also held the American Fine Arts Society, the influential Art Students League, and held exhibitions and events for the Architectural League and the National Academy of Design, among other organiza- tions. The American Fine Arts Building was frequently a venue for lectures on fine art and applied arts and sciences, color science included [8]. In short, Emily Noyes Vanderpoel was a remarkably independent Victorian woman with great access and much more than Virginia Woolf's requisite "money and a room of one's own."

At the turn of the 20th century, Vanderpoel published Color Problems, a Practical Manual for the Lay Student of Color, along with two other works: the 465-page first volume of Chronicles of a Pioneer School, and a set of charming and technically astute illustrations for the Tale of the Spinning Wheel by Cynthia Barney Buell [9]. She continued to author books and exhibit paintings into her last decade, before her death at the age of 96 [10]. Vanderpoel had a foot firmly in both centuries. She experienced the quickening of the 1800s into the speeding 1900s.

The World's Columbian Exposition, ushering in the new century, presented possibilities and means for the final distribution of the industrial revolution out of the factory and into homes, workshops, and classrooms, for the betterment of daily life. Her participation there seems to have inspired the long project of Color Problems. Vanderpoel would have been impressed by the advancements in science and technology, as well as the comprehensive displays of historical and contemporary fine arts found at the fair. Crafts from worlwide cultures were also on display at the Fair, which was attended by nearly a quarter of the nation's population. It was there that she may have been introduced to the inventor and publisher of arts educational materials Milton Bradley, who was displaying his Color Machine, patented that same year [11]. Many informed hands would be needed to direct the technological and aesthetic promise of the coming century.

Despite the future-oriented work in many of the Columbian Exposition's displays, the architecture and planning of the greatly influential "White City", as the campus was known, was itself a study in neoclassical Beaux Arts composition, an historical revival style that was on the rise in architecture and urban planning. In the fine and decorative arts, such historicism had already begun its long decline, amidst the nascent beginnings of new styles not yet precisely nameable. Developments that this book has become an important early example of.

While Mr. Bradley's work went on to educate future public school teachers about color and its science [12], Vanderpoel engaged her passion for craft production, the valuable work of women, the ornamental and the exotic. Her aim was to teach color to the non-artist and the non-arts-educator. It was intended for those in the practical arts and for the common citizen making things, especially women whose hands were being made idle by the rise of household technologies. [13] In this two-part book, she accomplished more than that.

One won't find a more concise summary of the contemporary technical literature on color than what is given in the first part of this book. However, in the creation of her own method to teach the practical observation and notation of color, Vanderpoel achieves a wholly original and thoroughly modern series of works: The 54 "Color Analyses" and the 15 freeform "Color Notes" we find in the book's 117 color plates. The Analyses are observations mainly of inanimate decorative objects and are of a more interior nature, described in the chapter "Historic Color", while the Notes are observations of more fleeting moments and natural phenomena outdoors, described in the chapter "Natural Color".

The freeform Notes might be said to be highly influenced by the works of the prolific art teacher and color theorist Mary Gartside, who was working at the transition of the 18th to 19th Centuries. Vanderpoel's Notes are significantly different, however, in that they are not only illustrations of the production of effects of adjacent colors coming from theory, but are abstract paintings of observed scenic color.

In the case of the unprecedented Color Analyses, Vanderpoel's invention is a highly synthetic method. By careful observation of a part or whole of an object using a subjective fram-
ing device—the Color Isolation Card found in the in the back cover [14]—students are instructed to separate the object's color from its form to appreciate colors and their adjacencies in and of themselves.
The observation, refined to just the quantity, quality and adjacency of color, is painted into the matrix of a 10 x 10 grid. The analysis, then, performs as a kind of memory device composed of its 100 pixels to capture the essence of the scanned color experience.

Vanderpoel's grids liberate the measured color arrangements to be used at another scale or in another medium. No longer part of the observed Mummy Case, or confined to be a Celtic Ornament or Panel of the Taj Mahal, the new compositions are free to be interpreted and repurposed at will. They can be viewed in the context of textile pattern, flower arrangement, parlor decoration, or hat design. They can be seen as space plans or cross sections at the scale of a room, building or town. The color adjacencies create space within the matrix as colors and color fields advance or retreat in relation to each other. The observer and interpreter are assured of the value in a measured practice of color understanding. [15]

The abstraction of the Analyses enables this cross-discipline, trans-media transfer. [16] The object can be liberated from its name while its valuable visual essence remains. Their use of a square format enables further distancing from source by allowing free rotation, erasing any trace of up and down. The method produces a modernist axiom associated with the great living artist Robert Irwin, that "seeing is forgetting the name of the thing one sees." [17]
One will find colors organized in grids in the previous technical literature: square ones, round ones, triangular. But one won't find the use of grids in the manner that they are employed here...analogous to the arrangement of the rods and cones of the retina, or sensor in a digital camera, though at another resolution and just as subjective as the camera lens of photography. If the appearance of the grid in art was a unique declaration of modernity, as the eminent Rosalind Krause theorizes, "appearing nowhere, nowhere at all in the art of [the 19th century]", then maybe in retrospect Vanderpoel's grids could be considered a candidate for such an appearance . [18]

It wouldn't be until a few years after the 1902 publication of Color Problems that artists and designers, from diverse locations and disciplines would coalesce, using abstraction as a lingua franca in their quest to give a visual language to their shared experience, renouncing representation and declaring themselves, their art and their era "modern." [19]

It took until the 1929 founding of the Bauhaus in Germany before such approaches to art, craft, and design pedagogy were systematically developed into an institutional force. The Bauhaus entirely changed the landscape of art and design, and its influence is in part why it's possible for us to now see Vanderpoel's remarkable works in a way she herself could not, though her passion and pleasure in the work is plainly apparent. [20]

We don't know if any of the later modernists knew of this work, although running across it in a library was a distinct possibility, especially in an English-speaking country. It doesn't appear in the library records of the Bauhaus, nor of the American experimental design school Black Mountain College, for instance. Renowned artist and color teacher Josef Albers, whose works have such an affinity for work like Vanderpoel's, was inspired by but not beholden to the same color theory sources that she was: Johann Wolfgang von Goethe, Michel Eugène Chevruel, James Clerk Maxwell, and Ogden Rood—her colleague in the Watercolor Club whose color science influenced Georges Seurat as well as Wilhelm Ostwald at the Bauhaus.

How the book was received in its time is unknown, other than appreciative reviews by booksellers. It doesn't appear to have had much influence on its stated lay audience. The numerous color plates made it expensive and in its two printings the book seems to have been distributed mainly to collectors and institutional libraries. Complete printing records and whatever correspondence [21] that may have remained from the process of its publication and distribution were lost to the blitz of World War II at the London-based publisher. What records there may be of Boston publishing partner Rockwell and Churchill Press also haven't been found [22].

Vanderpoel went on painting conventionally representational watercolors, never again producing abstractions like those found in Color Problems. She did not write of them again, or exhibit them in an art context that we know of. A 1927 watercolor of black cubic automobiles jostling up and down a rainy Fifth Avenue under the direction of its first traffic lights does seem to bear some fruit of the Analyses. [23]

A series of photographs taken after her 1907 move from Park Avenue to a townhouse on Gramercy Park reveals something of a dual nature in the character of Vanderpoel. There was a Downstairs Emily and an Upstairs Emily. While the photos documenting the downstairs salon are furnished in a respectable unassuming period correctness, the photographs of her fourth floor studio reveal a private world entirely different.

Dressed in a full-length silk Chinese robe, her hand resting on a stone carved elephant trunk supporting the mantelpiece, Vanderpoel presides over a large bear skin rug. The room's walls carry an oceanic theme adorned by fields of shell-encrusted panels framed by finely crafted Japanese-inspired woodwork. The aperture of the large square skylight above is draped with finely woven fish netting. A winsome expression is on her face.

This lovely, mysterious book is an introduction to that colorful upstairs world, Emily Noyes Vanderpoel, and her eye-opening, all but forgotten work.

—Alan Bruton, 2018

Notes:

1. Regarded as the first structure of national importance to be designed by a woman and run by women. Designed by Boston architect Sophia Hayden, with the program curated by the Board of Lady Managers, which included women of both the progressively conservative rear-guard and the progressively liberal vote-getting avant-guard. See Weimann, Jeanne M. The Fair Women: [the Story of the Woman's Building, World's Columbian Exposition, Chicago 1893]. Chicago: Academy, 1981. Across the Exposition, the top 20 percent of exhibitors in each category were awarded the bronze medal. In the Woman's Building this grouping was in the Hall of Honor. See World's Columbian Exposition, 1893 : Official Catalogue : pt. XIV, Woman's Building, Pg 45.

2. The painting The Spirit of the 19th Century is in the collection of the Litchfield Historical Society.

3. This painting is referred to in Vanderpoel's New York Times obituary as well as in a letter from a descendant to a researcher in the 1970's.

4. Lynne Brickman, PhD., conversation, 2010. Dr. Brickman discovered the destruction of the personal effects during research on Vanderpoel in conversation with a descendant.

5. In Lynne Brickman's essay in the catalog of the Litchfield Historical Society 1993 exhibition To Ornament their Minds: Sarah Pierce's Litchfield Female Academy 1792-1823, p.36, we learn that "every hour of the week must be occupied" for the young women of the academy that Vanderpoel admiringly documented in Chronicles of a Pioneer School. "Inclined to be a tartar, but she knew what she was doing." was the opinion of William Lampson Warren, 1896/1998, a longtime Connecticut resident and former director of the Litchfield Historical Society. Documented in 1971 Letter the Dr Clark S Marlor of Adelphi University.

6. Her primary known philanthropy, very substantial, was for the Litchfield Historical Society. In Litchfield she helped organize the local chapter of the D.A.R. (Daughters of the American Revolution) in 1899, and her continuous work on the documenting of girl's education and particularly their education in the arts and crafts is thoroughly demonstrated in the two volumes of her books Chronicles of a Pioneer School and in her book American Lace and Lace Makers. She donated most of her large collection of artifacts to the Slater Museum in Norwich, Connecticut. The Litchfield Historical Society received much of her ceramic collection.

7. The public record shows Emily Noyes (1842-1938) married John Aaron Vanderpoel (1842-1866), the youngest of the prominent Kinderhook, NY family, 22 May 1865. He died 12 April 1866 before the birth of their son John Arent Vanderpoel, born 4 June 1866. No obituary has been found for husband John Aaron, graduate of Columbia, listed in some records as an author. Their son's

Boston Chronicle obituary reports he died in a hotel there 28 January 1901, as Color Problems was being copyrighted. Just prior to his death he was involved in a high profile divorce from his Washington DC society wife. Correspondences archived at the Litchfield Historical Society show that mother and son had a congenial relationship. All that is known of her formal art education is that she is said to have been a student of the American painters Robert Swain Gifford (1840 –1905) , who wrote the introduction to Color Problems, and William Sartain (1843 – 1924).

8. Physicist Ogden Rood, an amateur painter and member of the New York Watercolor Club, is listed in the New York Times to have lectured on Maxwell's spinning color disks, for instance (which were later improved upon by the metrication device of the Milton Bradley Color Machine.)

9. In the Tale of the Spinning Wheel, p.35, there is an illustration "Woman with Hetchel, 15thCentury" of a spinner preparing flax on a tool called a hetchel that has a remarkable likeness to a person looking through the 15th century device of a Sighting Grid. The nature of the Tale being told is how women of the revolution won the Revolutionary War through their weaving and other necessary and fine crafts, as it says has been throughout history.

10. A 1928 clipping from the Metropolitan Museum of Art Vertical File reports her exhibition at the Community House of the Connecticut Agricultural College of nine watercolors, brought there by the Met, none of which remain in their collection. The titles were: The Long Hill, Japanese Color, Over the Dark Valley, The Green Mug, The Bronze Home, Early Morning, The Cliff, Moonrise, and The Ledge.

11. World's Columbian Exhibition Catalog, 1893 Department L, Liberal Arts, Gallery I, Primary Secondary Superior Education, Z-13, page 215 lists several likely possibilities for such presentation of the Color Machine.

12. Bradley, Milton. Elementary Color. Milton Bradley co, 1895. Print

13. See for instance the article Women as Consumers, Women as Producers in Lupton, Ellen, and J A. Miller. Design Writing Research: Writing on Graphic Design. London: Phaidon, 2008. Print. pp178-79.

14. Vanderpoel demonstrates the method in Plates LXXXI, An Antique Rug, and LXXXV, its Analysis. Note the asymmetry in the analysis which has color quantity winning over formal quality.

15. Vanderpoel tells us these Analyses are not merely pixelated representations, fixed in scale, material, name and meaning on page 109 of Color Problems where she projects onto PLATE LIV, Color Analysis from Mummy Plate her re-interpretation of the matrix as a "gayly feathered parrot". Thus, the grids could be considered "continuous sites of emergence of material thought", as per Carol Armstrong's analysis on the dialog between painting (in the work of Seurat) and other media ( textile craft in the work of Anni Albers.) in Arm-

strong, Carol. "Seurat's Media, or Matrix of Materialities." Grey Room. 58 (2015) 6-25. Print. P18. Vanderpoel also here refers to "those who made [the plates]" as if they were her students or someone else, but no record of her teaching the method or somehow stumbling upon it as the work of someone else exist.

16. In the introduction to the catalog of the exhibition Ornament and Abstraction, at the Beyeler Foundation, (pp16-26), Markus Bruderlin introduces questions in the discourse about abstract art's continuation of the history of ornament that Vanderpoel's work engages.

17. A quote attributed to the French poet Paul Valery, and the title of Lawrence Weschlers 1982 biography Robert Irwin's titled "Seeing is Forgetting the Name of the Thing One Sees."

18. Krauss, Rosalind. "Grids." October. 9 (1979): 51-64. Print.

19. Dickerman, Leah, and Matthew Affron. Inventing Abstraction, 1910-1925: How a Radical Idea Changed Modern Art. New York: Museum of Modern Art, 2012. Print. pp13-14. For an institutional definition of what is Abstract Art verses what is abstract otherwise, refer to the catalog of the Museum of Modern Art's exhibition Inventing Abstraction: "Scores of earlier images from other Western disciplines — chromatic studies, theosophical and mediumistic images, cosmogonic images, scientific images—may resemble abstract art. But these are not at all, for despite any formal similarity they are meant to produce meanings in other discursive frameworks....[they] do not declare a break with subject matter." Vanderpoel certainly generates an ambiguity if not a "declared break" with subject matter.

20. Bergdoll, Barry, and Leah Dickerman. Bauhaus 1919-1933: Workshops for Modernity. New York: Museum of Modern Art, 2009. Print.p.21 On the "Grid logic" that developed in the Bauhaus: "the grid became a structural tool allowing for the creation of spaces that integrated disparate mediums into overarching designs - painting, furniture, and textiles into architecture...city planning... the computer-like punch cards used in the Jacquard looms."

21. Correspondence with Reading University, 2010, archive of publisher Longman's and Green.

22. Correspondence with Pearson Press, 2010, successor to Longman's and Green.

23. New York Historical Society, Object #35.66, gift of Emily Vanderpoel. In Color Problems, Vandepoel often positions her interest in color in relation to personal and public well being, even safety: color blindness as a primarily male trait would be dangerous for railroad engineers and drivers of automobiles in relation to choreographing color signals.

24. Collection of New York Historical Society.

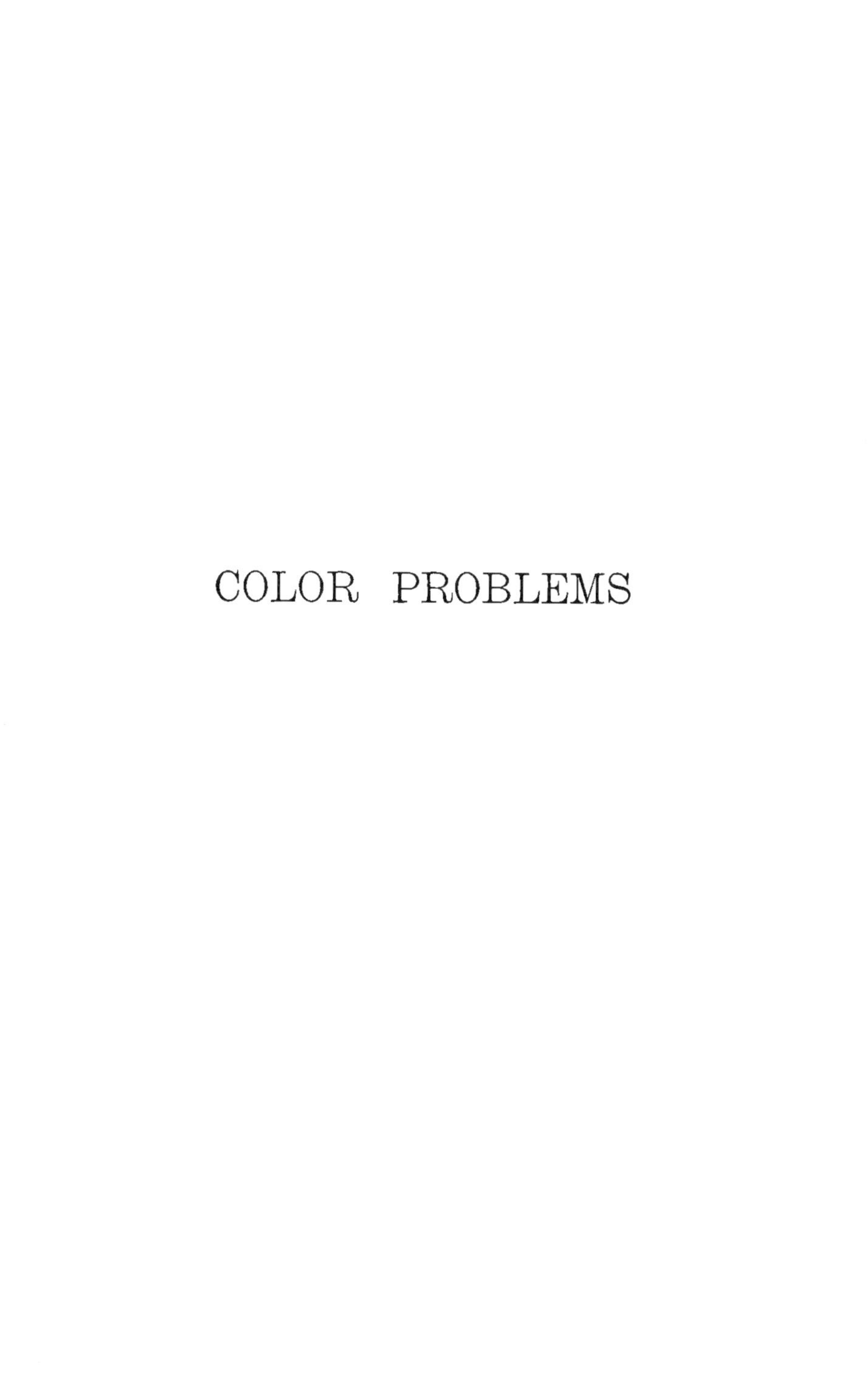

# COLOR PROBLEMS

# COLOR PROBLEMS

A PRACTICAL MANUAL FOR THE LAY STUDENT OF COLOR

By

EMILY NOYES VANDERPOEL

*WITH ONE HUNDRED AND SEVENTEEN COLORED PLATES*

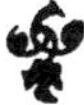

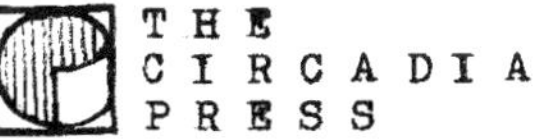


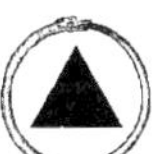

First Edition, January, 1902.
Reprinted, January, 1903.
Reprinted, October, 2018.

Rockwell and Churchill Press
BOSTON, U.S.A.

*To*

*My Father*

WILLIAM CURTIS NOYES

# PREFACE

FROM a scientific standpoint admirable works on color have been written, but they demand more time and study than many can give to them, and are too theoretical to be easily understood; while those written from an artistic standpoint may be useful to those who paint pictures but are not of much benefit to larger classes of people who are artists in other occupations. Painters of pictures must study color as well as lines and composition; but a better understanding of color would also be of great value to decorators, designers, lithographers, florists, dressmakers, and milliners; women in their dress and home decoration, and many others. For such, to combine the essential results of the scientific and artistic study of color in a concise, practical manual, and to classify the study of color in individual eyes, in light, in history and in nature, has been the aim of the author of this book. Also, as color cannot be fully appreciated by any written description, the text has been made as brief as possible, the plates full and elaborate.

It has been asked by artists who have given years of study to form, perspective and composition, why it should be necessary to study color if one has a good eye for it, to which another question may serve as answer. Suppose a person intending to make art his life work has a good eye for form, will he, therefore, begin to paint pictures before learning to draw, or without going through a thorough drill in perspective? Later, having some subject in his mind which he wishes to put on canvas, he does not stop to review all the rules he studied of form and perspective; the knowledge and facility he gained in that study will enable him unconsciously to crystallize his thought into better shape on his canvas. Does the possessor of a naturally fine voice think he can dispense with the time and trouble of cultivating it? The same reasoning may well be applied to color and its study.

E. N. V.

# INTRODUCTION

FOR some years I have known of the study and research the author of this book has devoted to problems in Color, and its uses in the arts of Design and Decoration, and it is gratifying to me that the result of much of this work is to be given to the public for the use of those who are interested in the subject.

A great deal will be found in these pages that will be of practical service, particularly to those who have not been able to read the works of Chevreul, Von Bezold, Rood, Church, and others. Indeed, even in these, careful study would be necessary to select passages describing combinations that could be applied to special work.

Much attention is here given to contrasts of modified or subdued colors, such colors as would be required constantly in decorative designs covering large spaces, against which points of more positive color would be placed. One of the greatest difficulties in arranging a color design is in determining the *qualities* and *quantities* of color in an effective and agreeable way, and very few works give the useful hints on this subject contained in this book. Under the heading of "Historic Color" are some very interesting and original diagrams, presented in a way easily to be understood and made use of in actual practice.

The study of color from the scientific side has very little attraction for the layman, and it is even difficult for a painter to get out of such study much that will help him in his work; but the presentation of some of the salient points of the scientific side, by one who has also borne in mind the artistic side, cannot fail to make this book attractive and useful to a great number who wish to know something of the laws that underlie agreeable arrangements of color.

R. SWAIN GIFFORD.

# CONTENTS

# LIST OF PLATES

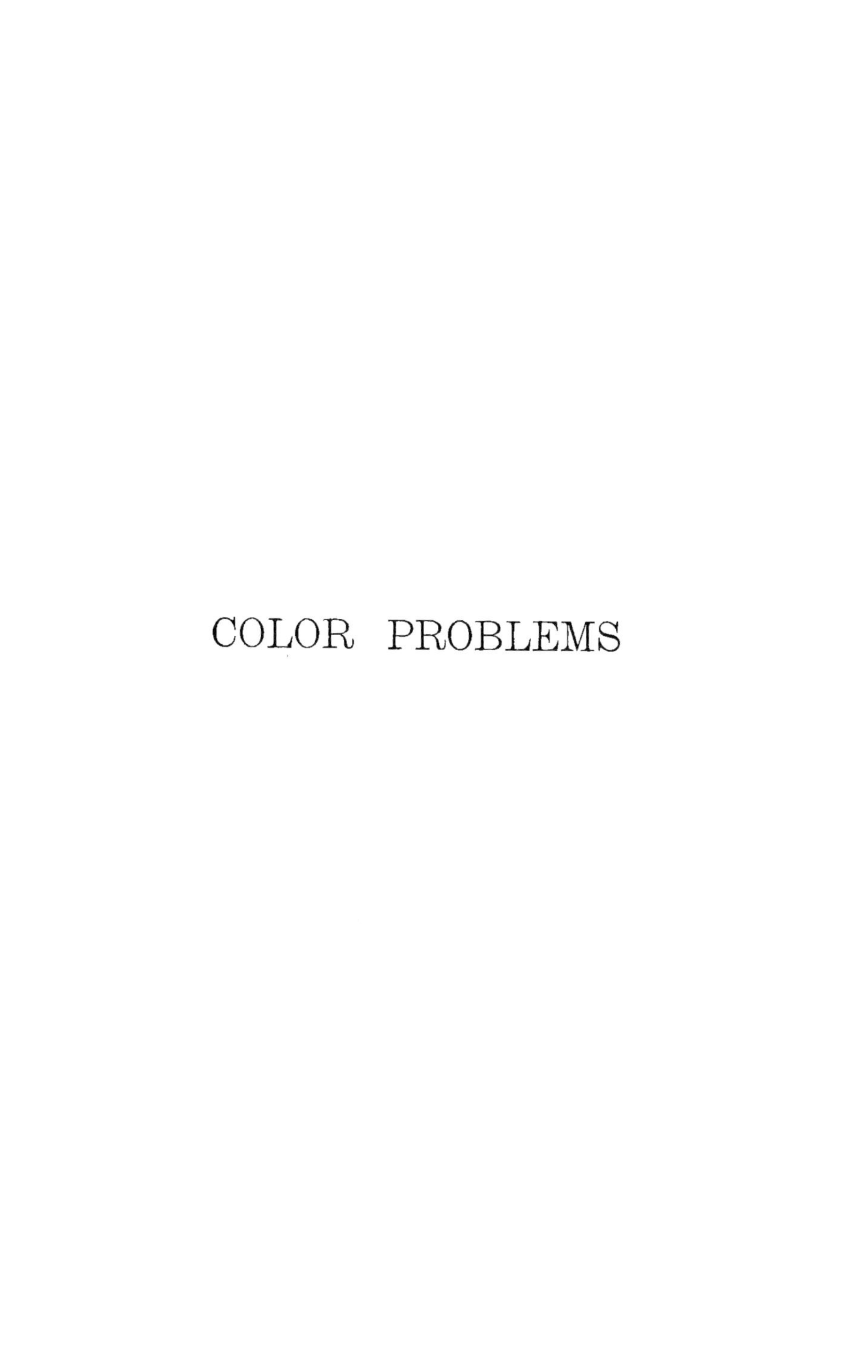

# COLOR PROBLEMS

# COLOR PROBLEMS

## CHAPTER I

### COLOR-BLINDNESS

THE relation of color to light is much the same as that of music to sound. Color has its many hues, its long scales of tints and shades, its true and its false chords. Mere sound gives us but little pleasure; when developed, however, into its highest form, music, we are thrilled, as by the song of a bird, a favorite ballad, or a Beethoven Symphony. So in light, our enjoyment culminates at the glories of color in a flower or a sunset, at the shadows that play over the hills, or at the varied hues of a salt marsh. Hence we may aptly term color *the music of light*; and when we think of the wonderful ways in which it has been used and combined by painters and designers for hundreds of years, it must seem strange to us that *its* harmonies have not been as thoroughly studied and classified as those of sound.

Furthermore, color has come to be so closely

connected with all the occupations and enjoyments of mankind that it is hard for us to realize that many persons are wholly or partially blind to its beauties. It is well known that there are some individuals with such perfect organs of hearing that they are able to distinguish the slightest sounds, who yet are so utterly unable to distinguish between two tones or between the harmonies and discords of music that they are said to have "no ear." So there are those whose eyes are as well formed for seeing all and distant objects, but who are unable to see *color* as it is seen by people with normal eyes. Such individuals may be said to have "no eye" for color, and are scientifically termed "color-blind."

This fact is not so well known; and, in view of it, any one interested in color will understand the wisdom of beginning a study of color with some knowledge of color-blindness, and, if possible, with having his eyes examined by an expert. Such an examination is a short and simple matter. Dr. William Thomson of Philadelphia has devised what he calls a "color stick," on which colored wools are so hung and numbered that it is not even necessary to be an expert to use it, and with the help of which color-blindness can easily be detected. It has been used with great success over some fifty thousand miles of railroad. From the same hand has lately come a newer and simpler form of the same invention.

Color-blindness is seldom a total want of the power to see colors, but is rather a want of the true normal perception of colors, and it is more common than is generally supposed. The most common form of the defect, which has been called by some "red-blindness," is that of not seeing red, but of confusing it with green, as, for instance, being unable to see any difference between the red flower of a geranium and the green of its foliage; between green grass and red autumn leaves. A color-blind person will sort variously colored wools in the strangest way, putting the reds among the greens, and mixing the blues and the violets together.

Plate I shows part of the result of an examination of a color-blind man by Doctor Thomson. The patient was given one hundred and fifty different-colored wools to sort in little heaps according as he saw them to be red, blue, green, etc.; he seemed to hesitate over but few of them. These he put by themselves in a heap called neutral. To a normal eye the result is almost incomprehensible, as he mixed green with all the other colors and made other as strange combinations. Di-chromatic vision has been suggested as a fitting term for such defective color perception, as colors to red-blind persons amount to but two, *viz.*, yellow and blue, with a long range of neutral grays between.

There are other forms of color-blindness which are less common. Some persons seem to see but red and blue, classing yellow and green with red. A less common defect is that of not seeing violet, while there are a few cases on record where all sensation of color is wanting, everything appearing in differing degrees of gray. One such instance coming under the notice of the writer occurred temporarily from over-strained nerves in a person gifted with an abnormally fine color-sense. No doubt some people are born color-blind, but the defect is also brought on by disease, by the excessive use of tobacco, alcohol, and other stimulants, and may, or may not, prove permanent. According to Abney, the disease begins in the centre of the eye, so that those suffering from its early stages can match colored wools correctly, but when given instead small colored pellets to match make many mistakes, because a pellet may happen to be directly before the small blind spot that is insensible to its color, while the larger mass of wool extends before the whole retina. Doctor Charcot and his school in Paris have made many examinations into visual disturbances, and through these examinations much of the peculiar coloring and mannerism of some of the modern painters of the so-called impressionist, tachist, mosaist, gray-in-gray, violet colorist, archaic, vibraist, and color orgiast schools has been explained. The artists tell the truth when they say that nature looks to them as they paint it, but they are suffering from hysteria or from other nervous derangements by which their sight is affected.

For a long time railroad engineers would not believe that examinations for color-blindness were necessary, but when shown the results of such an examination the surprise of those with normal eyes was intense. They realized what it would be to travel on a train in charge of an engineer who did not know when the red danger signal had been put in place of the usual green one. In other spheres of life correct knowledge of color is not so vitally necessary, yet to artisans of many kinds — decorators, florists, manufacturers, dressmakers, milliners, etc. — it is both useful and important.

As to the extent of color-blindness, it has been estimated that in England about one person in eighteen is more or less afflicted with it. In 1873 and 1875 Dr. Farre examined in France one thousand and fifty officials of various grades, and found among them ninety-eight color-blind, or nine and thirty-five hundredths per cent. In 1876 Professor Holmgren examined in Sweden two hundred and sixty-five persons on the Upsala

Gefle line, with the result that thirteen were found to be color-blind. Seebach found five young persons out of forty-one in a gymnasium who were color-blind. None of them had been at all conscious of the defect.

Among the visitors to the International Health Association in London, in 1884, Mr. F. Galton found a large number of men and a small number of women with more or less defective color-perception. In this country, examinations in the army and navy and among railroad engineers reveal that color-blindness, if not as general as in England, is quite common. Dr. Thomson states that as far as has been gathered from statistics generally, the percentage of color-blind men in the civilized world is four per cent., or one in twenty-five, — among women one in four thousand. While he has seen a great number of color-blind men he has never met a woman with the defect.

Singularly enough this color-blindness — the confounding of one color with another, or the want of perception of certain colors — does not prevent great enjoyment of both nature and art. A person so color-blind as to see no difference between the scarlet of a geranium blossom and the green of its leaves, or who buys a pair of bright green gloves supposing them to be brown, is still an enthusiastic and seemingly an intelligent admirer of landscape and art. One cannot say from what the enjoyment arises, but it is certainly there.

There is a noted instance of a man who learned in later life that he was color-blind, and then first understood why he had never been able to pick as many strawberries as his boy companions, because with his defect he saw no difference between the colors of the berry and that of its leaf.

There is, however, a very simple way in which it is possible for some color-blind persons to correct in a measure their erroneous impressions. If they have something green to match and fear they may mistake red for the green, by looking at their samples through a green or red glass they can prove whether or not they are correct. Through a green glass the green will keep its color, while the red will look nearly black. Through a red glass the red will remain unchanged and the green will seem nearly black.

Color-blind people can have colored glasses mounted as spectacles at small cost, which will almost entirely relieve their defect and be of great help in their work.

How far the eye of a color-blind person is susceptible of education is still uncertain. Sufficient experiment has not been made in that direction, but the fact that women notice color more than do men and are, as a general rule, more correct in their judgment of color, points to the fact that the eye is unconsciously educated by its surroundings. The constant discrimination in choice of dress and home decoration which enters early into a girl's life gives an education which men, in Europe and America at least, are deprived of, from generally wearing black or quiet colors.

That an eye normal in its perceptions of colors is capable of cultivation cannot be doubted. "It does not admit of doubt that individual sensibility to color admits of large variations, and that it is susceptible of immense improvement. This cultivation of the sense of color is, however, rather psychological than physiological, rather mental than physical. It is not that the organ of vision is improved, but our power of interpreting and coördinating the senses which it transmits to the brain. And here it is that the effects of association come most prominently, though often unconsciously, into play. We try to trace out the causes of the vast numbers of color sensations which we are continually receiving, but we constantly find that the cold methods of analysis fail to explain the mental appreciation with which we regard the astounding fertility of nature in its gifts of color."[1]

[1] Church, *Colour*.

Artists often find that when the eyes are overstimulated by false lights or colors, or want of balance in the colors looked at, the nerves are so irritated that a confusion of color and complementary tones takes place. If continued to any length of time the nerves become so fatigued that the color sense is lost, and the eye responds only to gradations of black and white.

That there are also subtle shades of difference in the sensibility to color even of good, normal eyes, no one who has paid any attention to art can fail to know. These shades of difference it is impossible to gauge, and they can only be known by the differing qualities of work produced. In a studio where perhaps a dozen pupils may be painting from one piece of still life, a vase, or bit of drapery, such differences can be clearly seen. One pair of eyes may have a tendency to see more violet than the others, another pair sees everything more brilliantly or in a higher key than the others. One student may have more difficulty in harmonizing on his canvas the different colors of the model than the rest, while another with perhaps less skill in using the paint may have such a fine eye for harmony as by the mere charm of his color to delight every one in the room.

There comes with advancing years a subtle change in the condition of the eye which it is well to understand. With age the lens of the eye loses its purity or whiteness and becomes tinged with yellow. This is not generally known, and the change is not always strongly marked, but it produces a decided effect upon the perception of blue and bluish colors. The case of the English painter Mulready may be cited as a good instance. His pictures in his later years were different in color from his earlier ones, being much colder in tone, that is bluer or less yellow. If, however, they were looked at through a piece of slightly yellow glass they appeared of the same coloring as his earlier work, painted when his eyes were normal.

## CHAPTER II

### COLOR THEORIES

A FULL review of the theories held about color is not necessary in a work of this nature, and those who have more time for and further interest in the subject will find mentioned in Appendix B to this volume the titles of a number of admirable works and treatises.

The sensation of color is first and preëminently produced by light. But an electric discharge, internal causes, or even pressure on the eyeball may also cause it; just how, we do not know. In fact, the whole subject of color, its causes, and its mechanism, is still in the region of speculation, although of speculation that may be useful.

Leaving aside the theory of color production by other causes, we will give our attention to that color sensation caused by the light of the sun, and briefly to that produced by artificial light.

The cut on page 14 shows the construction of the eye viewed from the side. We see that light enters the front of the eye through the cornea and lens and strikes the interior coating, which is the retina.

This is a wonderful membrane, very thin, but composed, as we see in the next illustration, magnified many times (page 15), of a marvellous network made of minute nerves and blood vessels ending on the innermost surface in tiny rods and cones. These rods and cones in some mysterious way are acted upon by light, and, like the outposts of an army, send messages of form and color to the brain.

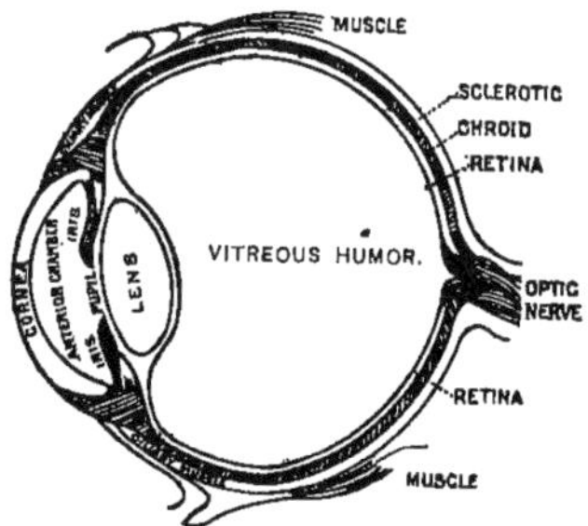


THE CONSTRUCTION OF THE HUMAN EYE AS VIEWED FROM THE SIDE.
(Nearly life size.)

Color is therefore spoken of as "an internal sensation," and is fine or poor as are the eyes and brain of the person who sees it.

What is light, we ask? Scientists answer that it is something which comes to us from a luminous or light-giving body. Sir Isaac Newton pronounced it to consist of fine atoms moving toward us rapidly. A later theory is called the *wave theory* — that there exists throughout space a fine impalpable medium, "the light-bearing ether," — that this ether moves in waves, which, beating upon the retinas of our eyes as ocean waves beat upon the shore, produce what we call *light.*

Sunlight compared to candle or gas light appears to be white; this white was proved by Sir Isaac Newton in 1672 to consist of many colors com-

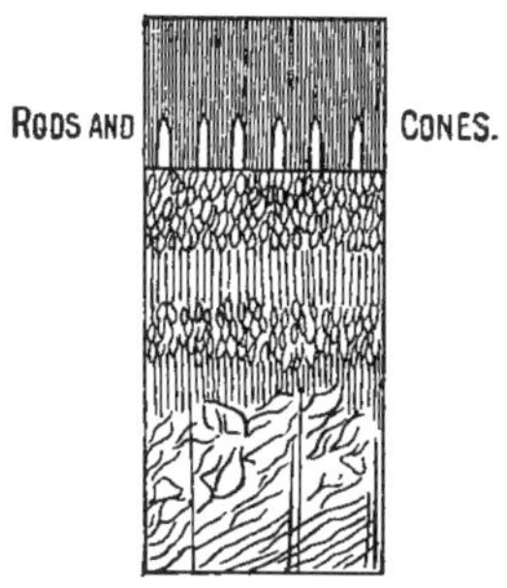


CROSS-SECTION OF THE RETINA, SHOWING THE RODS AND CONES.
(Very much magnified.)

bined in one ray. He was the first to divide such a ray of sunlight, which he did by letting it fall through a slit in the window of a darkened room, then through a prism, or three-sided piece of glass, on white paper. If this experiment be repeated there will be seen "a long streak of pure and beautiful colors which blend into each other by gentle gradations." Any one who has seen a rainbow has seen the same separation of colors, as the raindrops act in the same way as the prism and divide the rays of sunlight into their component colors.

The "spectrum" is the name given to the streak of colors when produced by the help of the prism, and it and the rainbow contain the same colors in the same order. The experiment has also been made of passing this streak of colors through a second prism, when they again unite and the ray of simple white light reappears.

An instrument called a "spectroscope" has been invented, and is constantly used by scientific students of color, which analyzes a ray of light still better than the simple prism. With its aid, early in this century, Wollaston and Fraunhofer discovered that the spectrum of sunlight, in addition to its colors, was crossed by many fine, dark, fixed lines. These have been named Fraunhofer lines, and are most useful in dividing and mapping out the limits of the different colors. Still a later invention called a "diffraction grating," made either of speculum metal or of glass silvered on the back and ruled with fine parallel lines, sometimes as many as eighteen thousand to the English inch, is used in place of a prism. With the use of improved methods Professor Rowland of Johns Hopkins University has made one ruled with some fifty or sixty thousand lines.

A ray of sunlight can be divided by this without the disadvantage of crowding the colors in the middle, as is unavoidable by the wedge-shaped glass of the prism.

Plate II shows a solar spectrum as produced by a prism and also one as shown by a diffraction grating. They both give the colors and the main Fraunhofer lines, the latter being numbered.

Although not essential to the practical use of this manual, we will now return to the theories of the primary colors, so called, upon which differing views have been held. Sir David Brewster's theory of three primaries — red, yellow, and blue — has been the most popular, because of the ease with which the three so-called secondary colors may be made by mixing paint of the three primaries, as follows: red and blue, violet; blue and yellow, green; yellow and red, orange. Artists have generally adopted it; Chevreul, the great director of the Gobelin tapestries, based his whole color system on the theory of three primary colors — red, yellow, and blue; three secondary colors made by combinations of the first three — orange, green, and violet; and three tertiary colors made from combinations of the second three — olive, russet, and citrine. We must, however, discriminate carefully between pigments, paints, and light. By experiment we prove that yellow and blue light do not make green, but white; that red and green light make yellow; and so on, so that the theory of Thomas Young is now more generally followed by scientists. As Rood gives it in his *Modern Chromatics*, "there can be in an objective sense no such thing as three fundamental colors, or three primary kinds of colored light. In a totally different sense, however, something of this kind is not only possible, but, as the recent advances of science show, highly probable. We have already seen in a previous chapter that in the solar spectrum the eye can distinguish no less than a thousand different hues. Every small, minute, almost invisible portion of the retina possesses this power, which leads us to ask whether each atom of the retina is supplied with an immense number of nerve fibrils for the reception and conveyance of this vast number of sensations.

"According to the theory of the celebrated Thomas Young, each minute elementary portion of the retina is capable of receiving and transmitting three different sensations; or we may say that each elementary portion of its surface is supplied with three nerve fibrils, adapted for the reception of three sensations. One set of these nerves is strongly acted on by long waves of light and produces the sensation we call red; another set responds most powerfully to waves of medium length, producing the sensation we call green; finally, the third set is strongly stimulated by short waves, and generates the sensation known as violet." (This might perhaps rather be called violet blue, as scientists differ as to the exact shade.) "The red of the spectrum, then, acts powerfully on the first set of these nerves; but according to Young's theory, it also acts on the

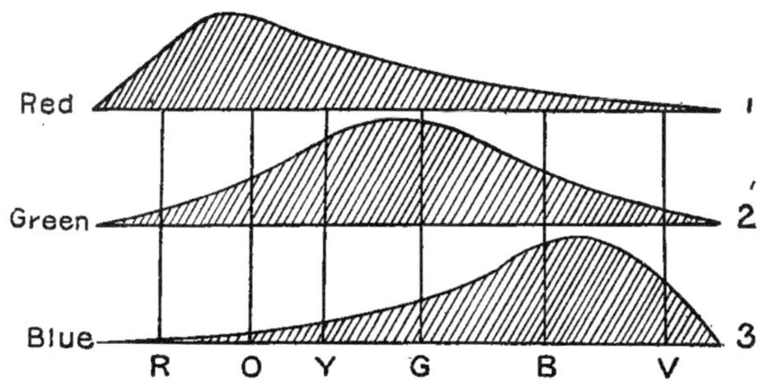


DIAGRAM ILLUSTRATING THE YOUNG–HELMHOLTZ THEORY OF COLOR SENSATION.

two other sets, but with less energy. The same is true of the green and violet rays of the spectrum; they each act on all three sets of nerves, but most powerfully on those specially designed for their reception." All this will be better understood by the aid of the accompanying diagram, which is taken from Helmholtz's great work, *Physiological Optics*. In this figure, along the horizontal lines 1, 2, 3 are placed the colors of the spectrum properly arranged, and the curves above them indicate the degree to which the three kinds of nerves are acted on by these colors. Thus we see that nerves of the first kind are powerfully stimulated by red light, are much less affected by yellow, still less by green, and very little by violet light. Nerves of the second kind are much affected by green light, less by yellow and blue, still less by red and violet. The third kind of nerves answer readily to violet light, and are successively less affected by other kinds of light in the following order: blue, green, yellow, orange, red. The next point in the theory is that if all three sets of nerves are simultaneously stimulated to about the same degree the sensation which we call white will be produced. This result would almost lead us into calling white a color — and the most brilliant one of all. These are the main points of Young's theory, which was published as long ago as 1802, and more fully in 1807. Attention has been called to it within the last few years by Helmholtz, and it is mainly owing to his labors and those of Maxwell that it now commands such respectful attention. Thus far the study of color-blindness has furnished evidence in favor of the theory of Young, and its phenomena are more easily explained by this than by any other theory.

A recent invention by Frederick E. Ives of Philadelphia has also been cited in its support. Through the use of what he calls a photo-chromoscopic camera he takes through three color screens — a red, a green, and a blue one — three negatives. These negatives, placed in an instrument called by him a stereo-photo-chromo-scope (which resembles a stereoscope, and which also holds three screens of the same colors), produce to the eyes an image so perfect in color and relief that "people have been seen to place their hand in front of it before they were convinced that they did not see a direct reflection." Various sets of three hues, or modified hues, might be used to produce the same effect.

In 1878, having re-investigated the subject thoroughly, Hering published in Vienna a paper advocating another theory. According to this "the retina is provided with three visual substances, and the fundamental sensations are not three, but six, —

Black and white,
Red and green,
Blue and yellow.

Each of these three pairs corresponds to an assimilation or diassimilation process in one of the visual substances; thus red light acts on the red-green substance in exactly the opposite way from green light, and when both kinds of light are present in suitable proportions a balance is effected, and both sensations, red and green, vanish."[1]

One of the latest accounts of these theories (of Young-Helmholtz and Hering), written in English, is to be found in Dr. Foster's *Text-book of Physiology*. It contains a full and clear discussion of the merits and demerits of both theories from a scientific standpoint. From it we give the accompany-

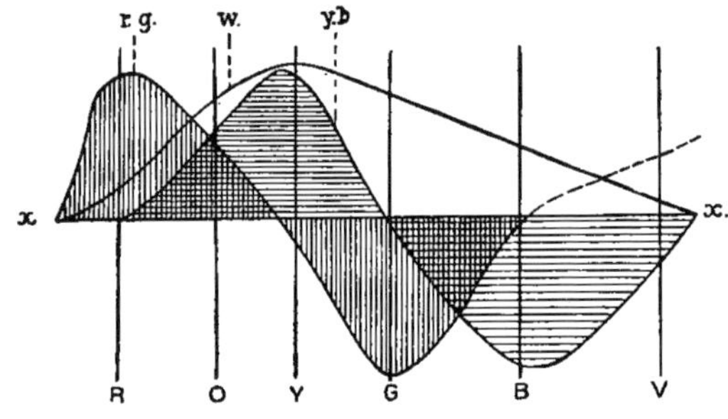


DIAGRAM ILLUSTRATING HERING'S THEORY OF COLOR SENSATION.

ing diagram illustrating Hering's theory of color vision.

Edridge Green also discusses both theories fully in connection with color-blindness.

On one point all these theories agree, which is that perfect or normal color vision is made up of three factors, or as Foster says, it is "*tri-chromic,*

[1] Rood, *Modern Chromatics.*

based on three or the equivalent of three primary sensations." The first, the Brewster theory, states that they are red, yellow, and blue colors; the second, the Young-Helmholtz theory, that there are three kinds of nerve fibrils in the retina, affected respectively by red, blue, and green, and their combinations of the spectrum; while that of Hering is that in the eye there are three changeable visual substances which are increased or diminished accordingly as the rays of black and white, yellow and blue, or red and green, fall upon them.

Le Conte, in his work *Sight*, says of the latter part of this theory, "according to Hering, complementary colors are the result of opposite affections of the retina, so that there are only two essentially distinct color affections of the retina, which, with their opposites, produce two pairs of complementary colors; the one with its opposite produces red and green; the other with its opposite, yellow and blue. This, though more doubtful, seems a probable cause of complementariness." Also, "Stanley Hall . . . believes that color is perceived by the cones (in the retina) alone; further, that different parts of the same cone vibrate with different degrees of rapidity, and therefore respond to different colors, and the conical form is adapted for this purpose. In order to gain a clearer conception we may imagine each cone to be made up of a number of buttons of graduated sizes joined together. These buttons, on account of their different sizes, would vibrate with different degrees of rapidity, and therefore co-vibrate with different colors. White light, he supposes, vibrates the whole series; red light the thicker, and violet the thinner portion of the series; or, taking Hering's view of the primary colors, we may imagine that red and green rays affect one portion and yellow and blue rays another portion of the same cone."

From the fact that in 1876 F. Boll discovered that the retina contained a red or purple substance that quickly disappeared on exposure to light, Kuhne elaborated, after further experiments with light upon that substance, a still later theory of color vision which supposes that the light waves produce in the retina different compounds that give rise to the sensation of the different colors.

Mrs. Franklin of Baltimore has lately given us a theory of "light sensation," as she prefers to call it, which has been favorably received.[1] The question of the specific uses of the rods and cones in the retina has been a puzzling one, and she suggests that they may be of the same nature, but in different stages of development, — in other words, that the rods are undeveloped cones. As there are more cones than rods in the middle of the

[1] "Mind," n.s., Vol. II. 1893.

retina, and as color is seen more vividly there, the inference is that the cones are susceptible to both light and color, while the rods are only sensitive to light. Such a theory seems to explain the results of many experiments heretofore made by scientists. Some discussion of the subtile and beautiful colors produced by interference, refraction, absorption, and polarization, as well as by opalescence, fluorescence, and phosphorescence, might aptly follow here, but that such discussion hardly comes within the scope of this mainly practical book. Readers who wish to understand and experiment with them are referred to the works of Rood, Church, and Dove.

# CHAPTER III

## COLOR QUALITIES

### HUE, PURITY, LUMINOSITY — COLD AND WARM COLORS — TINTS, SHADES, BROKEN TINTS

COLORS have three principal qualities, called scientifically "constants of color," which should be studied as a preparation for the study of the harmony of colors. These qualities are hue, purity, and luminosity. To make these as clear as possible, we will for the present, at least, ignore the delicate divisions of the spectrum made by both scientists and artists of which about one thousand have been counted, and divide it arbitrarily into six pure spectral colors differing from each other by their hues as by their wave lengths; the wave lengths we give according to Rood, expressed in ten-millionths of a millimetre ($\frac{1}{10000000}$). (See Plate III.) These six divisions can be placed beside and compared with flowers and colored materials, and are printed to imitate colored light as nearly as pigments and paper can give them. At best, any such imitation falls far short of nature.

The first quality or constant of colors is *hue*,

this term being generally agreed upon by scientists to mean color pure and simple, according to its wave length in the spectrum. Plate III gives us six hues — violet, blue, green, yellow, orange, and red. Each of these is quite different from the next one, as the violet hue is from the blue hue, the blue hue from the green hue.

The second quality or constant of colors is *purity*, that is, its lack of any mixture of white, black, or any other color. These not only weaken the color but change its character, as will be found by mixing white paint with vermilion paint, which will be seen to grow more pink, as well as lighter, as the white is added.

The third quality or constant of colors is their *luminosity* or *brightness*, also sometimes called *clearness*. It is measured by the total amount of light reflected to the eye, and is therefore independent of hue and purity. The amount of luminosity of a color can be determined correctly by means of an invention called Maxwell's Disks. These disks date back to the time of Ptolemy, but were brought into use early in this century by Maxwell. A disk, or round piece of cardboard, painted with the color to be tested, is put behind two smaller disks, one of white and one of black, which can be so adjusted that on turning them all rapidly the gray formed by the mingling of black and white matches in luminosity the one back of it.

From such experiments we see that a room papered or painted in yellow will give you the lightest room, because it will reflect more light to the eye than any of the other colors; one done in orange will come next, and so on through the list. A practical knowledge of these different luminosities is most useful in decoration, both on account of the contrast between colors for this reason as well as for their hues. Also for the ability to lighten a dark part of a room by placing there a piece of luminous coloring, and *vice versa* to darken what is too bright. We must here add that these terms, purity of color and luminosity, are used by artists in quite a different sense, as they call paintings noticeable for purity of color, meaning only that the tints in them have no tendency to look dull or dirty, but not at all implying the absence of white or gray light. They call color in a painting luminous simply because it actually recalls to the mind the impression of light, not because it actually reflects much light to the eye. Plate No. IV gives the six spectral colors in their order of luminosity.

We will now take up in turn each of the six hues by itself and study it in its variations towards its neighboring hues.

That we do not appreciate the influence of color upon man as well as upon the lower animals, is true; but color has not been studied by us as it probably will be in the near future. The powers of attraction of different colors for ants and bees have occupied the time and close observation of Sir John Lubbock and of many other scientists, and now the effect of different colors is being tried on the children in some schools and on the patients in certain insane asylums. A few facts are enough to show that there is still much to learn in that direction, and that these questions can be investigated with profit. One of these facts is that a certain shade of purple always produced the condition of the skin commonly known as "goose-flesh" upon a girl in a normal condition of health.

Goethe in his *Theory of Colour*, as translated by Sir Charles Eastlake, records observations and experiments of the most minute character with regard to light and colors — of a character hardly touched upon by others. His suggestion of using colored glass for study in colors is very valuable. He says, "People experience a great delight in color generally. The eye requires it as much as it requires light. We have only to remember the refreshing sensation we experience, if on a cloudy day the sun illumines a single portion of the scene before us and displays its colors. That healing powers were ascribed to colored gems may have arisen from the experience of this indefinable pleasure.

"From some of our earlier observations we can conclude that general impressions produced by single colors cannot be changed, that they act specifically and must produce definite specific states in the living organ.

"They likewise produce a corresponding influence on the mind. Experience teaches us that particular colors excite particular states of feeling. It is related of a witty Frenchman, "Il pretendoit que son ton de conversation avec Madame étoit changé depuis qu'elle avait changé en cramoisi le meuble de son cabinet, qui étoit bleu." (He imagined that the tone of his conversation with Madame was changed since she had changed the coloring of her sitting-room from blue to crimson.)

"In order to experience these influences completely, the eye should be entirely surrounded with one color; we should be in a room of one color, or look through a colored glass. We are then identified with the hue, it attunes the eye and mind in mere unison with itself.[1]

"The colors on the *plus* side are yellow, red-yel-

[1] The use of this suggestion as to colored glass is strongly urged by the author, as it is a capital way of seeing how the world would look were everything in it blue, or any other color.

low and yellow-red. The feelings they excite are quick, lively, and aspiring.

"The colors on the *minus* side are blue, red-blue and blue-red. They produce a restless, susceptible, anxious impression."

Each of these six hues can be divided roughly into three, as they are pure or tend toward their neighboring hues. So violet, of which we have pure normal or spectral violet, with red-violet on one hand, blue-violet on the other; or yellow, of which we have pure normal or spectral yellow, with orange-yellow on one side, green-yellow on the other.

Violet is a cold color, red-violet warmer than blue-violet. It is grave, dignified, as compared with the other colors. Being a retiring color, it will serve well as a background, as it will throw forward any more luminous color put upon it. In flowers we have examples of this color in its variety in violets, lilacs, asters, sweet peas, and morning-glories. In the latter it is exquisitely shaded from one extreme to the other. The wild Eupatorium furnishes a fine example of red-violet, the cultivated variety an equally good one of the blue-violet, almost cold enough for a blue. There is no sound pigment which can be used alone to paint this color. The violet in the originals for these plates was made with French blue and crimson lake, and crimson lake is not considered a permanent color. Violet of all kinds suffers from artificial light, losing much of its blue, and becoming more red and dull.

Blue is a cold color, and a retiring one, especially suited for backgrounds, as one will notice in studying a blue sky, against which the landscape stands out with great beauty. In flowers, examples of this color are more rare than of others. The blue gentian is not a true blue, it is so close on blue-violet. Forget-me-nots, chicory, centaureas, and larkspur give us blue in differing varieties. The sky from the deep violet blue of a winter's night to the pale, greenish tones near the horizon on a summer's day shows us an unsurpassed scale of this hue.

Goethe says of it, "It may be said that blue brings a principle of darkness with it.

"This color has a peculiar and almost indescribable effect on the eye. As a hue it is powerful, but it is on the negative side, and in its highest purity is, as it were, a stimulating negation. Its appearance, then, is a kind of contradiction between excitement and repose.

"As the upper sky and distant mountains appear blue, so a blue surface seems to retire from us.

"But as we readily follow an agreeable object that flies from us, so we love to contemplate blue, not because it advances to us, but because it draws us after it.

"Blue gives us an impression of cold, and thus again reminds us of shade. We have before spoken of its affinity with black.

"Rooms which are hung with pure blue appear in some degree larger, but at the same time empty and cold.

"The appearance of objects seen through a blue glass is gloomy and melancholy.

"When blue partakes in some measure of the *plus* side the effect is not disagreeable; sea-green is rather a pleasing color."

Genuine ultramarine is an expensive but very pure blue paint made from lapis-lazuli. Artificial ultramarine generally inclines towards violet. A good deal of green and violet light is reflected from cobalt blue. There is some green in Prussian blue, in indigo, and in cerulean blue. Prussian blue, if used quite thickly, reflects some red. The blue for the original of Plate X was made of French blue (artificial ultramarine), tinged on the violet end with crimson lake, and on the greenish end with emerald green, which latter is not a permanent color, but which approaches nearest of any pigment to the green hue in the spectrum. Blue is one of the colors most used in decoration.

Green may be cold or warm, retiring or advancing according as it approaches blue or yellow, although pure spectral green is of a cold nature.

When one studies the great scale of greens as seen in a landscape lit up with full sunshine, and notices the intense yellow green where the sun shines through the leaves, the pale gray greens produced by the sun's glancing over the polished surfaces of others, and the rich dark green in the shadows, it seems as if no other color would admit of so varied a scale or be more restful to the eye.

Goethe says: "The eye experiences a distinctly grateful impression from this color. The beholder has neither a wish nor the power to imagine a state beyond it. Hence for rooms to live in constantly, the green color is most generally selected." This assertion may be doubted, many persons objecting to green, the truth probably being that it has been found difficult to use, and not having been understood or well treated has not been appreciated. Its healthfulness cannot be doubted if one considers how refreshing the surroundings of trees and grass are to an invalid who has been surrounded by city bricks and stones. Can we not derive a like benefit from this color by decorating our city rooms with varying tones of soft gray greens, like nature, relieved here and there with a touch of brightness, as flowers, birds, and butterflies gleam amid the foliage in their native haunts? The rules for heightening these contrasts with certain varieties of green will be given in the chapter on contrasts. The extremes of green blend better than those of other colors. Emerald green has been used as being the best paint with which to imitate the normal green of the spectrum, but it must be remembered that it is a trifle bluer than it should be to be exact.

Of yellow Goethe writes, "This is the color nearest the light.

"In its highest purity it always carries with it the nature of brightness, and has a serene, gay, softly exciting character.

"In this state applied to dress, hangings, carpets, etc., it is agreeable. Gold in its perfectly unmixed state, especially when the effect of polish is superadded, gives us a new and high idea of this color; in like manner, a strong yellow, as it appears on satin, has a magnificent and noble effect.

"We find from experience again that yellow excites a warm and agreeable impression. Hence in painting it belongs to the illumined and emphatic side.

"This impression of warmth may be experienced in a very lively manner if we look at a landscape through a yellow glass, particularly on a gray winter's day. The eye is gladdened, the heart expanded and cheered, a glow seems at once to breathe towards us."

Yellow is both a warm and an advancing color, especially useful to apply as ornament on other colors, as gold embroidery is beautiful on any color. With the exception of white there are more yellow flowers than of any other color. In Moorish decorations, which are some of the finest in the world, gold is used as ornament on blue and red grounds; in fact, throughout the history of ornament, yellow is more often used in that way than as a groundwork.

A thin wash of Aurora yellow gave the color for the original of Plate XII. This paint, when put on thickly, tends too much toward orange to imitate well the very narrow band of yellow in the spectrum. It is made from cadmium, and, according to Church,[1] the deep or orange cadmiums are all more lasting than the pale or lemon-colored kinds.

Orange is still a warmer color than yellow, and is also an advancing color. Goethe says, "All that we have said of yellow is applicable here in a higher degree. The red-yellow (orange) gives an impression of warmth and gladness, since it represents the hue of the intenser glow of fire, and of the milder radiance of the setting sun." Orange is perhaps the most intense color and should be used sparingly in decoration, as it needs great care as to the quality and quantity of other colors to balance it. Orange cadmium was used for the original of Plate XI.

[1] *The Chemistry of Paints and Painting.*

Red is a warm color and an advancing one. Goethe says, "The agreeable, cheerful sensation which red-yellow excites increases to an intolerably powerful impression in bright yellow-red.

"The active side is here in its highest energy, and it is not to be wondered at that impetuous, robust, uneducated men should be especially pleased with this color. Among savage nations the inclination for it has been universally remarked, and when children left to themselves begin to use tints (paints), they never spare vermilion and minium.

"In looking steadfastly at a perfectly yellow-red surface, the color seems actually to penetrate the organ. It produces an extreme excitement, and still acts thus when somewhat darkened. A yellow-red (scarlet) cloth disturbs and enrages animals. I have known men of education to whom its effect was intolerable if they chanced to see a person dressed in a scarlet cloak on a gray, cloudy day." In nature we have red only in small portions, a few red birds or those with throats or spots of red; almost no butterflies, but many flowers. The rose, which leads in beauty the long procession of flowers, contains an immense scale of this color on the violet side, from the palest blush to the deepest crimson, almost purple. There being less of red in nature than of any other color, it becomes by contrast the decorative color. It has also the quality of changing less with lessening light than any other color, and is particularly fine in combination with blue. Vermilion and carmine were used to make the spectral red of Plate XIV, though they are far from reproducing the vivid quality of the original. Vermilion used with oil is much more permanent than with water. Of the lakes, Church says in his *Chemistry of Paints and Painting:* "No artist who cares for his work, and hopes for its permanency, should ever employ them."

There is another quality shown in Plate III by which colors may be divided into the warm and cold classes. The six spectral colors we have so far been studying in this chapter may be roughly divided as follows:

| COLD. | WARM. |
|---|---|
| Violet | Yellow |
| Blue | Orange |
| Green | Red |

although some varieties of green may be classed among the cold colors because of the large amount of blue they seem to contain, and others may be classed among the warm ones from their seeming to contain so large an amount of yellow.

It is well to remember that cold colors seem to retire or go back from the eye, while the warm ones seem to come forward, and that the right use of these qualities greatly affects architecture and decoration. (See Plates V and VI.)

To recapitulate, we have first, three qualities or constants of *colors:* hue, purity, luminosity; then the qualities of being warm or cold. Following upon these are divisions of the tones into three other groups or scales of tints, shades, and gray or broken tints.

These scales have been confined to six for the sake of simplicity, but the reader may multiply them infinitely to correspond with the infinite gradations in nature.

1. Tints. — "The reduced scale — that is, the normal hue mixed with progressive increments (additions) of white, thus forming *tints.*" The spectral hue of the color weakened by white. Plate VII.

2. Shades. — "The darkened scale — that is, the normal hue mixed with progressive increments (additions) of black, thus forming *shades.*" The spectral hue of the color darkened with black. Plate VIII.

3. "The dulled scale — that is, the normal hue mixed with progressive increments of gray, thus forming broken tints commonly called grays." The spectral hue of the color changed by black and white. Besides these regular scales which can be approximately rendered in paint or colored inks there is an infinite variety of what we might call

irregular scales which can never be given save in nature. They are those in which a color is changed or neutralized by one or more of the other colors. These cannot even be named, for their multitude.

With the aid of a color wheel on which he used disks of black, white, and the six prismatic colors, Professor Rood has drawn up and formulated the proportions of 488 of these compound or neutralized colors. With the formulæ a number of them have been printed in color quite successfully. It is probably the first attempt to establish standard colors, and a most valuable one, which it is hoped may bear fruit. If those and the arbitrary terms for colors and their different states could come into general use it would greatly help all descriptions of color harmonies.

Having become familiar with the six colors, we now arrive at the object for which we have gone through the previous study; namely, the first kind of *color harmony*, one-color combinations, also called combinations of self-tones, the simplest and the preliminary harmony to that of combined colors. The first rule to be observed in making one-color combinations is to avoid putting together what we may call, borrowing the term from the language of music, the large intervals, or extremes, of a color in their pure spectral hues. For example, in arranging a basket of flowers, never put those of a crimson or violet-red, such as an American Beauty rose, next to a scarlet or orange-red flower, such as a scarlet geranium. These are too unlike each other, being at the large intervals of the hue. They injure each other and are therefore disagreeable.

As a second rule, all colors, even those above-named, may be combined in one harmony, but this harmony must be produced from the fact that tints, or shades, or both combined, are used, rather than the simple spectral hues. In fact, nature uses pure colors most sparingly; they appear, if you will remember, in small bright spots in jewels, in somewhat larger quantities in flowers and fruit, in the wings of butterflies and the plumage of birds, to relieve and ornament the more subdued great masses of neutral greens and grays that make up the ordinary garb of nature.

But to return to the combinations of larger intervals of color we were considering. For instance, while scarlet (orange-red) and crimson (violet-red) do not combine well, at a French sea-shore resort was seen the combination of a pink (that is, a tint of violet-red) dress, shaded by a brilliant scarlet (orange-red) parasol carried by its wearer. It was as daring a combination as could be made; its success was complete owing to the pale tint of the dress and the correspondingly correct hue of the scarlet of the parasol. The effect was helped and complemented by the large mass of the sea as background. No rule can prescribe these tints or shades exactly, a gifted eye only can combine them with success; but the fact might serve as a hint to those who find by examination and experiment that they have such an eye.

Besides the use of tints and shades to help us in combining what would otherwise be inharmonious color, gradation is another means we can employ to serve our purpose. For instance, considering different blues, which are not agreeable together, we will look at a cloudless sky; we find that above us it may be of a deep blue verging on violet blue, while, as we let the eye follow it down through the infinite and exquisite gradations it contains, near the horizon we come gently upon our other blue, the greenish one, and feel no discord. The rainbow, which is, in fact, a kind of spectrum, is the best possible example of the great use of gradation; there we have all the pure colors, one differing immensely from the other, but the gradations between them are so fine and complete as to prevent the least discord. In opals and pearl shells, in peacock's feathers and soap bubbles, such coloring is also seen enhanced by being broken by soft grays and greens. It is caused by what is scientifically called interference; that is, the thin layers of the material interfere or break up the waves of light and so produce the color.

Reflection in colored materials can be used to help greatly in harmonizing them. Look at a piece of red sealing-wax. Hold it up by a window and the high gloss on it will reflect so much light as to make the side toward the light appear almost white. On another side the true or local color, the brilliant red, will be seen, and the side in shadow will be of another color still, darker and more crimson or violet-red. Red satin will have the same varieties in its high lights, middle, and shaded parts, and these whiter lights and shaded parts really gray and subdue the color of the material. A woollen cloth of the same color which has less power of reflection will therefore have less of the gray about it. With practice, fine and beautiful one-color combinations, greatly varied, can be made by using materials of different textures but of the same color.

What has been said so far of colors applies to them as seen in ordinary daylight, but we must also know how they are affected by lessened, increased, and artificial light. Rood made many elaborate experiments in this direction, too numerous to be given here. With these in view, Church gives the following table of the main changes that occur in colored objects from the changing of the light in which they are commonly seen:

| If Light | | Increase, — | Diminish. |
|---|---|---|---|
| Red | becomes | Scarlet . . . . | Purplish. |
| Scarlet | " | Orange . . . . | Red. |
| Orange | " | Yellow . . . . | Brown. |
| Yellow | " | Paler . . . . | Olive-green. |
| Yellow-green | " | Yellower . | Greener. |
| Blue-green | " | More blue . . . | Greener. |
| Art'f. ultramarine | becomes | Blue . . . . | More violet. |
| Violet | " | More blue . . | Purple. |
| Purple | " | Redder . . | More violet. |

We must also note the effect produced by double light; as, for instance, at sunset when we find in one direction the cool light from the blue of the sky, in another the warm light from the setting sun. This is more complicated and difficult to understand.

Reflections from near objects produce similar effects; as, for instance, in the city, the light reflected from a red brick wall and that from a blue sky. An artist painted a portrait in which the likeness was spoiled by the unnatural amount of red in the complexion. On examination it was found to have been put there rightly, inasmuch as the artist certainly saw it; the error lay in choosing a place for the subject where the red reflection from a brick wall was thrown on his face. In a room, a yellow wall paper and a curtain of some other color may throw combined and confusing though perhaps at the same time most interesting reflections on some object. The combined effects of daylight and gas or lamp light are similar.

We will next consider the effect upon colored objects of a light, itself colored, — of what is called a dominant light. (See Plate VI, with instructions.)

Chevreul made many experiments with these. Church gives them to us, with modifications, in the following concise form:

| | | | | | |
|---|---|---|---|---|---|
| Red | rays falling | on white | make it | appear | red. |
| " | " | " red | " | " | deeper red. |
| " | " | " orange | " | " | redder. |
| " | " | " yellow | " | " | orange. |
| " | " | " green | " | " | yellowish-gray. |
| " | " | " blue | " | " | violet. |
| " | " | " violet | " | " | purple. |
| " | " | " black | " | " | rusty black. |
| Orange | " | " white | " | " | orange. |
| " | " | " red | " | " | reddish-orange. |
| " | " | " orange | " | " | deeper orange. |
| " | " | " yellow | " | " | orange-yellow. |
| " | " | " green | " | " | dark yellow-green. |
| " | " | " blue | " | " | dark reddish-gray. |
| " | " | " violet | " | " | dark purplish-gray. |
| " | " | " black | " | " | brownish-black. |
| Yellow | " | " white | " | " | yellow. |
| " | " | " red | " | " | orange-brown. |
| " | " | " orange | " | " | orange-yellow. |
| " | " | " yellow | " | " | deeper yellow. |
| " | " | " green | " | " | yellowish-green. |
| " | " | " blue | " | " | slaty-gray. |
| " | " | " violet | " | " | purplish-gray. |
| " | " | " black | " | " | olive-black. |
| Green | " | " white | " | " | green. |

| | | | | |
|---|---|---|---|---|
| Green | rays falling on | red | make it appear | yellowish-brown. |
| " | " | " orange | " " | grayish-leaf-green. |
| " | " | " yellow | " " | yellowish-green. |
| " | " | " green | " " | deeper green. |
| " | " | " blue | " " | bluish-green. |
| " | " | " violet | " " | bluish-gray. |
| " | " | " black | " " | dark greenish-gray. |
| Blue | " | " white | " " | blue. |
| " | " | " red | " " | purple. |
| " | " | " orange | " " | plum-brown. |
| " | " | " yellow | " " | yellowish-gray. |
| " | " | " green | " " | bluish-green. |
| " | " | " blue | " " | deeper blue. |
| " | " | " violet | " " | bluer. |
| " | " | " black | " " | bluish-black. |
| Violet | " | " white | " " | violet. |
| " | " | " red | " " | purple. |
| " | " | " orange | " " | reddish-gray. |
| " | " | " yellow | " " | purplish-gray. |
| " | " | " green | " " | bluish-gray. |
| " | " | " blue | " " | bluish-violet. |
| " | " | " violet | " " | deeper violet. |
| " | " | " black | " " | violet-black. |

In this table the effect of yellow light gives us the effect of gas or lamp light on colors, as they are yellow in character. To make his experiments with artificial light as sure as possible, Rood, or Chevreul, in daylight, threw the light from a gas burner on colors set in a camera so as to judge at the same time of the effects of the two kinds of light, for we must remember that commonly when we see colors by gas or lamp light we are so surrounded ourselves by the same yellow light that everything is tinged by it, and our judgment is affected; all we see being yellower, yellow objects will look less yellow for want of the contrast seen in daylight. This effect is now understood and provided for by dry goods merchants, who have for some time shown materials for evening dresses in rooms lighted by gas. A fairly good idea of the appearance which pictures, colored materials, articles of dress and decoration will make by gas or lamp light can be had by looking at them through a piece of pale orange-yellow glass.

Electric and calcium lights, being much whiter than that of gas or oil, make less difference in colors, but their intensity being different from that of ordinary diffused daylight, it produces different and more intense effects.

# CHAPTER IV

## CONTRASTS AND COMPLEMENTS

GIVEN a certain amount of any color, say normal or spectral red, and wishing to make it look as bright as it can, what color shall we put with it, and how much of that color, to attain our purpose? To answer that question correctly, having in the last chapter studied the harmony possible in what have been called self-tones, or one-color combinations, we will take up contrasts, of which we have several kinds, as follows:

Simultaneous contrasts of tone, neutral.
Simultaneous contrasts of color on neutral grounds.
Successive contrasts.
Mixed contrasts.
Contrasts of complements.
Contrasts of other hues or lesser contrasts.
Contrasts of brightness.
Contrasts of purity.
Contrasts of cold and warm colors.

The first point to understand clearly is the law of simultaneous contrast of tone as studied and written about by Chevreul in his elaborate work on color. Church explains this law: "Contrast caused by difference in brightness is commonly called contrast of tone. This kind of contrast may occur alone or it may be associated with contrast of hue and contrast of purity. It will be well to consider first the simplest cases, in which contrast of tone is not accompanied by other contrasts. It is impossible, however, to reduce experiments on tone-contrast to their simplest expressions, because a third element always comes in, namely, the background on which the pair of tones is placed for examination. Whether this background be black, white, gray, or colored, it must necessarily differ in some one direction from one or both the trial pieces, and will therefore itself produce a contrast. To minimize the complication thus introduced we may try an experiment for producing the phenomena of tone-contrast in three ways, using three backgrounds with identical trial pieces on each. We first take two strips of light gray paper, A and A, in Plate XV, and place them a few inches apart on a large sheet of (white) paper in a good light. We then prepare two similar strips of a considerably darker shade of gray, B and B′, and place them, as shown in the diagram, B′ alongside of A′ and the other the same distance from B′ as A is from A′. On close observation it will be seen that A′ close to B′ appears lighter than A, which lies at some distance, while B appears correspondingly darker than B′. The effect of contrast in enhancing differences of tone may be studied thus: Make such openings, five in number, in a piece of card, as will serve to divide each of the strips A and B into three portions. When viewed through this card, held between the trial pieces and the eye, it will be found that the two adjoining parts of the strip are most contrasted in tone, and the others less so in proportion to their distance from the line of contact. The experiment should now be repeated with a background of black velvet, and again with a background of gray paper lighter in tone than either of the strips. The effect of contrast of tone is still better seen in a series of toned strips placed next each other. In such a case the effect on all the strips save the end ones is that of *double* contrast. For the second strip or second tone has one side of it made apparently darker by reason of the contiguity of the lighter tone of strip, while the other side seems lighter, owing to the contiguity of the darker tone of strip 3. The general result of these double contrasts is that the whole series or scale of tones gives the appearance of a number of hollows, although, in fact, the apparent hollows are perfectly flat areas of uniform shade. The effect of this experiment is approximately represented in Plate XV, where the real flatness of each tone of the six may be verified by covering up all the others by a card. Tones of any one color instead of gray may be thus employed to illustrate this kind of simultaneous contrast, but its characteristic effect is not seen unless the contrasting tones differ considerably in intensity, increase by regular gradations, and are near each other, or in absolute contact. However, if tones of a color, whether in tints or shades, be used, there is generally a complication introduced, owing to the difficulty of getting a series of such tones which shall be the same in hue.

"This phenomenon of simultaneous contrast of tone of course largely affects . . . all drawings in black and white and in monochrome."

Following upon the law of simultaneous contrast of tone is the law of simultaneous contrast of color formulated by Chevreul, as follows: "In the case where the eye sees at the same time two contiguous (or adjoining) colors, they will appear as dissimilar as possible, both in their optical composition and the height of their tone. We have, then, at the same time simultaneous contrast of color, properly so called, and contrast of tone." Plate XVI gives the simplest examples of this simultaneous contrast of color, the six spectral colors we have been studying on grounds of white, black, and gray. The colors seem brighter on the black ground and darker on the white, while with the gray the yellow alone is much affected, it seeming to grow brighter. The following plates (Nos. XVII, XVIII, and XIX) give the same coloring, but reversed, the white, black, and gray being in spots or disks on the six colored grounds. By covering the squares on Plate XIX. with the prepared sheet of paper having a square opening just large enough to allow but one of its six divisions to be seen at a time, we shall find that each one of the disks or spots looks, not pure gray, but tinged with another color. This result gives us our first hint of what is called a complementary color. In the case of the gray on blue the gray will appear rusty or yellowish, yellow being the complement of blue; the gray on yellow will appear bluer, blue being the complement of yellow; on the green the gray will look purplish-red, on the orange greenish-blue, on red bluish-green, and on the violet yellowish-green.

Black lace over colors is always affected by them in a similar way. Over yellow, its complement being blue, the lace will look at its best, that is, blackest; over blue, the lace will tend to yellow, and will lose something of its strength and the fulness of its black; over greens, it will partake of their complement, red, and tend to look rusty.

In connection with this tinging of black with the color complementary to that of the color of the ground on which it is placed, Chevreul tells an interesting anecdote. A manufacturer was given black and colored wools with which to make some goods, the pattern to be black on colored grounds. When they were delivered the man who had ordered the goods complained that he had not been given the same black wool, that the blacks were not pure and clear. The manufacturer declared he had used the same wools. A lawsuit followed, in the course of which Chevreul was called upon to give his testimony as to color, when he proved that, according to the law of simultaneous contrast of color, the black wool was the same, but when woven in figures, as for instance, black on blue, the complementary color to blue, namely, yellow, being called up by the eye, made the black look a rusty-brownish black instead of pure clear black. He added that the only way to make the black on blue look pure would be to color it with a little of the blue so as to overcome its yellowish complement.

This delicate impression of the color complementary to the one we are looking at, is called up involuntarily by the eye, of which the nerve fibrils become fatigued by the strong color, and incline to see the extreme opposite or complementary color. The complement of a color may also be called up or produced by looking fixedly at a round spot like that on Plate XX for some time. After a while there may be seen a faint image of its complement on the white paper around it. A still better way of seeing the complement of a color is by looking fixedly for some time at a disk of the selected color placed on white paper (Use Plate XXI); then suddenly slip a sheet of white paper over it, and, continuing to look at the place where it was, the same-sized image of its complement will be seen. Here we have the answer to the question at the beginning of the chapter: bluish-green is the color complementary to spectral red. The eye becomes tired with looking at the red, and the nerve fibrils excited by it incline to see its complement, bluish-green. We can, however, prove this conclusion most correctly by means of what are called Maxwell's disks. If we cut out a disk or circular piece of cardboard and paint it spectral red, then cut a second one just like it but paint it bluish-green, cutting a slit in both from the edge to the middle so we can slip one into the other as shown in Plate XXII, and then turn them rapidly, the color in both will seem to fade away until, when turning fast enough, we shall see no color at all, — simply a complete disk of light gray. That result proves that spectral red and bluish-green are true complements of each other, because a certain number of parts of red neutralize a certain number of parts of bluish-green. If, instead of using paints and paper we were able to use colored light, the result would be even better; we should have white light as the result of mixing the red and the bluish-green in the right quantities. Pigments are so dull or non-luminous compared with light that with them we can only produce gray, or as it has been called, dark white, or white in shadow. To be quite sure that we have gray, let us add in front of our disks two smaller ones of black and white, and we will find the gray produced by the mixture of the black and white to match perfectly the gray made of spectral red and bluish-green. To measure the quantity of each color necessary, we can put behind the two disks a white disk that is not slit, the circumference of which is divided, as in Plates XXII, XXIII, XXIV, XXV, and XXVI, into one hundred parts. These are plates of the six specified spectral colors with their complements. The numbers give the quantity in one-hundredths of each color. The "number of luminosity" means the quantity of white in proportion to black, in one-hundredths, necessary to make the gray of that particular degree.

The Milton-Bradley Company, of Springfield, Massachusetts, make an excellent little machine, including several sets of disks of different sizes and good colors, and a stout frame on which to put the disks, with a crank by which to turn them. It can be set up and screwed on a table, so that any one can make for himself these delightful experiments. Plate XXVII is an illustration of this machine. There is hardly a limit to the number of the other complementary colors that can be made with this set of disks. Study of this set of complementary colors is most important as a foundation for all contrasts. Experiment has also proved that colors have more than one complement.

"Complementary colors of full brightness and purity afford the most striking examples of the effect called contrast. When each of a pair of such colors differs as much as possible from its fellow in hue, but is of the same degree of brightness, it is found, while the brightness of both is enhanced, that the hue of both is unchanged by the close neighborhood or contiguity of the two colors. But if the pair be not truly complementary, or if in brightness or purity one color differ from the other, then such difference will not be seen exactly as it is, but such dissimilarity as exists, whether it be of one hue, of purity, or of brightness, will be increased or enhanced by juxtaposition. This is the primary law of contrast, which embraces three varieties dependent respectively upon differences as to the three constants of color, namely, hue, purity, and brightness (or luminosity). If two adjacent colors differ in brightness, that which is the brighter, or, in other words, the more luminous, will increase in brightness, while the less luminous will have its brightness diminished. If two adjacent colors differ in hue, such difference will be increased, each hue tending to change as if it had been mixed with the complementary of the other. In the case of complementaries no increase of difference in hue is, however, possible."[1]

Plate XXVIII shows us the six spectral colors with their complements, not in quantity, but as a table. After thorough study of this table of first and simplest contrasts, the practical advantage of Plates XXII to XXVI will be apparent. To make it easier we give Plate XXIX, which shows the same set of complements. Here they are arranged in a circle in which each color is opposite its own complement. This circle leads us from the strongest contrasts of complements to *lesser contrasts*. This should also be studied till it can be remembered for future reference. Being in simple spectral colors, it is easier than the more numerous tints of shades of neutralized colors, and is also a key for under-

[1] Church.

standing and classifying them. It is well here to note how many complements are green or greenish in hue.

Concerning the law of simultaneous contrast, with regard more especially to lesser contrasts, Rood says: "When any two colors of the chromatic circle are brought into competition or contrasted, the effect produced is apparently to move them both farther apart. In the case, for example, of orange and yellow, the orange is moved toward the red, and assumes the appearance of reddish-orange; the yellow moves toward the green, and appears for the time to be greenish-yellow. Colors which are complementary are already as far apart in the chromatic circle as possible; hence they are not changed in hue, but merely appear more brilliant and saturated." Plate XXX will be found of great assistance[1] in comparing pairs of colors with each other. Here we have a diagram of a chromatic circle. By placing over it the transparent color screen found at the end of the book, and moving it slowly in the same direction, it will be seen that red when contrasted with greenish-blue causes this last color to move away from the centre of the circle in a straight line; hence, as the new point is on the same diameter, but farther from the centre, we know that the greenish-blue is not made more

[1] See note on page 72.

or less blue or green, but is simply caused to appear more saturated or brilliant. The new point for the red lies also on the same diameter, but is nearer the centre of the circle; that is, the color remains red, but appears duller or less saturated. Experience confirms this. If a considerable number of pieces of red cloth, for example, are examined in succession, the last one will appear duller and inferior in brilliancy to the others, but it will still appear red. Proceeding with the examination of the effects produced on the other colors, we find that the orange has been moved toward yellow and also toward the centre of the circle; hence our diagram tells us that red, when put into competition with orange, causes the latter to appear more yellowish and at the same time less intense. So we can go on comparing one color with another and find out the effect of each by moving the one circle over the other in different directions, always finding that the complements as moved away from each other only grow more brilliant but more changing in color. Church gives us a list of the changes due to the principal pairs of lesser contrasts from the observations of Chevreul, Rood, etc., as follows:

(It may be remarked that this table of changes as here given is more easily understood than in its original form as given by Church.)

| Pairs of Colors. | Change due to Simultaneous Contrast. |
|---|---|
| Red with orange | inclines to purple. |
| Orange with red | " yellow. |
| Red with yellow | " purple. |
| Yellow with red | " green. |
| Red with blue-green | becomes more brilliant. |
| Blue-green with red | " " |
| Red with blue | inclines to orange. |
| Blue with red | " green. |
| Red with violet | " orange. |
| Violet with red | " blue. |
| Red with purple | " orange. |
| Purple with red | " blue. |
| Orange with yellow | " red. |
| Yellow with orange | " green. |
| Orange with green | " red. |
| Green with orange | " blue-green. |
| Orange-yellow with turquoise | becomes more brilliant. |
| Turquoise with orange-yellow | " " |
| Orange with violet | inclines to yellow. |
| Violet with orange | " blue. |
| Orange with purple | " yellow. |
| Purple with orange | " blue. |
| Yellow with green | " orange. |
| Green with yellow | " blue-green. |
| Yellow with turquoise | " orange. |
| Turquoise with yellow | " blue. |
| Yellow with blue | becomes more brilliant. |
| Blue with yellow | " " |
| Green with blue | inclines to yellow-green |
| Blue with green | " violet. |
| Green with violet | " yellow-green |
| Violet with green | " purple. |

| PAIRS OF COLORS. | | CHANGE DUE TO SIMULTANEOUS CONTRAST. |
|---|---|---|
| Green with purple | . . . . . | becomes more brilliant. |
| Purple with green | . . . . . | " " |
| Blue with violet | . . . . . . | inclines to green. |
| Violet with blue | . . . . . . | " purple. |
| Violet with purple | . . . . . | " blue. |
| Purple with violet | . . . . . | " red. |

"It must not be imagined that the changes enumerated in the above table are at all equal to one another in amount. We have, indeed, always some change, but it varies much in the case of different pairs. When the chromatic interval (on the color-circle) is small, then the change of *hue*, in virtue of simultaneous contrast, is large; when the interval is large the change of hue is slight, but it is accompanied by change of brightness; when the interval is as large as possible there is no change of hue, but the brightness of both hues is increased."

After simultaneous contrasts Chevreul gives us successive contrasts, which latter "may be observed when we tire one set of retinal fibrils by gazing for some time on a surface of a very decided color and brightness. Afterward, on looking at a colorless surface of white, gray, or black, it will be found to be tinctured with the complementary of the first color." If we stare at a piece of bright red paper and then look at white paper we will see blue-green, the complement of the red. So, if we look at a series of pieces of red cloth the first will appear the brightest, the second less so, the third still less, but if the eye is rested by looking at a piece of bluish-green cloth the red will then be seen of its original brightness. When a black spot laid on red cloth is looked at steadily for some time, then is taken suddenly away, the place where the black spot was will appear to be of a brighter red than that around it on account of the less fatigue there has been to that part of the retina. A salesman who understood complementary colors could use this law of successive contrasts with great effect in showing goods.

Still another form of contrast is called *mixed contrast.* "The distinction of simultaneous and successive contrast renders it easy to comprehend a phenomenon which we may call mixed contrast; because it results from the fact that the eye, having seen for a time a certain color, acquires an aptitude to see for another period the complementary of that color and also a new color, presented to it by an exterior object; the sensation then perceived is that which results from this new color and the complementary of the first. The following is a very simple method of observing this mixed contrast: One eye being closed, the right for instance, let the left eye regard fixedly a piece of paper of the color A; when this color appears dimmed, immediately direct the eye upon a sheet of paper colored B; then we have the impression which results from the mixture of this color B with the complementary color, C, of the color A. To be satisfied of this mixed impression it is sufficient to close the left eye, and to look at the color B with the right: not only is the impression that produced by the color B, but it may appear modified in a direction contrary to the mixed impression C+B, or, what comes to the same thing, it appears to be more A+B."[1]

That the complementary of a color exists in its shadow may be seen by watching a stretch of snow when the sun is hidden by a cloud: the snow is white, the shadow gray. When the cloud passes away, the light on the snow makes it look yellow; the shadow will also be seen to be more or less blue as the atmosphere is more or less clear and free from the moisture which veils the sunlight. The same result in a greater or less degree exists in all shadows, which shows how useful study of the complementary colors is for painters.

The purple or violet shadows of the "impressionists" are in many cases exaggerations. On snow, dust, or sand, violet shadows are to be found

[1] Chevreul.

in certain conditions of the atmosphere, but "impressionists" often do not seem to take into sufficient account the color called by artists "local color" of the substance or material on which the shadow is thrown, or the color of the sky reflected in the shadow. A true colorist detects these subtle varieties. An artist who has not a fine eye for color uses the pure colors given by scientists, thus making the crude, harsh pictures so much criticised. They are true to a great extent scientifically, but are cold and glaring, and without the true spirit of nature.

In studying the complements of these six spectral hues we come across the theory that because a color and its complement together make white, therefore they must prove to be an agreeable harmony. Now, is that true? At first sight we answer, No. We do know that if we wish to make a color as brilliant as possible, we must add to it its complement. Under certain circumstances that may give us a good result, but artistic taste declares that a pure spectral color and its complement make a combination so strong and vivid as almost to amount to crudeness, and to jar on a sensitive eye. Still, the theory that complementary colors make a true and perfect harmony is well considered in the following extract from Eastlake:

"Every treatise on the harmonious combination of colors contains the diagram of the chromatic circle more or less elaborately constructed. These diagrams, if intended to exhibit the contrasts produced by the action and reaction of the retina, have one common defect. The opposite colors are made equal in intensity; whereas the complemental color pictured on the retina is always less vivid, and always darker or lighter than the original color. This variety undoubtedly accords more with harmonious effects in painting.

"The opposition of two pure hues of equal intensity, differing only in the abstract quality of color, would immediately be pronounced crude and inharmonious. It would not, however, be strictly correct to say that such a contrast is too violent; on the contrary, it appears the contrast is not carried far enough, for though differing in color, the two hues may be exactly similar in purity and intensity. Complete contrast, on the other hand, supposes dissimilarity in all respects. In addition to the mere difference of hue, the eye, it seems, requires difference in the lightness or darkness of the hue. The spectrum of a color relieved as a dark on a light ground is a light color on a dark ground, and *vice versa*. Thus, if we look at a bright red wafer on the whitish surface, the complemental image will be still lighter than the white surface; if the same wafer is placed on a black surface the complemental image will be still darker. The color of both these spectra may be called greenish (bluish-green), but it is evident that a color must be scarcely appreciable as such, if it is lighter than white and darker than black. It is, however, to be remarked, that the white surface round the light greenish image seems tinged with a reddish hue, and the black surface round the dark image becomes slightly illuminated with the same color, thus in both cases assisting to render the image apparent.

"The difficulty or impossibility of describing degrees of color in words has also had a tendency to mislead, by conveying the idea of more positive hues than the physiological contrast warrants. Thus, supposing scarlet to be relieved as a dark, the complemental color is so light in degree and so faint in color that it should be called a pearly gray; whereas the theorists, looking at the quality of color abstractedly, would call it a green-blue, and the diagram would falsely present such a hue equal in intensity to scarlet, or as nearly equal as possible.

"Even the difference of mass which good taste requires may be suggested by the physiological phenomena, for unless the complemental image is suffered to fall on a surface precisely as near to the eye as that on which the original color was displayed, it appears larger or smaller than the original object, and this in a rapidly increasing proportion. Lastly, the shape itself soon becomes changed. That vivid color demands the comparative absence of color, either on a lighter or darker scale, as its contrast, may be inferred again from the fact that bright colorless objects produce strongly colored spectra. In darkness the spectrum, which is first white, or nearly white, is followed by red; in light, the spectrum, which is first black, is followed by green. All color, as the author observes, is to be considered as half light, inasmuch as it is in every case lighter than black and darker than white. Hence no contrast of color with color, or even of color with black or white, can be so great (as regards lightness or darkness) as the contrast of black and white, or dark and light abstractedly. This distinction between the differences of degree and the differences of kind is important, since a just application of contrast in color may be counteracted by an undue difference in lightness or darkness. The mere contrast of color is happily employed in some of Guido's lighter pictures, but if intense dark had been opposed to his delicate carnations, their comparative whiteness would have been unpleasantly apparent. On the other hand, the flesh-color in

Giorgione, Sebastian del Piombo (his best imitator), and Titian, was sometimes so extremely glowing that the deepest colors and black were indispensable accompaniments. The manner of Titian, as distinguished from his imitation of Giorgione, is golden rather than fiery, and his biographers are quite correct in saying that he was fond of opposing red (lake) and blue to his flesh. The correspondence of these contrasts with the physiological phenomena will be immediately apparent, while the occasional practice of Rubens in opposing bright red to a still cooler flesh-color will be seen to be equally consistent. . . .

"It was before observed that the description of colors in words may often convey ideas of too positive a nature, and it may be remarked generally that the colors employed by the great masters are, in their ultimate effect, more or less subdued or broken. The physiological contrasts are, however, still applicable in the most comparatively neutral scale."

Chevreul gives us in his book, *Colour* (a work published in 1835, which has gone through many editions and translations, having finally been edited and republished in 1889 by his son), an elaborate system of color contrasts based upon the older theory of three primary colors, red, yellow, and blue. There followed upon this in 1890 one by Charles La Couture, *Répertoire Chromatique*, containing an ingenious and beautiful system of color scales also founded upon the Brewster theory of red, yellow, and blue as primary colors. Of these color charts it has been well said that they are only able to display the effects, not of mixing colored light, but colored pigments.

The following are rules to be used in regard to contrasting colors:

*Rule I.* — A pair of complementary colors in their pure spectral tones in the proportions in which they neutralize or complement each other, as in Plates XXII to XXVI, should only be used if you wish to produce a bold, striking, perhaps harsh effect; or if you wish to create a focus in your picture, your room, or your decoration. In the latter case it will be well to soften the effect (especially in the case of a picture) by repeating the same colors in tints or shades in some other part of the work.

*Rule II.* — Harmony of contrast exists only in proportion to the changes in quality or quantity in equal portions of pure spectral tones.

*Rule III.* — The more neutral you make the tint or shade of one of the pair of complements, so much the more may you add to its quantity. For instance, a small quantity of bright spectral red will balance a large quantity of pale blue-green.

*Rule IV.* — By using two or more tints, or shades and tints, of one of the pair of complements, so much the finer becomes the harmony. The artist Turner sent to an exhibition of the Royal Academy in England a marine which was accepted and hung, but which, being a quiet picture consisting mainly of pale, grayish sea-greens, attracted little attention. On varnishing day, however, he went to the Academy and painted in the foreground of his picture a scarlet buoy, when to the surprise of every one, owing to the correct balance of the quality and quantity of his complementary contrast, the scarlet and blue green so intensified each other that the picture became a striking one, dulling the others around it and drawing constant admiration.

From a dinner table set out at a flower show in the Madison Square Garden, which took a first prize, Plate XXXI is taken. It was a harmony of yellow and blue.

1. Yellow chrysanthemums.
2. Yellow lamp-shades.
3. Yellow satin centrepiece.
4. Yellow candies.
5. Yellow candies.
6. Yellow candies.
7. Yellow-brown almonds.

8. Gold ornament on glass, china, and candies.
9. Dark purple-blue grapes.

In this case some of the yellow was in pure spectral tones, the blue very strong, dark, and neutralized.

*Rule VI.* — The finest harmony of contrast will be found where tints and shades of both the pair of complements can be combined. Then a small amount of both in spectral tones may be introduced to give accent to the rest. Plate XXXII gives a blue and yellow harmony taken from an English china cup composed of two blues and two yellows, both neutral. The ground, being of a pale tint of yellow, is greater in quantity according to Rule III. The dainty pattern painted on it is in the two blues; the delicate stems holding and uniting the conventional leaves and flowers are of brown (or dark yellow). The brown, being the darkest color, is the smallest in quantity, as the harmony is intended to be light and cheerful.

Harmonies in blue and yellow have been used with great success in old decoration, when blended, modified, and interchanged with each other, and are one of the most useful combinations of colors that can be made. They are largely used in Italian and Spanish tiles and other porcelains. They are complementary colors strongly opposed to each other, but the reason for their being more agreeable than other pairs of complements seems to arise from the fact that one, the yellow, is so much more luminous (or lighter) than the other that it affords a greater contrast than appears in the other pairs of complements.

*Rule VII.* — Even pure spectral colors may be used with good effect by blending them in small portions, as in what are technically called diaper patterns.

We have still a further power of adding to our harmony of contrasts by the use of different materials, such as paper, paint, plaster, silk, satin, velvet, plush, and metals, in which the variety of surfaces gives an infinite number of tones, absorbing and reflecting, etc. These will be considered in the chapter on color-harmonies, and seem really inexhaustible. In that chapter is given a list of pairs of the lesser contrasting colors, such as have been found by observation of historic color to be the most agreeable to the eye.

---

*Note.* — As a transparent screen colored like Plate XXIX. could not well be made, Plate XXX. has been added. It represents the same color circle as Plate XXIX. except that the colors are only given by name. The reader is to suppose that Plate XXX. and the celluloid screen at the end of the book are the same as Plate XXIX. and then follow the directions for use given on page 58.

# CHAPTER V

## COLOR–HARMONIES

### HARMONIES OF COMPLEX OR VARIOUS COLORS

IT is said that the use of agreeable and harmonious colors tends to the sanity of the whole body by strengthening the nerves; so much so, that part of the treatment of insane patients in a European asylum consists in surrounding them with certain colors, and, probably, of changing these according to certain rules. From these facts we surely learn that there is reason beyond that of our mere enjoyment of colors to lead us to study color harmonies.

The most widely accepted division of these harmonies is that of Chevreul, who in his life of over one hundred years had time to formulate, revise, and amplify his laws of color, and, from his position as director of the manufacture of the Gobelin tapestries, great opportunities for experiment. The two chief groups, based respectively on analogy and on contrast, are resolved into three subdivisions each. These are quoted as follows from Church, who has added some explanations to them as given in *The Law of Simultaneous Contrast:*

"I. — HARMONIES OF ANALOGY.
"II. — HARMONIES OF CONTRAST.

"1. *The Harmony of Analogy of Scale.* — This harmony is essentially that of a series, the harmony of gradation. It includes those cases in which is presented a simultaneous view of three or more tones of the same scale, whether these tones be tints, or shades, or broken tones. It is obtained in various degrees of perfection, according to the number of tones present, and the value of the intervals between them. When the tones are not easily separable by the eye, and pass into one another, then the effect called 'shading' is produced.

"2. *The Harmony of Analogy of Tones.* — When two or more tones of the same depth, or of very nearly the same depth, but belonging to different but related or neighboring scales, are viewed together, the harmony of tone is produced. Many such assortments are, however, displeasing to the educated eye, unless the tones be so selected as to fall into a series with a gradually increasing quantity of some one of their color elements, when they may be arranged in the third kind of harmonies of analogy.

"3. *The Harmony of a Dominant Hue.* — An example of this harmony is afforded by viewing a contrasted color assortment, a bouquet of flowers, or even a landscape, through a piece of glass so slightly tinctured with a color as not to obliterate, but merely to modify, the various colors belonging to the arrangement or composition.

"1. *The Harmony of Contrast of Scale* is produced by the simultaneous view of two or more distant tones of the same scale.

"2. *The Harmony of Contrast of Tones* is produced by the simultaneous view of two or more tones of different depths belonging to neighboring or related scales.

"3. *The Harmony of Contrast of Hue* is produced by the simultaneous view of colors belonging to distant scales, and assorted in accordance with the laws of contrast. This kind of contrast includes also those cases in which the effect is still further enhanced by difference of tone as well as of color.

"The distinction between these two classes or groups of harmonies is somewhat arbitrary, for the collocation of any two tones or any two colors, whether its results be agreeable or otherwise, inevitably involves the element of contrast. Color-harmonies, so far as contrast is concerned, differ in degree and complexity, but Chevreul's harmonies of analogy pass by steps more or less marked into distinct and undoubted harmonies of contrast. In every harmony there is contrast of tone or of color, and therefore contrast cannot be employed as a criterion of classification. The two fundamental ideas underlying complex color-harmonies may perhaps be expressed as those of *gradual change* and of *abrupt change*. Instead of separating color-harmonies into two distinct groups, it would be better to arrange them in order upon the arc of a circle, placing at one extremity those harmonies on which the succession of contiguous tones or hues is marked by the smallest differences, and at the other extremity, those harmonies in which the elements of contrast are most strongly developed. About the middle of the arc will be arranged those transitional harmonies in which contrasts of tone, contrasts of color, and contrasts of tone and color combined, begin to make themselves felt as modifying the effect of the regular sequence of tones and related hues. According to this scheme, we may commence with harmonies in which the succession of tones is so gentle as to be barely perceptible, and we may end with those harmonies in which the change of hue and of tone is most abrupt. A list of illustrative examples will help to elucidate the scheme:

"1. The passage, by insensible differences, of the tints, shades, or broken tones of a single hue from light to dark.

"2. The passage, by small but regular, definite,

and perceptible steps, of the tints, shades, or broken tones of a single hue from light to dark.

"3. The passage, as in the preceding example (2), of the tones of one hue, from light to dark, when each step is separated by a neutral element, such as white, gray, or black.

"4. The passage, by insensible differences, of one hue, or of the tones of one hue into another related hue, or its tones.

"5. The passage, by definite steps, of one hue, or of the tones of one hue, into another related hue or its tones.

"6. The passage, as above (5), of related hues into each other, each step separated by a neutral element.

"7. The passage, by insensible differences, of one hue into another chromatically remote hue.

"8. The passage, by definite steps, of one hue into another chromatically remote hue.

"9. The passage, as above (8), of one hue into another, when each step is separated by a neutral element.

"10. The collocation of distant tones.

"11. The collocation of chromatically distant hues with or without the interposition of neutral elements.

"It will be noticed how the idea of seriation or gradation becomes more and more involved with that of change as we follow the sequence of the above examples. Gradually the notion of orderly succession, of a regular series with the presence of a pervading and dominant constituent, is lost by the abruptness of change caused by the introduction of foreign elements, or by the contiguity of distant tones and distant hues."

As both of these sets of rules for harmonies of colors are so elaborate as to amount almost to color charts, and would be difficult and complicated to print in colors, for our practical purpose we will roughly divide harmonies of colors under three heads; as follows (See Plate XXXIII):

Harmonies of one color.
Harmonies of contrast (of color).
Harmonies of complex or various colors.

This division is not strictly correct, because even in a harmony of one color the element of contrast will appear; as, for instance, when we combine a pale tint of yellow, say straw color, with brown, which is a dark shade of yellow. As, however, in this case it is contrast of tone, not contrast of color, we will not let that interfere with the order of our arbitrary classification. The first class, harmonies of one color, have been considered in Chapter III. When simple, refined color is wanted in either dress or decoration, or where from inexperience one is afraid to combine colors, it is best and safest to use this simplest kind of color harmony. With this class, as black and white are not colors, we will also include harmonies of one color combined with black, or white, or gray, or two or all three of these. From a book advertisement most successful in its clear, simple, and agreeable character we give Plate XXXIV. It was on white paper, the proportions as follows: Most white, less black, least yellow, this latter always outlined with black. The white also showed through the yellow in some places and served to lighten the design.

In decoration, when two tones of one color are used they are often separated with a fine line of white or black or gray. In Plate XXXV the useful effect of such a line of separation is shown. A light tint on a dark shade does not so much need an outline, but a dark shade on a light tint is much improved by white outlines. The white line increases the apparent strength of both tint and shade, while black will increase their brightness but diminish their purity.

"In the consideration of the specific effects of the association of white, gray, or black with a single color, we follow the order in which the colors succeed each other in the spectrum, adding purple at the end.

"1. Red. — *Red* with *white* becomes deeper, more saturated or purer, and less bright. The combination, as to intensity of contrast, is similar to that of green with white, being less than that of blue, violet, or purple with white, but more marked than that of orange or yellow with white.

"*Red* with *gray*, when the latter is moderately pale, becomes brighter and less saturated, sometimes acquiring an orange tinge.

"2. Orange. — *Orange* with *white* is rendered deeper, and perhaps a trifle more reddish. The contrast of tone between orange and white is much greater than that between yellow and white; the combination is consequently more effective.

"*Orange* with *gray*, when the latter is pale, is deepened and reddened. With dark tones of gray orange becomes lighter.

"*Orange* with *black* becomes brighter and slightly yellower.

"3. Yellow. — *Yellow* with *white* is rendered deeper, less bright, and less advancing, acquiring a slight greenish hue. The lighter the tone of the yellow the less pleasing is the combination.

"*Yellow* with *gray* is rendered brighter and perhaps slightly orange. The combination is satisfactory when the gray is rather dark.

"*Yellow* with *black* is rendered paler, brighter, and more advancing. The combination affords the most intense contrast of tone next to that of white with black. The blackness of the black is modified by acquiring a slight bluish hue which enriches it.

"4. GREEN. — *Green* with *white* becomes deeper and purer; the combination is capable of yielding very beautiful effects.

"*Green* with *gray* becomes deeper only when the gray is pale; if the gray be at all dark it acquires a purplish tinge.

"*Green* with *black* is rendered brighter and paler, while the black suffers, being tinged with a reddish or purplish hue.

"5. BLUE. — *Blue* with *white* constitutes a generally pleasing combination. The contrast of tone is very decided when the blue is at once pure and bright. The effect of strongly illuminated white clouds in deepening the tone of the blue of the sky bordering them is a good example of one of the chief characteristics of this combination; under such conditions the white often assumes a slightly yellowish tint.

"*Blue* with *gray*. Gray, if pale, deepens and purifies blue; the combination, though necessarily cold, is often most serviceable in pictorial as well as in ornamental art.

"*Blue* with *black*. This combination is less agreeable than that of blue with gray, or of violet with black, especially when the tone of the blue is deep. Light tones of blue are made still paler, but broken tones more saturated, by contiguity with black.

"6. VIOLET. — *Violet* with *white* affords a strong contrast of tone; the combination is an agreeable one, resembling that of blue with white.

"*Violet* with *gray*. The distinctive hue of violet makes itself felt strongly in this combination, which is a quiet and agreeable one.

"*Violet* with *black* gives but a slight contrast of tone when the violet is pure. The black acquires a rusty brown hue, which reduces its depth.

"7. PURPLE. — *Purple* with *white* affords a good contrast of tone. Pale purples and rosy tints form agreeable combinations with white.

"*Purple* with *gray* resembles in effect the combination of violet with gray; the gray, if of moderate area, becomes decidedly greenish.

"*Purple* with *black* is rarely a satisfactory combination; the black acquires a greenish hue."[1]

The second class, harmonies of contrast, have been studied in Chapter IV. Where bold, striking, emphatic color is needed the complementary colors may be used. The most prominent part of a picture, a room, or a decoration will be, as far as color is concerned, where some color and its com-

[1] COLOUR. By A. H. Church. Ch. X., p 116.

plement in nearly, or quite, spectral hues are given. This striking effect of contrast will lessen accordingly as the colors darken into shades, or lighten into tints, or become more and more neutral from the mixture with some other color. An eye untrained or inexperienced will find these complementary contrasts difficult to use, there being danger of producing a crude or harsh effect. Rules for their use are given in Chapter IV. Classifying the complementary pairs according to the pleasure we take in them we may put yellow and blue first, then orange and green-blue, red and blue-green, finally violet and green. Chevreul, Rood, Von Bezold, and Bruecke, having made many experiments and observations in their attempts to lay down rules for harmonious combinations, state that here we come upon problems that cannot be solved by purely scientific reasoning. By comparing the art of one country or of one period of one country with that of another, we find that throughout them all, certain pairs of colors have been preferred to certain others and we feel that æsthetic taste, which cannot be explained, influences us greatly in our liking for certain combinations. Beside taste, inheritance, training, environment, and contrast all have their unconscious effect upon these preferences. Church divides pairs of colors into three classes: Pairs of the small intervals, pairs of decided differences, and the extremes or complements. The latter we have considered in Chapter IV. Pairs of the small intervals are such as

> Orange-red and yellowish-orange,
> Reddish-orange and orange-yellow,
> Orange and yellow,

which, being so close to each other in the color scale in decoration, are apt to injure each other unless separated by outlines of black, white, gray, or gold. Rood gives the following table of small intervals:

| "DARKER. | LIGHTER. |
|---|---|
| Red | Orange-red. |
| Orange-red | Orange. |
| Orange | Orange-yellow. |
| Orange-yellow | Yellow. |
| Yellowish-green | Greenish-yellow. |
| Green | Yellowish-green. |
| Cyan-blue | Green. |
| Blue | Cyan-blue. |
| Ultramarine-blue | Blue. |
| Violet | Purple. |
| Purple | Red." |

Church gives us the following list of pairs as, from his and others' observations, they have been found to have been more or less agreeable:

"An asterisk attached to the name of a color

indicates that the mixture of gray or black with it improves the effect of its association. It may be further remarked that in many cases where two colors of full depth yield a bad or unsatisfactory assortment the reduction of the tone of one of them by a considerable addition of white often makes the combination agreeable.

| | | | |
|---|---|---|---|
| "Normal red | with | violet . . . . . | bad. |
| " " | " | blue . . . . . | excellent. |
| " " | " | blue-green . . . | good, but strong. |
| " " | " | green . . . . . . | good, but hard. |
| " " | " | green-yellow . . . | fair. |
| " " | " | yellow * . . . . | unpleasing. |
| Scarlet | " | violet . . . . | bad. |
| " | " | turquoise . . . . | good. |
| " | " | blue . . . . . . | good. |
| " | " | yellow . . . | unpleasing. |
| " | " | green . . . . | fair. |
| Orange-red | " | violet . . . . . | good. |
| " " | " | purple . . . . . | fair. |
| " " | " | blue . . . . | excellent. |
| " " | " | turquoise . . . . | good. |
| " " | " | blue-green . . | unpleasing. |
| " " | " | yellow-green . . | fair. |
| Orange | " | purple . . . . . | bad. |
| " | " | violet . . . . . . | good. |
| " | " | blue . . . . . . | good, but strong. |
| " | " | turquoise . . | good. |
| " | " | blue-green . . . | good. |
| " | " | green . . . . . . | fair. |
| Orange-yellow | " | purple . . . . . | good. |
| " " | " | violet . . . . | excellent. |

| | | | |
|---|---|---|---|
| Orange-yellow | with | blue | good. |
| " " | " | turquoise | fair. |
| " " | " | blue-green | moderate. |
| " " | " | green | bad. |
| Yellow | " | violet | excellent. |
| " | " | purple | good. |
| " | " | normal red | poor. |
| " | " | turquoise | moderate. |
| " | " | blue-green * | bad. |
| " | " | green * | bad. |
| Greenish-yellow | " | purple | good. |
| " " | " | violet | excellent. |
| " " | " | scarlet | strong, and hard. |
| " " | " | orange-red | fair. |
| " " | " | turquoise | bad. |
| " " | " | normal blue | good. |
| Yellowish-green | " | normal red | good, but hard. |
| " " | " | purple | difficult. |
| " " | " | blue-green | bad. |
| " " | " | blue | good. |
| Normal green | " | purple | strong, but hard. |
| " " | " | scarlet | difficult. |
| " " | " | orange-red | hard. |
| " " | " | turquoise | bad. |
| Blue-green | " | purple | fair. |
| " " | " | violet | good. |
| " " | " | blue | bad. |
| " " | " | green | bad. |
| " " | " | yellowish-green | bad. |
| " " | " | turquoise | bad. |

"The above list comprises fifty-five only of the very numerous combinations, in pairs, of some of the decided hues. . . . It is assumed that in our experiments on their chromatic effects, pleasing or otherwise, we have been using colored materials, which neither by any peculiarity of texture, nor quality, nor design, are capable of improving the results. Cloth and paper are suitable; silk, velvet, glass, and enamel, for various reasons, give results which are complicated by the introduction of new elements. Pairs in these latter materials, in consequence of the presence of lustre, translucency, or 'throbbing' hues, in varying degrees, will often become quite acceptable, while in prosaic cloth, or paper, they are just the reverse."

The third class, harmonies of complex or various colors, follows, and includes groups of three or more colors. The difficulties of combination increase as the number of colors increases. It is well to remember, if one is bewildered with these difficulties, that, however fine the harmony of many colors may be, it can hardly surpass the beauty of one made of but two or three, provided that these are well proportioned to each other in quantity and quality, suited to and combined in some good design, or made up of various materials with differing surfaces. As to triads, or three-color combinations, Rood gives us the following groups as having been most extensively used, and if we draw on our memory we may probably recall both paintings and decorations consisting of any one of these combinations. (See Plates XXXVI and XXXVII.)

> Spectral red, yellow, and blue.
> Purple-red, yellow, cyan-blue (greenish-blue like a turquoise).
> Orange, green, violet.
> Orange, green, purple-violet.

With regard to these he calls our attention to the fact that in them the colors are nearly, or quite, 120° apart on the chromatic circle, also that artists in their choice of these colors have been evidently guided by their wish to have two out of three warm colors. According to Bruecke:

*Carmine, yellow,* and *green,* a favorite combination during the middle ages, to us seems "somewhat hard and unrefined."

*Orange-yellow, violet,* and *bluish-green* are not so agreeable because two of the colors are cold. In the triad *vermilion, green,* and *violet-blue,* used greatly by the Italian schools, there seem at first to be two cold colors, but as the *green* was *olive* it might be called *vermilion, dark greenish-yellow,* and *violet-blue.*

Attempts have been made to give formulas of certain colors as they are supposed properly to balance one another, or to make "chromatic equivalents." Field elaborated this theory in his *Chromatography*, and it was adopted by Owen Jones in his *Grammar of Ornament*. Later writers on color, however, show that Field's experiments were not such as to justify his conclusions. The leading idea he tried to prove was, that to make a perfect harmony, each color in a given picture or design should bear such a mathematical relation to the whole that the combination of all should make, when seen at a distance, "a neutralized bloom, or a whitish-gray." He speaks, for instance, of red, yellow, and blue. This has a plausible sound, but cannot be correct, for with a color-wheel we find that red, yellow, and blue will not in *any* proportions make a "whitish-gray," also because almost all of the best works of good colorists have throughout them some dominant hue, more generally on the warm side, such as yellow, orange, or red. At the same time careful study of texture will be very useful, as different weaves reflect and absorb the colors so as to produce a sort of "neutralized bloom," such as Field speaks of.

That chromatic equivalents can be made is shown by Maxwell's disks; as, for instance, Church gives us the proportions of three colors which on being turned on the wheel rapidly produce a neutral gray, as follows:

"Red $36\frac{1}{2}$ + green $33\frac{3}{4}$ + blue $29\frac{3}{4} = 100$."

We have also already seen in the chapter on Contrasts that certain parts of one color require certain parts of another color to neutralize it and so make gray.

As there is no end to the possible combinations of colors we can only give certain rules for making them, leaving it to the student to follow up his previous practice with two colors and by experience to enlarge his knowledge and ability to use all colors with skill.

A full harmony, in fact a symphony, of colors can hardly be better explained than by describing one used in the trial scene in the "Merchant of Venice," as given by Mr. Mansfield. The tribune or desk behind which Portia delivered her speech was white, draped with a full-hued scarlet cloth. The black of her gown, the strongest contrast to white, and the brilliant red, were admirably used to focus the eye upon this part of the scene just as the ear was focused on the speech "The quality of mercy is not strained." The other principal actors, Shylock, Antonio, and Bassanio, wore red, yellow, blue; bright colors, but less bright and less contrasting than the white, black, and scarlet. The attendants and spectators were in more neutral and subdued colors, while away behind them all stretched a grayish blue sky seen between the pillars of a wide porch which formed a background well calculated to throw into relief the colors of the costumes.

From what we have learned we find the following ways of harmonizing colors:

*First.* BY GRADATION, that is, the gradual blending of one color into another, or one variety of one color into another variety of the same color, as in the morning-glory blossom, in which the different hues grade softly into one another from edge to heart; or as in a clear sunset sky, where the blue above changes into green, the green into yellow, and the yellow into red near the horizon, and where still we cannot find the exact boundary of any one of the colors. (See Plate XXXVIII.)

"These ever-present gentle changes of color in all natural objects give to the mind a sense of the richness and vastness of the resources of Nature; there is always something more to see, some new evanescent series of delicate tints to trace; and, even where there is no conscious study of color, it still produces its effect on the mind of the beholder, giving him the sense of the fulness of Nature, and a dim perception of the infinite series of gentle changes by which she constantly varies the aspects of the commonest objects. This orderly succession of tints, gently blending into one another, is one of the greatest sources of beauty that we are acquainted with, and the best artists constantly strive to introduce more and more of this element into their works, relying for their triumphs far more on gradation than on contrast. The greatest effects in oratory are also produced by corresponding means; it is the modulation of the tone and thought, far more than sharp contrasts, that is effective in deeply moving audiences. We are very sensitive to the matter of modulation even in ordinary speech, and instantly form a general judgment with regard to the degree of cultivation and refinement of a stranger from the mode in which a few words are pronounced. All this has its parallel in the use of color, not only in painting, but also in decoration. Ruskin, speaking of gradation of color, says: 'You will find in practice that brilliancy of hue and vigor of light, and even the aspect of transparency in shade, are essentially dependent on this character alone; hardness, coldness, and opacity resulting far more from *equality* of color than from nature of color.' In another place the same author, in giving advice to a beginner, says: 'And it does not matter how small the touch of color may be, though not larger than the smallest pin's head, if one part of it is not darker than the rest, it is a bad touch; for it is not merely because the natural fact is so that your color should be gradated; the preciousness and pleasantness of color depends more on this than on any other of its qualities, for gradation is to colors just what curvature is to lines, both being felt to be beautiful by the pure instinct of every human mind, and both, considered as types, expressing the law of gradual change and progress in the human soul itself. What the difference is in mere beauty between a gradated and ungradated color may be seen easily by laying an even tint of rose-color on paper, and putting a rose-leaf beside it. The victorious beauty of the rose as compared with other flowers depends wholly on the delicacy and quantity of its color-gradations, all other flowers being either less rich in gradation, not having so many folds of leaf, or less tender, being patched and veined instead of flushed.' "[1]

In connection with gradation, Church says: "There is one *quality* of good color which lies at the very root of all successful employment of vivid hues. It consists in minute variations of hue and tone within the same surface. A color must not be absolutely uniform, flat, and monotonous unless it be very pale, very dull, or very dark, when the absence of this 'throbbing' or 'palpitating' quality, though undesirable, is less observed. We

[1] Modern Chromatics. By Prof. O. N. Rood. Ch. XVI.

have before us, as we write, a fine old Chinese vase of turquoise crackle. Apart from the mosaic texture, resulting from the innumerable fissures in the glaze, what a number of variations in appearance does this turquoise color offer! Where the color is thinnest it is paler, and verges more upon green; where it is thickest, it is at once deeper, and more blue, and there are innumerable hues and tones. In painting, similar effects may be produced by unequal glazings and scumblings of one hue upon another, or by apposition of minute dots and patches of closely related colors."[1]

The following is a practical way of using this beauty of gradation: "For instance, in the morning glory and the sweet pea we may observe a perfectly beautiful combination of crimson, purple, and violet. Notice the charming gradation of color in the morning glory; one tone runs into the other with a subtlety which is quite wonderful, and all the colors merge into the luminous green white centre from absolute positivism to perfect delicacy with an ease which is surprising. Now let us try to mass a large group of crimson, purple, violet, and greenish-white asters together with the same result. Alas! what a task it is and how confused we become with the distracting color tones; but we must feel our way carefully and systematically. First, our most powerful color —

[1] COLOUR. By A. H. Church. Ch. XI., p. 144.

crimson or violet — must be grouped gracefully and placed in a prominent position; next, we must run our color tone either toward blue or crimson, as the case may be. If we have any gas-light near we must make use of it to accent our prominent group, and last, mingled slightly with the palest tones of dull pink and purplish-blue, we may group our greenish-white asters in some position where they will contrast well with the strong color group, and where they will be sure to have the intermediate blue and crimson tones act like a bridge to connect the color scheme. Nothing distracts the eye so much as violent transitions of color."[1]

A similar element of beauty in Oriental rugs, not always understood, and one in which they differ from those made by machinery, arises from the fact that being made by hand there are slight variations throughout, even in the dyeing of the wools. In an unusually fine specimen the rich green ground varied slightly in tone three or four times. To an uncultivated eye this might seem a defect; to an artistic one, the play of color, the variety in unity, is far finer than the even monotony of a perfectly matched surface.

*Second.* By Change of Quality; as from pure spectral colors to their tints or shades. The

[1] F. Schuyler Matthews.

greater we make this change either way, the more sure we may be of harmony, as a color scheme of very pale tints or very dark shades is almost sure to be good even if quite varied. In fact, contrast of tone, which is change of quality, will harmonize any two colors, as pale blue and dark green, or pale green and dark blue. Of pairs of contrasts which in pure spectral colors we have seen to be crude and harsh, Rood says, "Complementary colors are very valuable when the artist is obliged to use dark, dull, or pale colors, and still is desirous of obtaining a strong or brilliant effect." Another kind of change of quality helps us to make very beautiful combinations. It lies in the use of colors that are neither spectral, nor pure tints, nor shades, but of such as are neutralized by mixtures of other colors; as, for instance, if instead of using pure yellow, pure red, and pure blue, we use a yellow toned down by an admixture of a little red and blue, a red toned in the same way with blue and yellow, and a blue that has in it something of red and yellow; the colors will still be yellow, red, and blue, but in approaching each other will become more related and so far more harmonious. Still another change of quality allows us to put in the place of one or more of the colors the same amount of a tint or a shade of the same color which will improve the harmony by varying its luminosity and by bringing all nearer together. (See Plate XXXIX.)

*Third.* BY CHANGE OF QUANTITY; as of a large amount of one of the colors to a small amount of the other, so as to introduce another element of contrast. For want of the better balance as given by the fourth rule it is inferior to it. (See Plate XL.)

*Fourth.* BY CHANGE OF QUALITY AND QUANTITY; or by making a small amount of a dark shade of one color balance a much larger amount of a light tint of another color, or, *vice versa*, a small amount of a light tint to balance a much larger amount of a dark shade, or a small amount of a pure color to balance a large amount of a more neutral color. In this case the rule is that accordingly as you lower or raise the quality of your color so in proportion may you increase its quantity. (See Plate XLI.)

*Fifth.* BY THE ADDITION OF ANOTHER COLOR, however unobtrusive, which breaks the even balance between two colors, just as in form, where we may find two trees of the same size and shape make an unpleasant composition. There the effect can be much improved by the addition of a third tree of a different size and shape. For instance, with yellow and yellowish-green, the addition of violet would improve and harmonize them. This third color can be added in different ways, by outlines, small masses, etc. (See Plate XLII.)

*Sixth.* BY THE ADDITION OF BLACK, WHITE, GRAY, GOLD, OR SILVER. — When two colors are not quite harmonious a small quantity of black will much improve the combination. The strong contrast in depth between the black and the colors seems to bring them together and so make them more related. In Chinese coloring the happy effect of black should be noted, also in old Japanese prints where the black hair of the figures acts in the same way. This black, white, gray, gold, or silver may be added in outlines, as the brass in Japanese cloisonné, or in such lines as these | | | | | | | | drawn over the whole design, as seen in a wall paper, softening the colors and blending them with each other. It may be as in cement around and between the little bits of stone in mosaic, which produces much the same effect in throwing a sort of bloom over the colors. It may be in separating some part of the design from the other, as seen in a wall decoration where there was a rectangle of greenish-blue on a ground of dark violet-blue separated by white and gold, of which the result was excellent; or it may be by little dots over all the colors. (See Plate XLIII.)

*Seventh.* BY A DOMINANT HUE, which may run through all the design in outlines, although colored outlines are not so good as those of black, white, gray, gold, or silver, or those which may be added in small spots over all the colors ; or those which may be added in small quantities to all the colors, changing their quality, and so bringing them to a harmony of a dominant hue. To make this clear, look at Plate VI. In it we have pure spectral yellow, pure spectral blue, and pure spectral red. Put over it the blue screen found in the end of the book ; the blue will be seen to be bluer, the yellow will become a greenish-yellow, the red will have a violet tinge to it. It will have become a harmony of the dominant hue of blue, but as blue is a cold color the harmony will not have become much more agreeable for the change. Try what making the same colors a harmony of the dominant hue of yellow will do by putting over it the yellow screen. The colors will be seen to be quite different. The yellow will be changed very little, only growing slightly darker, the red from the pure spectral hue will be moved toward the orange, and the blue will be moved toward the green. This gives us a fine harmony, and a favorite one with artists. Harmonies of the dominant hues of red, orange, or yellow — warm colors — are much more generally liked than those of blue, green, or violet, the cold colors. Age has done much for old pictures by darkening and mellowing the paints and varnish so as to give them harmony of the dominant hue. Jean François Millet's have such harmony already, owing to his fine eye for color; it will be noticed that though he may have put many fairly bright colors, blue, red, green, and yellow on one canvas, they all blend wonderfully together. "Harmony" (we quote from Burnet on *Colour*, who speaks of Mengs) "he considers to consist in the true equilibrium of the different colors regulated by the general tone of light by which they are illuminated; thus, if the light is yellow, all the colors will appear tinged with the same hue, as the air interposed between them and the eye of the spectator is already tinged with that color." The harmony resulting from a dominant hue in nature may also be seen in a spray of young leaves in spring when many hues of green and yellow will be found connected and harmonized by the red of the stem, which color runs through it all, carrying the red into the greens and yellows. (See Plate XLIV.)

*Eighth.* BY INTERCHANGE. — If two unbroken masses of the same quantity of strong color are put side by side the result may be unbearable. By interchanging them, however, in this way, in what are called in design diaper patterns, they may blend so as to be quite agreeable. Or they may be blended in weaving by interchange, as if one thread be of green, the next of purple, then again green. (See Plate XLV.)

*Ninth.* BY COUNTERCHANGE. — Examples of fine decorative art may be found of two colors where the design and the ground change places at certain intervals. It is an ingenious and beautiful way of obtaining variety of coloring. To make it successful the amount of ground color should balance that of the design. Plate XLVI gives us a good example.

*Tenth.* BY FORM AND TEXTURE, as by the curves in a vase or any object which deepens the color as it goes away from the light and lightens it as it turns toward the light; as in a curtain of which the folds modify the color; as in rough and shaggy stuffs like plush, etc., which produce constant variation and vibration of color, and just so much added charm. The sparkle in jewels and colored glass, the sheen on satins, silks, and metals, and the down on fruit also come under this rule, as so many modifications of color tending to break up its flat surface and produce harmony.

*Eleventh.* BY OUTLINING a mass of flat color in a design with black or a dark color, then adding a second outline inside the first, but of either a light tint of the same color as the dark mass or of another color which harmonizes with it; then there will be found an agreeable result. In fact, this will give a velvety appearance to the color.

In making a complex color arrangement it is well to begin by planning first its leading parts; the additions will be much easier. Harmony of color must come not alone from the object we are planning for, but also from the place in which it is to be used, or the person who is to wear it. The color of an object may be beautiful in itself, but much of that beauty may be lost or neutralized by its surroundings. On the other hand, an object giving but one good, simple color note may be so appropriate to its position, may so exactly suit its surroundings, as to complete a perfect harmony.

Colors should also be adapted to the form of the object or designs on which they are to be used. Thus, when wishing to emphasize a part that retires from the eye, retiring colors should be used, and *vice versa*.

In addition to the above rules a few suggestions for making color-harmonies may be useful:

First, texture can be used to help the harmony.

Second, harmonies with warm colors predominating are preferred.

Third, if certain colors are to be used in any decoration it is wise to put them together first in paint, paper, or plain materials, for the reason that any unpleasant effect they may have on one another will show more quickly in such materials; for the better the material, the more readily the colors blend on account of the richer surfaces. In colored, not painted, glass, this can be appreciated. It will be noticed that the quality of the glass and the brilliancy of the light through it help to harmonize the colors.

Fourth, a simple pattern, if pattern at all, should be tried first, as the beauty of a good design may blind one to the quality of the coloring.

Fifth, remember that combinations in which warm colors prevail are more agreeable than those made mainly of cold colors, while it is also true that the finest harmony of complex or various colors is that in which there is a proper balance of both warm and cold colors, so used that they enhance each other.

Sixth, it is safe to affirm that any colors may be used together with success, provided that they are harmonized by the use of some of the rules here given.

Any one unused to working with colored materials would do wisely to begin cautiously, experimenting at first with simple combinations of one color according to the first rule on page 78 for such combinations. In some flowers we do see the two extremes of a color combined, as in a jonquil the centre is of orange-yellow, the outer petals of greenish-yellow, but they are rather the exception. Attention here should also be had to the suggestion as to the use of differing materials of one color. When some skill has been gained in the simplest kind of color harmony, a single note of the complementary color may be added. For example, see the dinner table harmony, page 69, of yellows with a strong note of dark blue. When the eye has become somewhat trained by practice of this kind, harmonies in triads or three colors may be tried. Constant practice in pairs and triads cannot be too fully recommended. Finally, trials may be made in complex combinations. One other way to begin working in color is by the use of neutral or grayed colors. Turner, the English artist, one of the greatest, if not the greatest, of modern landscape painters, began in this way, in the use of what are called "broken tints," using finally in his pictures the fullest palette of glowing colors.

Let us suppose three ways of being called upon to make a color harmony. The first, that a designer has an order for a bouquet, a dress, a curtain, or for the decoration of a room, but is limited by the terms of the order to the use of certain colors. Then let him begin by studying the qualities of those colors, and ask himself if they are cool or warm, tints or shades, bright or dull, whether they are tones of one color, contrasts or complex.

Again, suppose the order to be less limited in color, but that the bouquet is to be put in a room of certain coloring, or the dress to be worn by a person of such and such complexion and hair, or that the curtain is to be hung in a north room where warm color is needed, or perhaps in a light room where the southern sun needs to be toned down as it enters, to prevent a glare. The general coloring of the room must also be taken into account, but is it not seen that the answer must be different in each case? One colored flower would give quite a different effect from another, the dress that would suit a fair face with yellow hair would be quite unlike one becoming to a dark skin with black hair, while a curtain of soft yellow would tinge the northern light with some of the sunshine color that never enters the dull room, and in the sunny room a curtain of cool, non-luminous color would soften the glare and add to its comfort and harmony. The light and shade in the room should also be taken into account. The warm and cold tones can be arranged in such balance that color will glow from the shadows.

In a third supposable case the designer is given unlimited choice of colors. Then every resource can be called in, and the work resulting should be beautiful in proportion to the freedom of the order.

Furthermore, colors should be appropriate; for a quiet room, a quiet, commonplace person, for anything where quiet effect is desired, the designer should adhere to quiet, neutral combinations, or to combinations of one color. When a woman has a brilliant complexion, black eyes and dark hair, gay colors may be worn and seem all in harmony with the wearer, but these same gay colors would only emphasize the more commonplace character and coloring of others.

Plates XLVII and XLVIII have been added here to show the true character of *whites* so-called; as blue-white, which is really a very pale tint of blue; and how by *gradation*, one color changes into another in nature.

## CHAPTER VI

### HISTORIC COLOR

TO continue our color study we must next ask what has been done with it in the past and how it has been used and combined. Our knowledge would be incomplete without the experience of the past. The simplest and easiest way will be to consult the *Grammar of Ornament*, by Owen Jones, and *L'Ornement Polychrome*, by Racinet, the two best books of the kind, remembering, however, that there are several editions of each, varying in the quality of the coloring of the plates, and that even the best of these do not succeed in thoroughly reproducing the rare harmonies of color attained in the pictures, rugs, pottery, silks, metal, and jewel work that served as models. For these we must turn to the museums, and there is where the real lover of, and worker in, color must go for examples of the most skilful use of color by man up to this time. To many of them age has helped to give the great charm they possess, by fading and refining the colors so that they blend more perfectly with each other.

Unfortunately, no mention is made in the *Grammar of Ornament* of Japanese color, and Racinet gives but small space to it. Since the publication of these books we have become familiar with it even in the shop windows. We must bear in mind, however, that intercourse with western nations and the increasing demand for Japanese goods is already lowering their artistic standard, especially as they are making many goods entirely for western markets, so that for their best work we must look for old specimens made when Japan was a shut-in nation. As a whole, nothing finer can be found. For pure coloring, for the most complex and happiest combinations, they have no equals. Thorough study of these is one of the best schools for designers. The Japanese themselves are taught by being made to copy the best old works.

The Japanese love of color and their sense of fitness went so far that they even changed the ornaments of their rooms with the changing seasons. Nay, more, their women wore garments of which the embroidery harmonized with the different months: cherry, apple, pear blossoms when the fruit trees bloomed, colored leaves in the autumn, and so on, keeping in tune with the year, and getting great enjoyment out of things too little thought of by us.

At this point in his course the student will be wise to bear four things in mind: First, that as this is the study of color, not form, he should confine his attention to the colors as far as possible, as a fine design may tend to warp the judgment of them. Secondly, that different lights may vary what is really the same color. Thirdly, that if he isolates one color from another by means of such a card with a small opening in it as is to be found with the color screens at the end of this book, he will be greatly helped to understand it. Fourthly, that he should pay special attention to the proportions of the colors.

The following plates have been taken from specimens of color of different nations, and are given in simple proportions of quality and quantity, the latter in one-hundredths, as nearly as it is possible to measure, when the design may be much complicated and broken up. In studying these with reference to making the plates, it has seemed probable that those who made them took their color in many instances directly from nature; as, for instance, Plate LIV reminds one of the qualities and quantities of color of a gayly feathered parrot. It is hoped that these plates may help to create a taste for hard study of whatever originals may be at hand in books, shops, private houses, or museums.

Plate LXXXIV is a drawing of the antique rug from which Plate LXXXV is reduced. By comparison the student will see how these and the other plates have been made.

## CHAPTER VII

### NATURE COLOR

"AND you, painter, who are desirous of great practice, understand that if you do not rest it on the good foundation of Nature, you will labor with little honor and less profit; and if you do it on a good ground, your works will be many and good, to your great honor and advantage.

"A painter ought to study universal Nature, and reason much within himself on all he sees, making use of the most excellent parts that compose the species of every object before him. His mind will by this method be like a mirror, reflecting truly every object placed before it, and become, as it were, a second nature."

From the *Treatise on Painting*, by Leonardo da Vinci, we copy the above passages. May they serve as an introduction to the next branch of our color study, and prove a stimulus of the highest kind not only to painters, but to other artists. This final step in our study leads us to Nature, a step easy to make, but once made, it places us in a school as vast as it is great, and in one which we should never leave. Until our attention is called to it, we are unconscious what apparently unpromising material may yield new and beautiful motives for color-harmonies.

"We do not sufficiently study from nature; we ought to draw and study vegetable forms, shells, fishes, birds, beasts. A continual use of your note-book should enable you to lay up an inexhaustible store of artistic materials and suggestions. . . . Then, again, the study of the arrangement of color of natural objects is almost entirely ignored; yet how pregnant would it be with the most valuable and original suggestions. There is hardly anything in nature that is not perfect in color. A dead sparrow would enable you to arrange the marquetrie of a cabinet with faultless harmony. Then, again, the varied tints of any color in light, shade, and half tint are always harmonious. The gradations of color in a flower, if properly studied, would teach a lady to dress with a taste that would be the envy of her sex. That dress is not, more than it is, the study and recognized province of an artist, is a matter of wonder."[1]

Following closely upon this advice of Mr. Moody, an artist tells us that in Algiers he has seen the Arab girls working the beautiful embroideries so much admired with boxes of butterflies beside them, that from their harmonious blending of colors they may gain fresh enthusiasm

[1] Lectures and Lessons on Art. F. W. Moody. P. 131.

and inspiration for their work. Those who are not privileged to go to foreign lands in search of color motives can find them in our own country, and those who can leave the city's walls for but a day's holiday may find in the suburbs much that is new and helpful. Why not make excursions for the purpose ? A color hunt would surely be as cheap and harmless as it would be enjoyable and helpful. In New York City itself, the Museum of Natural History holds case upon case of birds, butterflies, shells, and minerals that can give an infinite number of novel motives, the florists' shops contain many more, and, if one keeps his eyes about him, even in the street he may meet with good and unexpected combinations, as, for instance, Plate C, which is from the flange of a propeller, of which the discoloration of the metal gave a fine color motive.

The Japanese have always been distinguished for their intense sympathy with nature, and we find that a large part of the enjoyment of their lives the year round comes from their constant study and observation of nature, the result, of course, showing itself in their art.

Condor says, in *The Flowers of Japan*, "Flower-viewing excursions, together with such pastimes as shell-gathering, mushroom-picking, and moon-viewing, form the favorite occupations of the holiday seeker throughout the year," and

" Snow-viewing is included as one of the flower festivals of the year."

One caution must be given to those looking to nature for color motives, which is this: to make allowance for the modifications of form, contrast, composition, gradation, and atmosphere which may deceive us as to the true color of our object. It can be more truly judged by being looked at through a card with an opening in it, which thus isolates it from the adjoining colors. "We should be cautious in basing our conclusions even on observations made directly from nature itself; for here our judgment is liable to be warped by the presence of beautiful form, good composition, exquisite gradation, and high luminosity."[1] A few plates made directly from nature are given, not for the sake of the imitation, but to suggest some of the many directions in which to look for fresh inspiration in color-designing.

Students in art and science are constantly bidden to go to nature for the abundant secrets she is ready to reveal to those who seek and prize them, and why should not workers in simpler, if not lower, occupations, be sent to the same source, which is so bountiful as to contain something for every one, and so, profiting by her fulness, learn at the same time to find contentment and joy in their work?

[1] Rood.

## CHAPTER VIII

### SPECIAL SUGGESTIONS

AFTER having carried the study of color as far as the limits of our plan allow, a few simple, practical suggestions may not come amiss.

Students of painting and design will find Rood's many experiments with colors in his *Modern Chromatics* minute and valuable, especially those on the effects of mixing paints and their consequent loss of luminosity. If their time for the scientific study of color be limited, *Colour*, by Church, is well adapted for their purpose, being small, clear, and admirably illustrated. It gives briefly the gist of what has been written heretofore on the subject.

Burnet, in *Colour in Painting*, is helpful on the artistic side. He says, "Harmony arising from the reflection of one color upon the adjoining, so as to produce a blending and union of the several hues, has been practised with the greatest success by many of the Dutch school, producing a chain of connections between the two extremes of hot and cold."

As to materials for painting, Church's *Chem-*

*istry of Paints and Painting* gives much useful information as to their substance, permanence, adulteration, and effect upon one another. Recollecting, as we do from experiments with Maxwell's disks, that neutral colors are simply any one of the six colors diluted or changed by black or white, or black and white, or other colors, it is interesting to know that an ingeniously illustrated book, published in Paris by E. Guichard, *La Grammaire de la Couleur*, gives abundant examples of neutral colors, and printed beside them samples of the colors of which they are made. The author suggests that in embroidery any of these combinations can be made by twisting together threads of each of the colors required to make the neutral color, as by Plates CXVI and CXVII.

In the matter of the choice of draperies and any kind of still life to be used to paint from, one of our leading artists advised his pupils generally to select *old* things as being usually finer than new ones, because age mellows and refines colors; and also that objects of *one country* harmonize better with each other than those of different countries, and those of *one period* of *one country* still better.

Florists, gardeners, and fruit-dealers will find a large part of Chevreul's book devoted to color as applied to horticulture, with notes of his experiments in the arrangement of plants and flowers.

While other nations love flowers and use and cultivate them, the Japanese, along with their great skill in growing them, have elaborated an art of arranging them, of which art a full and clear account, admirably illustrated, is given in *The Flowers of Japan, and the Art of Floral Arrangement*, a recent work published in Tokio. Many features of this art are very attractive, and much can be learned from them even if we do not wish to carry it to the same extent of form and ceremony. They make much of common flowers, and while our admiration is mainly given to the blossoms, they value every part of the plant, using stem, leaf, and bud in their arrangements so as to display each to advantage, with the flower as the crowning beauty of the whole. The author writes, "The arrangement of flowers has always been regarded in Japan as an occupation befitting learned men and literati. Ladies of the aristocracy have practised it, as they have other arts, but it is by no means considered as an effeminate accomplishment. Priests, philosophers, and men of rank who have retired from public life have been its most enthusiastic followers. Various virtues are attributed to professors of the art, who are considered to belong to a sort of aristocracy of talent, enjoying privileges of rank and precedence in society to which they are not by birth entitled. A religious spirit, self-denial, gentleness, and forgetfulness of cares are some of the virtues said to follow from a habitual practice of the art of arrangement of flowers."[1]

The fact that flowers usually make a focus wherever they may be placed, — on a table, in a room, or in a landscape, — on account of their comparative purity and luminosity of color, increases their beauty and shows the skill of the person who arranges them, but there is also a corresponding disadvantage that if discord there be, the arrangement is all the more prominent, the eye being called to it immediately.

While we speak of the "comparative purity and luminosity" of colors we may at the same time quote from one of a series of interesting articles by F. Schuyler Matthews:[2]

"Even our anxiety to obtain definite names for definite colors is completely overshadowed by the stronger wish to understand the secret of their harmonious relationship.

"Now let us try to discover if we can some small portion of this secret. Why is it that nature nearly always puts yellow stamens in her white flowers? Why is it that nearly all of her white flowers are *not* a colorless pure white? Why is it difficult for us to find a positively blue or positively yellow flower? What is the reason that

[1] FLORAL ART OF JAPAN. By Condor. [2] In THE AMERICAN FLORIST.

there is such a multitude, such an infinity of color tones in the flowers, on the earth, over the sea, in the sky, everywhere? What a perplexing, changeable, evasive thing the whole world of color is! What is the reason of it all? Simply this: Nature abhors the commonplace — she despises crude red, yellow, and blue. Variety she *will* have; harmony she insists upon; positivism she only employs to emphasize her love of the infinite. Thus we have one rather questionably perfect yellow marigold and a dozen others which have more orange in them than yellow; one scarlet-lake colored gladiolus and an infinity of red roses, which cannot be called anything which is an approach to the pure red color which scarlet-lake nearest resembles. We have the forget-me-not, which is nearly a true blue, but we have a host of so-called blue flowers, every one of which has barely fifty per cent. of the true sky blue in its composition."

It seems as though in the face of these facts it would be hardly possible to designate any special flowers which possess the prismatic colors in an absolutely pure form.

The rules for making harmonies can be made to apply to the arrangements of gardens, shop windows, bouquets and other decorations, as well as to the catalogues of florists, etc. A recently issued catalogue strikes a true color chord in its cover. It shows a bunch of sweet peas and leaves of agreeable colors well balanced by the background of pale neutralized green, thus making a true and tempting harmony to lovers of flowers and color.

Salesmen and women would be helped in their line of work by studying particularly the qualities of colors, and the effect on them of different kinds of artificial light. Knowledge of the contrasts of color will help greatly in showing goods to advantage, as one color may be made to heighten the color of another, and counters and shop windows may be well arranged according to the rules given for different classes of harmonies.

Women in their dress, embroidery, and house decorations have immense opportunities; no art is finer or higher for a woman however placed than that of being a harmonious whole herself, and of making or adding to a harmonious home, in which the unconscious influence of good color holds a large share. To do this it must not be thought that much money is necessary; it adds, of course, to the ability of choice among fine goods, but cheap materials of good colors wisely combined may produce a far happier, we may even say healthier, result, than an unlimited purse without knowledge and taste. This is difficult to overestimate. No woman has a right to say she has no influence, conscious or unconscious, on the world around her. Does not much of the influence for good or ill come from a woman's dress? It may be cheap, it may be plain, but it should be, and can be, in good taste and in harmony with the character and position of the person who wears it, and knowledge of one's own coloring and of that suited to it is one of the most important details.

Women in their dress, milliners and dress-makers, would do well to realize that a dress or bonnet may be good in color in itself, when it is a whole, but when worn it becomes only part of a whole and will be harmonious and becoming, or inharmonious and unbecoming, as it does, or does not, suit the coloring of the wearer. To wear anything simply because it is beautiful is unwise; it should first of all be suitable. Study of the law of contrast of color will here help immensely.

For instance, according to that law, red and yellow next to each other make the yellow seem more yellow, the red more red, so if a woman with a sallow, colorless complexion wears pink roses or pink ribbons, the yellow in her skin is intensified and the small amount of pink in her cheeks is lost. As blue is the complement of yellow, a bright blue will have a still worse effect, but let her try a shade of not too intense yellow; the skin will seem to lose *its* yellow, and whatever pink there may be will be brought out by the contrast. So other peculiarities may be softened or increased by contrast or harmony of color. White hair is made to seem whiter by the contrast of black or a very dark color; black hair and rosy cheeks are made more brilliant by a white surrounding; delicate blonde coloring will be made insipid and colorless by too strong colors, and a plain face may be made attractive by surrounding it with harmonizing coloring.

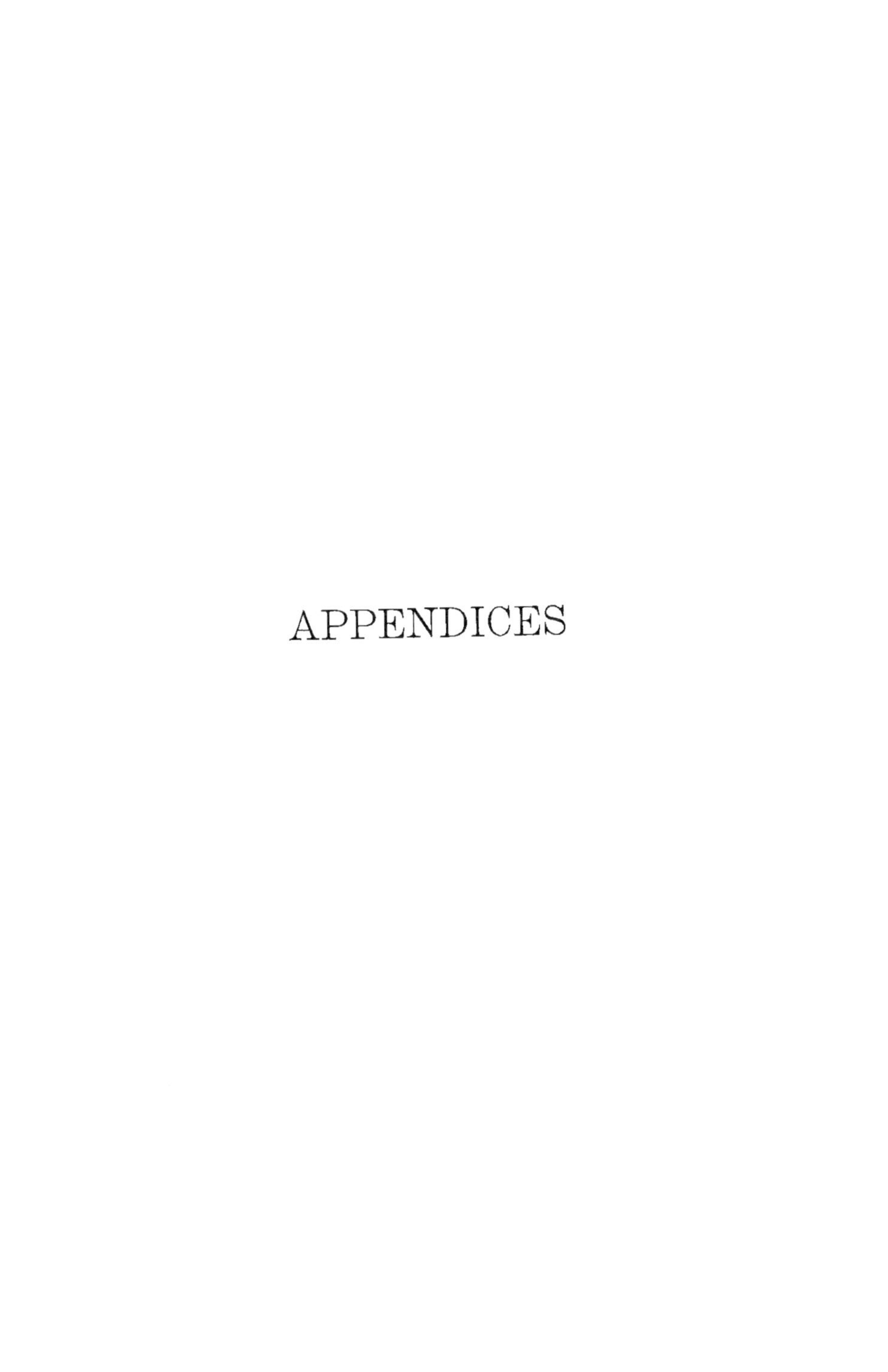

# APPENDICES

# APPENDIX A

## DEFINITIONS

ABSOLUTE COLORS: *see* Local Colors.

ADVANCING COLORS: those of the longer wave lengths; those that seem to come forward; but each color only advances or recedes according to its relation to some other color. *See* Luminosity.

ANALOGOUS HARMONY: *see* Harmony.

BEAM OF LIGHT: a linear portion * of light made of a number of rays.

BRIGHTNESS: *see* Luminosity.

BROKEN COLOR: a color changed by the addition of black and white or gray.

COLD COLORS: those of the shorter wave lengths, such as green, blue, and violet.

COLOR: an internal sensation, produced by various causes, chiefly by waves of incomplete light acting on the eye; as used by artists, the rich, harmonious effect, or full appearance produced by certain combinations of colors.

COLOR CHART: a systematic arrangement of colors in a geometrical design such that every variation and

---

* NOTE. — " A streak of light." — *Rood.*

combination of hue, tint, and shade is in its proper place and in correct relation to all other hues, tints, and shades.

| | | | | | |
|---|---|---|---|---|---|
| *Advancing* | | *Colors,* | see | under | Advancing; |
| *Bright* | | " | " | " | Brightness; |
| *Broken* | | " | " | " | Broken; |
| *Cold* | | " | " | " | Cold; |
| *Complementary* | | " | " | " | Complement; |
| *Complements of* | | " | " | " | " |
| *Constants* | " | " | " | " | Constants; |
| *Contrast* | " | " | " | " | Contrast; |
| *Harmony* | " | " | " | " | Harmony; |
| *Hue* | " | " | " | " | Hue; |
| *Intense* | | " | " | " | Saturated; |
| *Local* | | " | " | " | Local; |
| *Luminosity* | " | " | " | " | Brightness; |
| *Luminous* | | " | " | " | Luminous; |
| *Neutral* | | " | " | " | Neutral; |
| *Normal* | | " | " | " | Normal; |
| *Opaque* | | " | " | " | Opaque; |
| *Pigment* | | " | " | " | Pigment; |
| *Primary* | | " | " | " | Primary; |
| *Prismatic* | | " | " | " | Prismatic; |
| *Pure* | | " | " | " | Pure; |
| *Quality of* | | " | " | " | Constants; |
| *Saturated* | | " | " | " | Saturated; |
| *Secondary* | | " | " | " | Secondary; |
| *Spectral* | | " | " | " | Normal; |

| | | | | |
|---|---|---|---|---|
| *Tertiary* | *Colors,* see under | | | Tertiary; |
| *Transparent* | " | " | " | Transparent; |
| *Value of* | " | " | " | Values; |
| *Warm* | " | " | " | Warm. |

COMPLEMENTS or
COMPLEMENTARY COLORS: any color and the color of its after-image; any two colors which when mixed make white.

COMPOUND or MIXED COLOR: a color changed or neutralized by the addition of another color or colors.

CONSTANTS or QUALITIES OF COLORS: Hue, Purity, and Luminosity.

CONTRAST: *see* Simultaneous Contrast, page 53.

CONTRASTED HARMONY: *see* Harmony.

DIFFRACTION GRATING: a polished metal or brass surface ruled with fine lines and used instead of a prism to divide a ray of light and produce a spectrum.

DOMINANT HARMONY: *see* Harmony.

DOMINANT HUE: *see* Hue.

HARMONY: the pleasing effect due to the action upon each other of colors improved and made more beautiful by being put together; such an agreement between the different hues, tints, or shades of a design as will produce unity of effect.

*Analogous Harmony:* an agreeable combination of colors that are related to a fundamental color.

*Complex Harmony:* an agreeable combination of three

or more colors, or with the addition of black or white, or gray, or gold, or silver, or any or all of them.

*Contrasted or Complementary Harmony:* an agreeable combination of any pair of complementary colors, or of their tints or shades, or tints and shades.

*Dominant Harmony:* an agreeable combination of colors in which one color predominates by modifying all the other colors, by serving as a ground, or by being added in small portions all over the design.

*One-color Harmony, also called a Harmony of Self-tones:* an agreeable combination of one color used in tints or shades, or tints and shades, or hue and tints, or hue and shades, or hue, tints, and shades.

HUE: color, by wave length, much the same as color; the chief quality by which one color differs from another color, as red differs from blue or green.

*Dominant Hue:* the hue which predominates through the larger part of a design or composition.

INTENSE: *see* Saturated.

LIGHT: the chief agent that produces vision.

LOCAL COLOR: the actual color of an object unaffected by shadows or reflected lights.

LUMINOSITY: the strength of the light sent to the eye by any color; a luminous color sends more than a non-luminous one.

LUMINOUS COLORS: those which reflect light in large quantities; the colors of the long wave lengths are more luminous than those of the short ones.

NEUTRAL COLORS: a term often incorrectly applied to black, white, gray, gold, and silver.

NORMAL, SPECTRAL, PRIMITIVE, or PRISMATIC COLORS: those seen in the rainbow and the solar spectrum are generally accepted as such and are used as the standard for the study of colors. Pigment colors can only imitate these colors imperfectly.

OIL COLORS: pigments ground in oil.

OPAQUE COLORS: pigment colors which are so thick that paper or canvas cannot be seen through them.

PIGMENTS: materials from which paints, inks, dyes, and stains are made.

PIGMENT COLORS: paints, inks, dyes, and stains used in the fine and industrial arts.

PRIMARY COLORS: red, blue, and yellow; so called because it was supposed that all other colors could be made from them.

PRIMITIVE COLORS: *see* Normal Colors.

PRISM: a triangular or three-sided bar of clear glass.

PRISMATIC COLORS: those that appear when a ray of white light shines through a prism. *See* Normal Colors.

PURE COLORS: those unmixed with white light or any other color; those of the spectrum.

PURITY OF COLORS: the absence of an admixture of any other color or colors, or white or black.

QUALITIES OF COLORS: *see* Constants of Colors.

RAY OF LIGHT: a small linear portion or streak of light which may be white or any color.

RECEDING COLORS: those which seem to retire or recede from the eye; those of the short wave lengths.

RETINA: a thin inner lining of the eye. *See* page 20.

SATURATED or INTENSE COLORS: colors that are pure and luminous to their greatest extent; without any mixture of white light.

SECONDARY COLORS: orange, green, and violet; so called because it has been thought they were made from combinations of the primary colors.

SELF-TONES: *see* Tone.

SHADE: a tone of a color darkened by the addition of black pigments to paints, inks, dyes, and stains, or by the action of diminished light on immaterial colors.

SHADOW: about the same as *shade*, as generally used, but for the sake of clearness it is best to designate by *shadow* those parts of an object which do not receive any direct rays of light, while those surfaces which receive but little direct light, and are thus intermediate in value between the light and the shadow, are called *shade surfaces*. Then the term *cast-shadow* denotes the shadow projected by one body on another body or surface.

SOLAR SPECTRUM: *see* Spectrum.

SPECTRAL COLORS: *see* Normal Colors.

SPECTRUM: the result of the decomposition of a ray of sunlight into all the colors which form it; the streak of colors formed by a ray of light that has passed through a prism or over a Diffraction Grating.

STANDARD COLORS: those of the spectrum.

TERTIARY COLORS: citrine, olive, and russet, so called because it has been thought that they were made from combinations of the secondary colors.

TINT: a tone of a color produced by the addition of white to oil, water to water, and white light to immaterial colors.

TONE: the given state of a color as it may be pure, luminous, broken, compound, a tint, or a shade.

*Self-tones:* tones of the same color.

TRANSPARENT COLORS: those in which the color tints the paper or canvas, which shows through the color, thus helping to produce the effect.

VALUES: the relative amount of light contained in the different colors of a picture, design, or composition; the lightest or most luminous being called the highest in value.

WARM COLORS: those of the longer wave lengths, as yellow, orange, and red.

WATER COLORS: pigments prepared to be used with water.

WAVE LENGTHS OF COLORS: objects having no color in themselves possess the power of reflecting waves of light; waves of light of varying lengths give us the effect of color. Either the amount of motion of the ether, or *height* of the wave, produces the intensity or brightness of the light, and the *length* of the wave produces the color; *red* has a wave length of about $\frac{7000}{250,000,000}$ of an inch, *orange* $\frac{5979}{250,000,000}$, *yellow* $\frac{5802}{250,000,000}$, *green* $\frac{5272}{250,000,000}$, *blue* $\frac{4782}{250,000,000}$, and *violet* $\frac{4059}{250,000,000}$.

# APPENDIX B

AS whatever may be of value in this little work on a theme so large and complex as color must of necessity be drawn largely from what has been written before, the following list of books and authors is given, partly as having been referred to during its preparation, and partly as a suggestion for further reading to any student of color who can afford the time and labor necessary to the acquisition of a larger and wider comprehension of a subject which can be treated only scantily enough within the scope of a single small volume.

Although no pretence is here made to completeness as bibliography, yet it is believed that the fifty works enumerated below fairly cover the history of color and of its ever-growing relation to Art and Manufacture. For the sake of convenience the list is chronologically arranged.

A Treatise on Painting. By Leonardo da Vinci. (London, 1835: Nichols & Sons.) (Translation.)

Colour. By M. E. Chevreul. (London, 1839: Geo. Bell & Sons.) (Translation.)

Theory of Colour. By J. W. von Goethe. (London, 1840: J. Murray.) (Translation, with notes, by Sir Chas. Eastlake.)

Rudiments of the Painter's Art; or a Grammar of Colouring. By George Field. (London, 1850: Weale.)

Darstellung der Farbenlehre und optische Studien. By W. H. Dove. (Berlin, 1853.)

Researches on Colour-blindness. By G. Wilson. (Edinb., 1855: Sutherland & Knox.)

Grammar of Ornament. By Owen Jones. (London, 1856.)

On Colour (etc.). By Sir J. S. Wilkinson. (London, 1858: J. Murray.)

Die Farbenharmonie in ihrer Anwendung auf die Damentoilette. By R. Adams. (Leipzig, 1862: J. J. Weber.)

Practical Hints on Colour in Painting. By John Burnet. (London, 1865: J. & J. Leighton.)

Des Couleurs au Point de Vue Physique, Physiologique, Artistique et Industriel. By Ernst Bruecke. (Paris, 1866: J. B. Baillière & fils.)

The Principles of the Science of Colour. By William Benson. (London, 1868: Chapman & Hall.)

Color. By M. É. Cavé. (New York, 1869.) (Translation.)

Manual of the Science of Colour. By W. Benson. (London, 1871: Chapman & Hall.)

THE THEORY OF COLOURING. By J. Bacon. (London, 1872: G. Rowney & Company.)

L'ORNEMENT POLYCHROME. By A. Racinet. 2 vols. F°. (Paris, 1873–86: Firmin Didot.)

A GRAMMAR OF COLOURING APPLIED TO DECORATIVE PAINTING AND THE ARTS. By George Field. (London, 1875: Lockwood & Company.)

THEORY OF COLOR. By Dr. Wilhelm von Bezold. (Boston, 1876: L. Prang & Company.) (Translation.)

DIE GESCHICHTLICHE ENTWICKELUNG DES FARBENSINNES. By Hugo Magnus. (Leipzig, 1877: Veit.)

THE PRINCIPLES OF LIGHT AND COLOR. By E. D. Babbitt. (New York, 1878: Babbitt & Company.)

COMPLÉMENT DES ÉTUDES SUR LA VISION DES COULEURS PAR E. CHEVREUL. By M. E. Chevreul. (*In* Institut de France. *Académie des Sciences* — Memoires. T. 41, partie 2.) (Paris, 1879.) (English translations exist.)

MODERN CHROMATICS, WITH APPLICATION TO ART AND INDUSTRY. By O. N. Rood. (New York, 1879: D. Appleton.)

THE COLOUR SENSE: ITS ORIGIN AND DEVELOPMENT. By Grant Allen. (London, 1879: Trübner & Company.)

COLOR BLINDNESS. By B. Joy Jeffries. (London, 1879.)

A HANDBOOK FOR PAINTERS AND ART STUDENTS ON THE CHARACTER AND USE OF COLOURS. By W. J. Muckley. (London, 1880: T. & C. Baillière.)

SIGHT; AN EXPOSITION OF MONOCULAR AND BINOCULAR VISION. By Joseph Le Conte. (New York, 1881: D. Appleton & Company.)

Untersuchungen über den Farbencontrast vermittelst rotirender Scheiben. By G. B. T. Schmerler. (Leipzig, 1882: W. Engelmann.)

La Grammaire de la Couleur. By E. Guichard. 3 vols. (Paris, 1882: H. Cagnon.)

Die Farbenwelt. By Max Schasler. (Berlin, 1883: C. Habel.)

The Laws of Contrast of Colour and Their Application to the Arts and Manufactures. By M. E. Chevreul. (London, 1883: Routledge.) (Translation.)

Colour. By A. H. Church. (London, 1887: Cassell & Company.)

Il Libro dei Colori. Segreti del Secolo XV. Da O. Guerrini & C. Ricci. (Bologna, 1887: Romagnoli Dall' Acqua.)

Colour, An Elementary Treatise. By C. T. Whitmell. (Cardiff, 1888: W. Lewis.)

F. C. Schroeder's "Systematic Index." By F. C. Schroeder. (Boston, 1888: F. C. Schroeder.)

Iris: Studies in Colour and Talks about Flowers. By A. F. Dielitzsch. (Edinburgh, 1889: T. & T. Clark.) (Translation.)

Repertoire Chromatique. By Charles La Couture. (Paris, 1890: Gauthier, Villars & Fils.)

The Chemistry of Paints and Painting. By A. H. Church. (London, 1890: Seeley & Company.)

Colour in Woven Design. By R. Beaumont. (London, 1890: Whittaker & Company.)

Colour-Blindness and Colour-Perception. By F. W. Edridge Green. (London, 1891: Kegan Paul, Trench, Trübner & Company.)

A Text-Book of Physiology. By M. Foster. (London, 1891: Macmillan & Company.)

Flowers of Japan and the Art of Floral Arrangement. By Condor. (Yokohama, 1891: Kelly & Walsh.)

Colour Measurement and Mixture. By W. de W. Abney. (London, 1891.)

Harmonious Colouring. 3 vols. F°. By C. H. Wilkinson. (Manchester, 1891: Harmonious Colouring Company.)

Colour Vision. By E. Hunt. (Glasgow, 1892: Smith.)

On a Color System. By O. N. Rood. (New Haven, 1892.)

Students' Text-Book of Color; or, Modern Chromatics. By O. N. Rood. (New York, 1892: D. Appleton & Company.)

Colour Vision. By W. de W. Abney. (London, 1895: Low.)

Color-Vision and Color-Blindness. By J. E. Jennings. (Phila., 1896: Davis Company.)

Colour in Nature. A Study in Biology. By M. I. Newbegin. (London, 1898: J. Murray.)

PLATE I

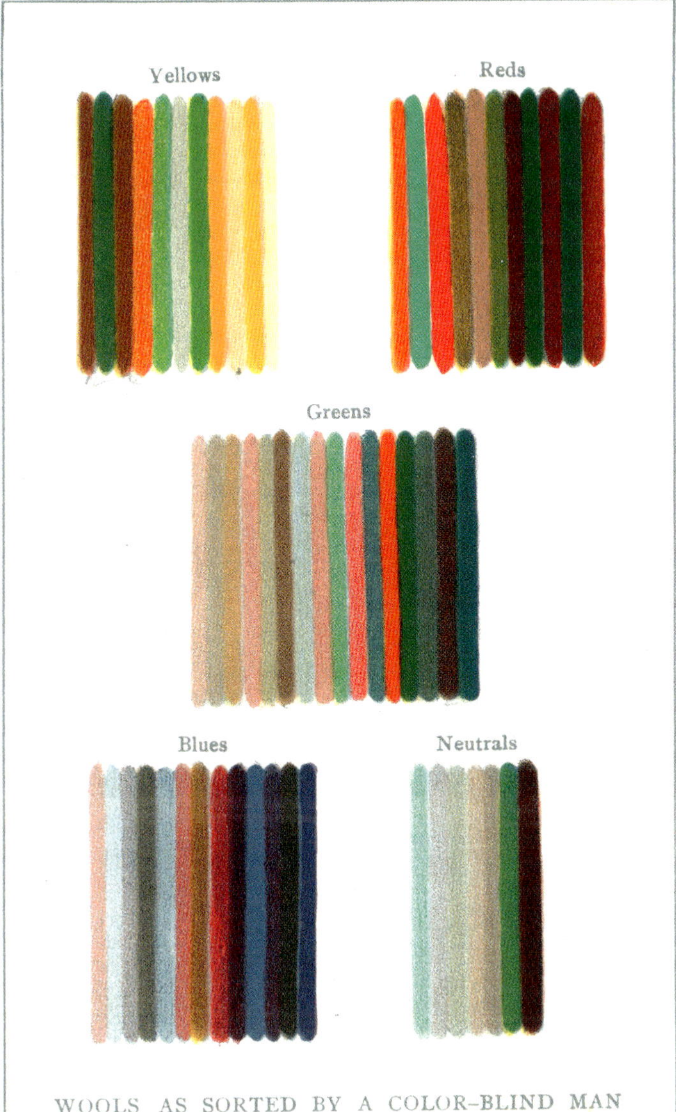


WOOLS AS SORTED BY A COLOR-BLIND MAN

PLATE II

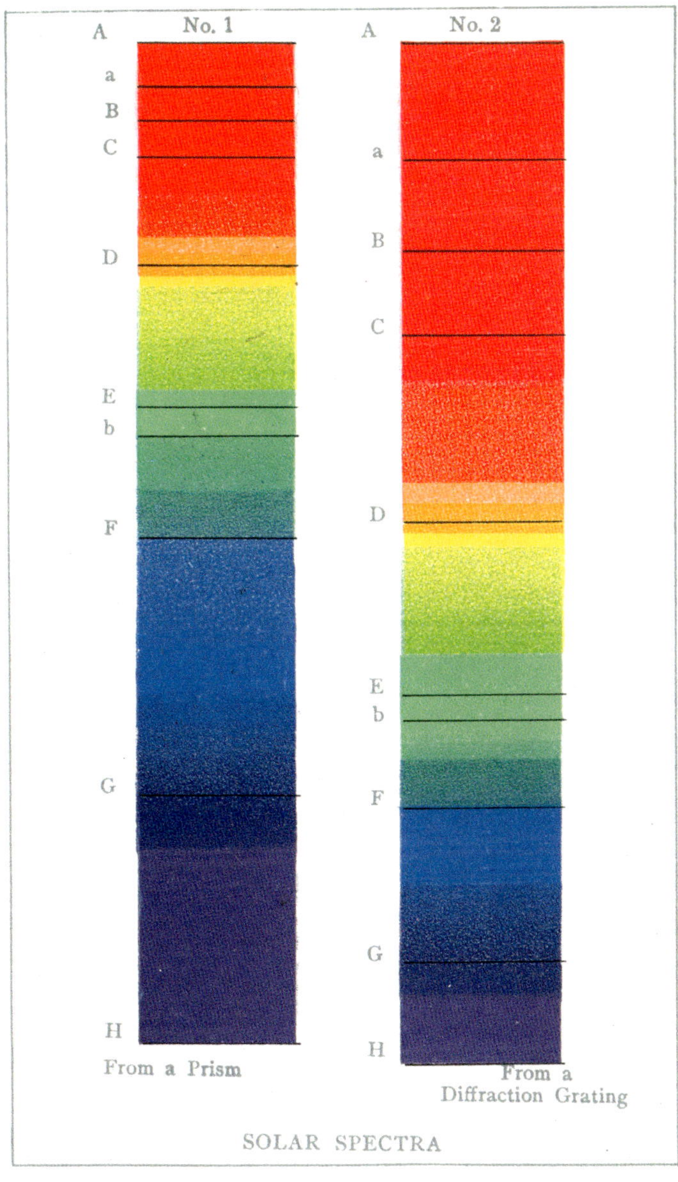


SOLAR SPECTRA

# Plate III

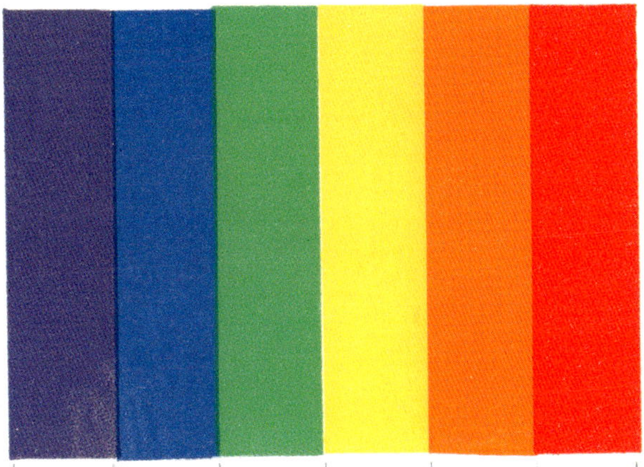

| Names | Paints used | Wave length | Purity | Luminosity | Warm or Cold |
|---|---|---|---|---|---|
| Violet | French Blue and Crimson Lake | 4.059 | As great as can be given by pigments | 6 | Cold |
| Blue | French Blue | 4.732 | | 5 | Cold |
| Green | Emerald Green | 5.271 | | 3 | Cold |
| Yellow | Aurora Yellow | 5.808 | | 1 | Warm |
| Orange | Vermilion and Cadmium | 5.972 | | 2 | Warm |
| Red | Vermilion and Crimson Lake | 7.000 | | 4 | Warm |

TABLE OF SPECTRAL COLORS

Plate IV

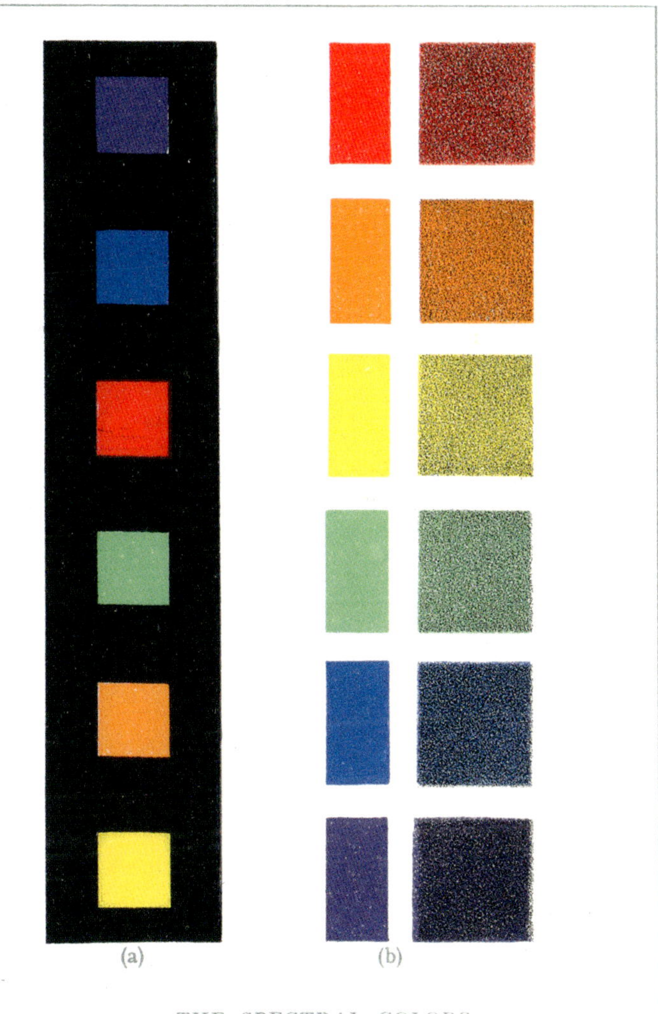


THE SPECTRAL COLORS

(a) In their order of Luminosity
(b) Pure and Grayed

PLATE V

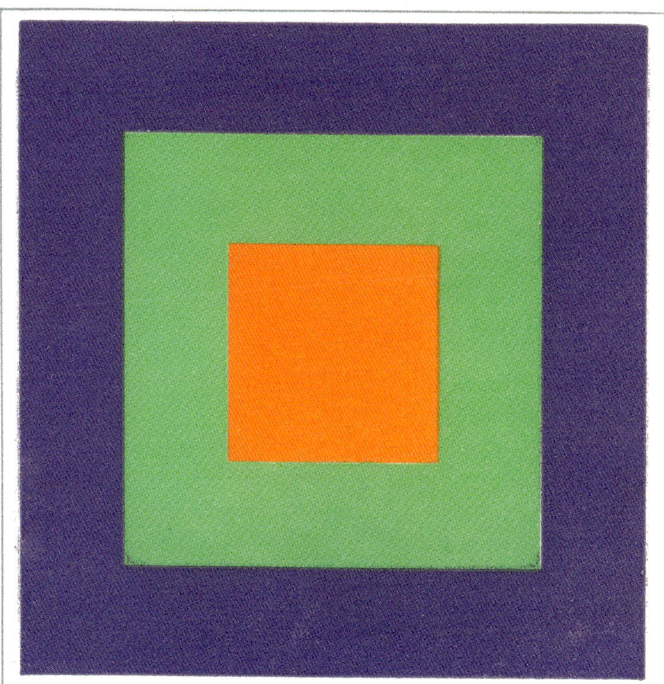

ADVANCING AND RETIRING COLORS

Plate VI

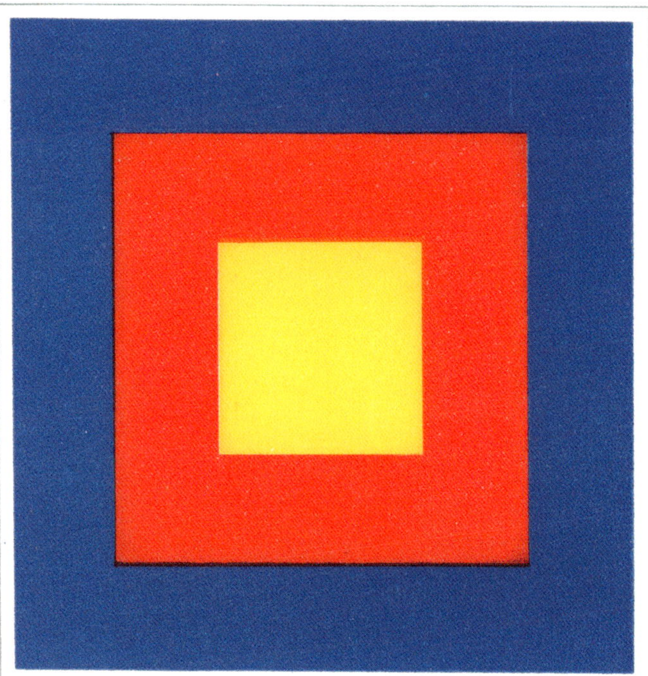

ADVANCING AND RETIRING COLORS

See page 99. The color screens at end of volume are for use with this plate.

Plate VII

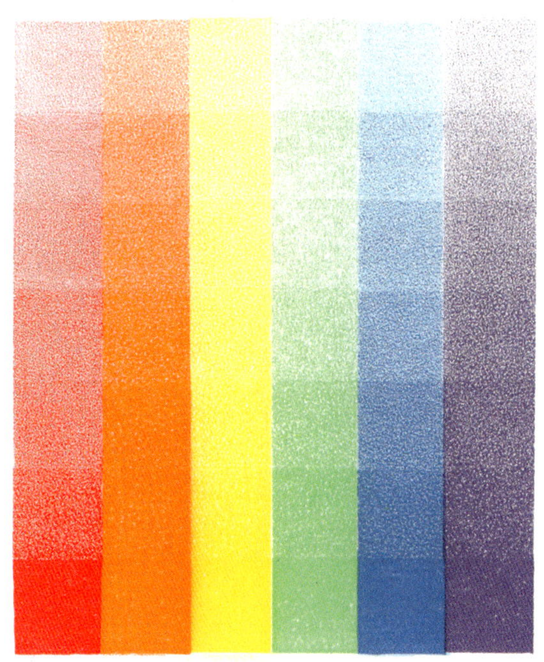

TINTS

Plate VIII

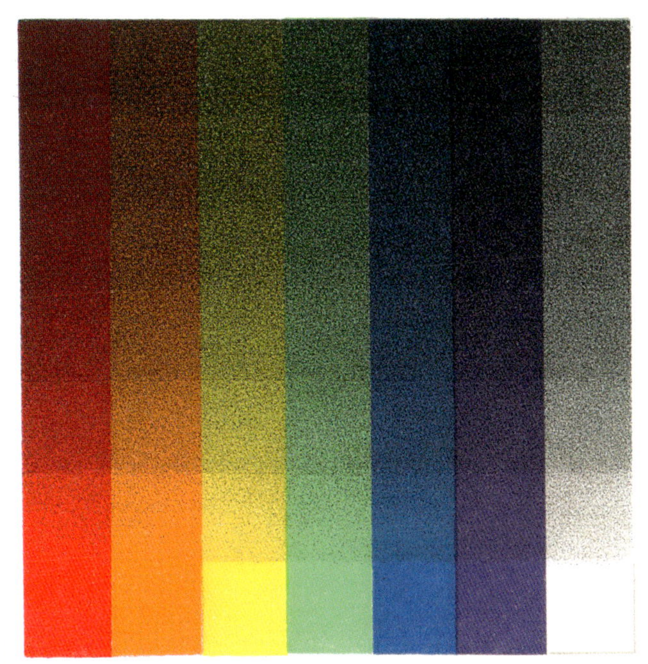

SHADES

PLATE IX

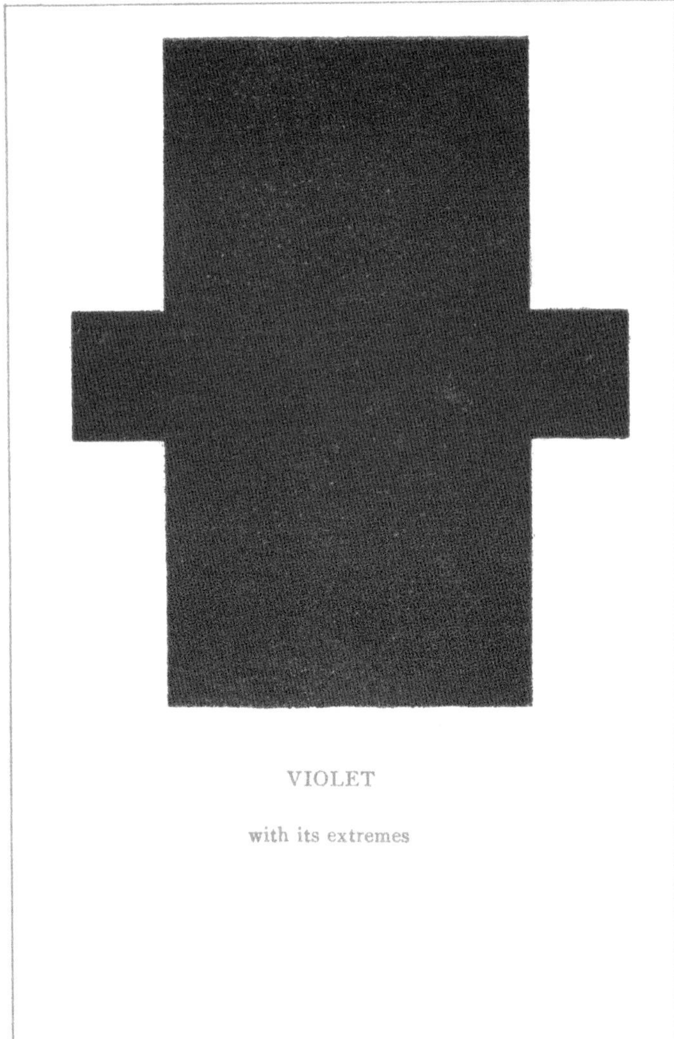

VIOLET

with its extremes

Plate X

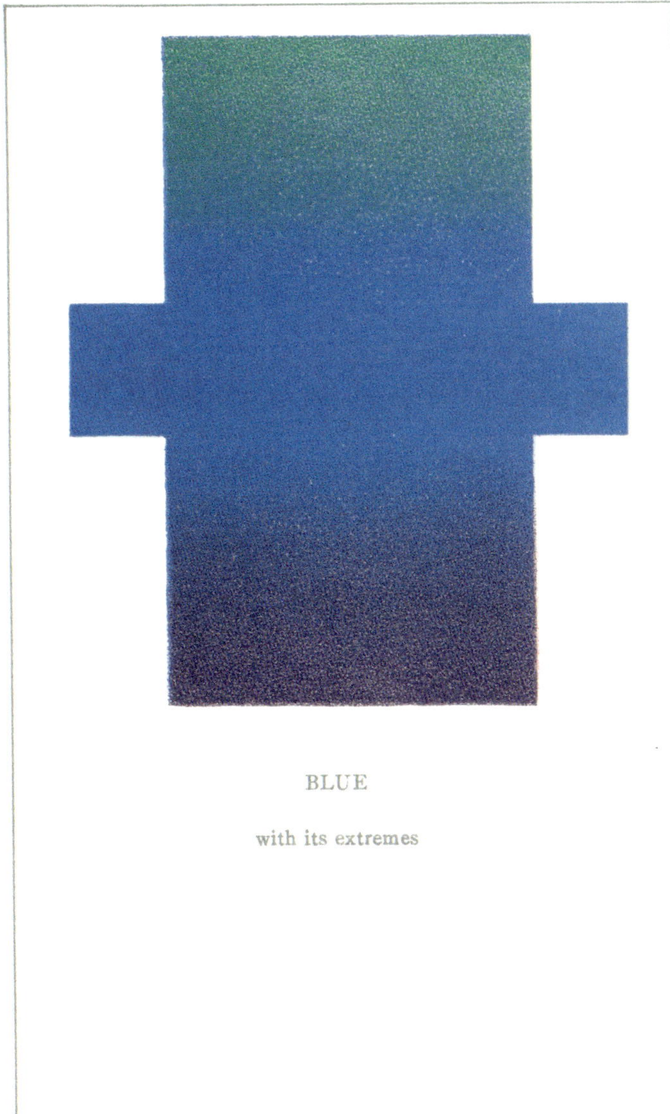

BLUE

with its extremes

Plate XI

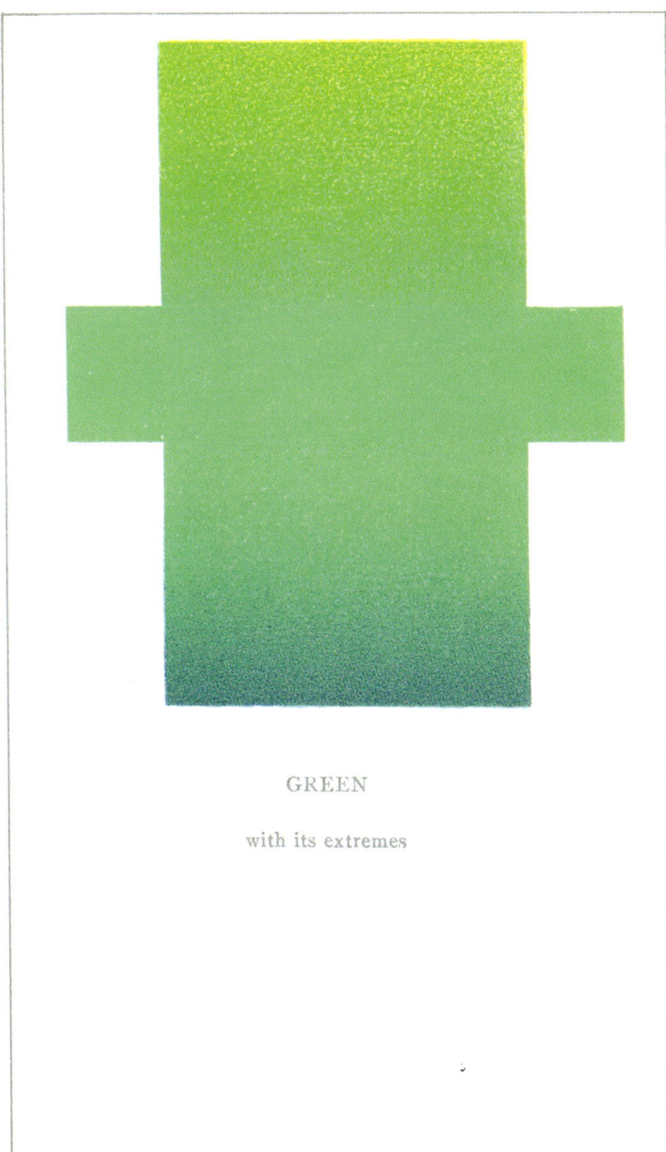

GREEN

with its extremes

Plate XII

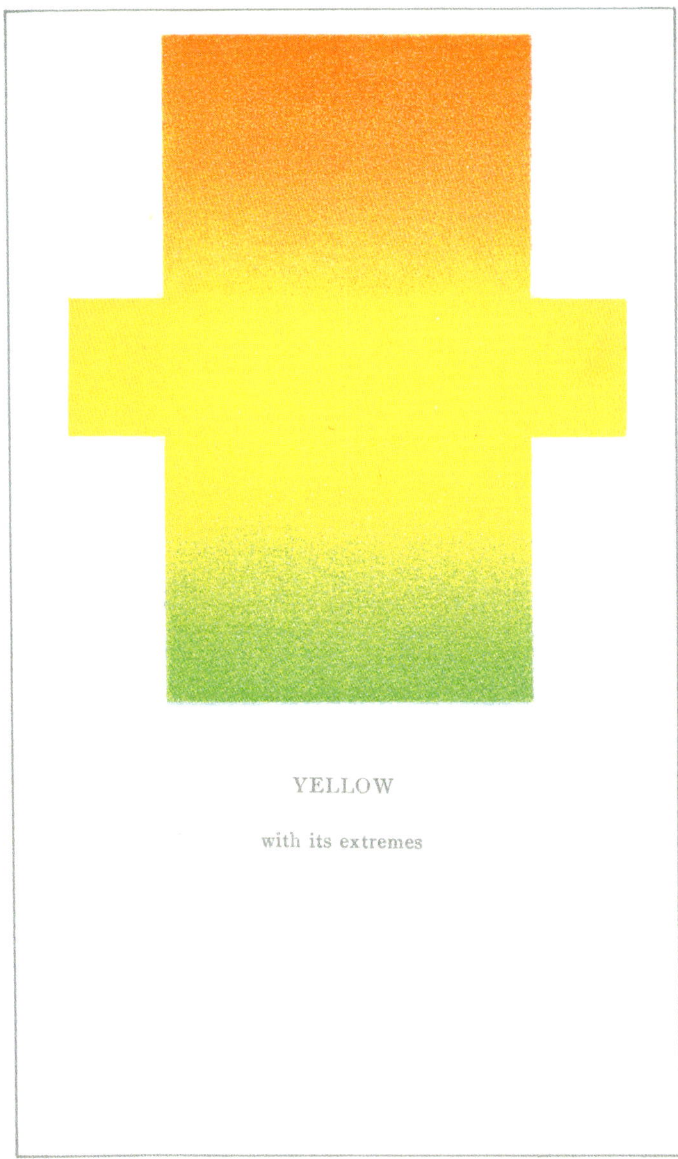

YELLOW

with its extremes

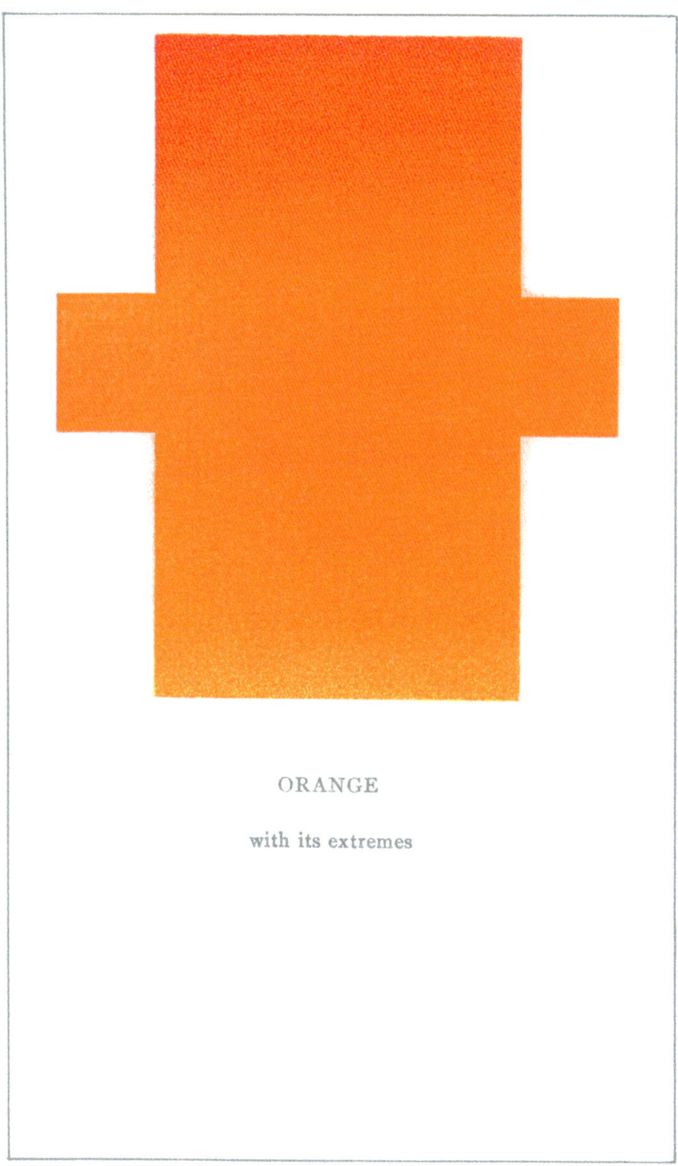

ORANGE

with its extremes

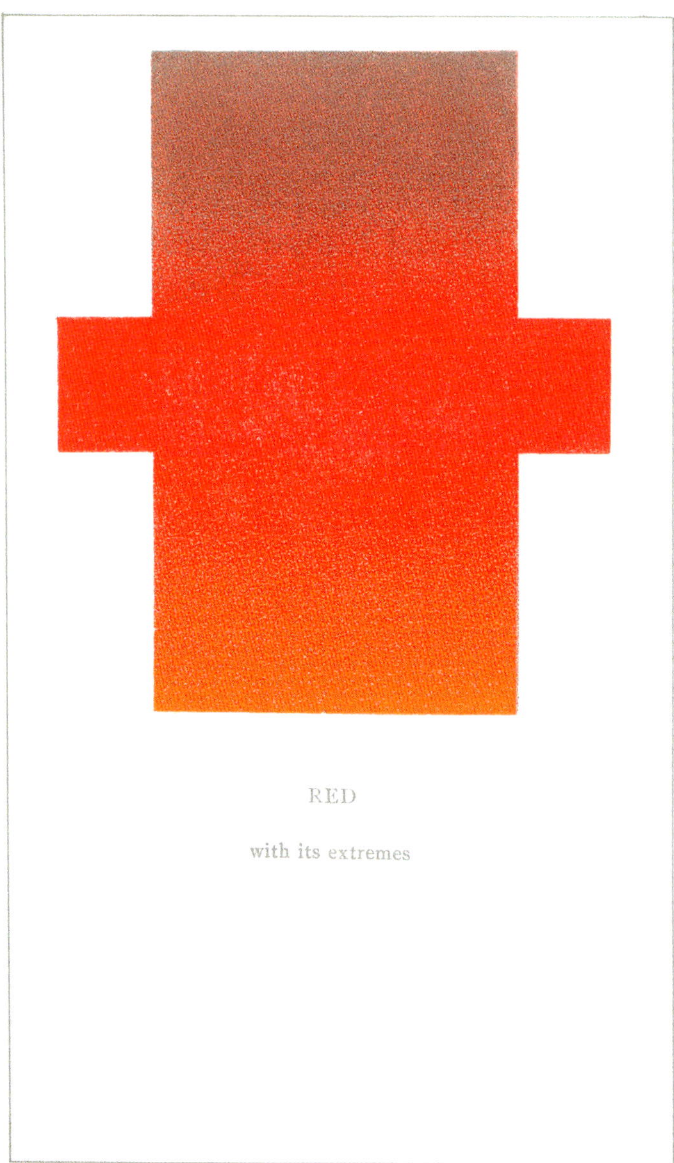

RED

with its extremes

Plate XV

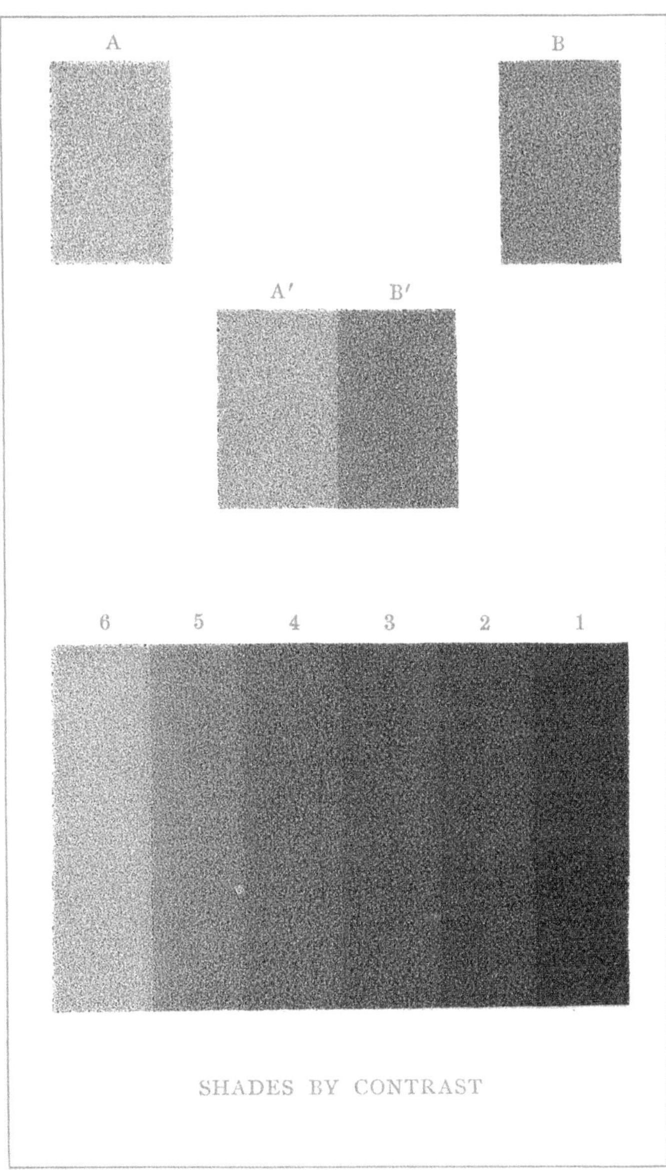


SHADES BY CONTRAST

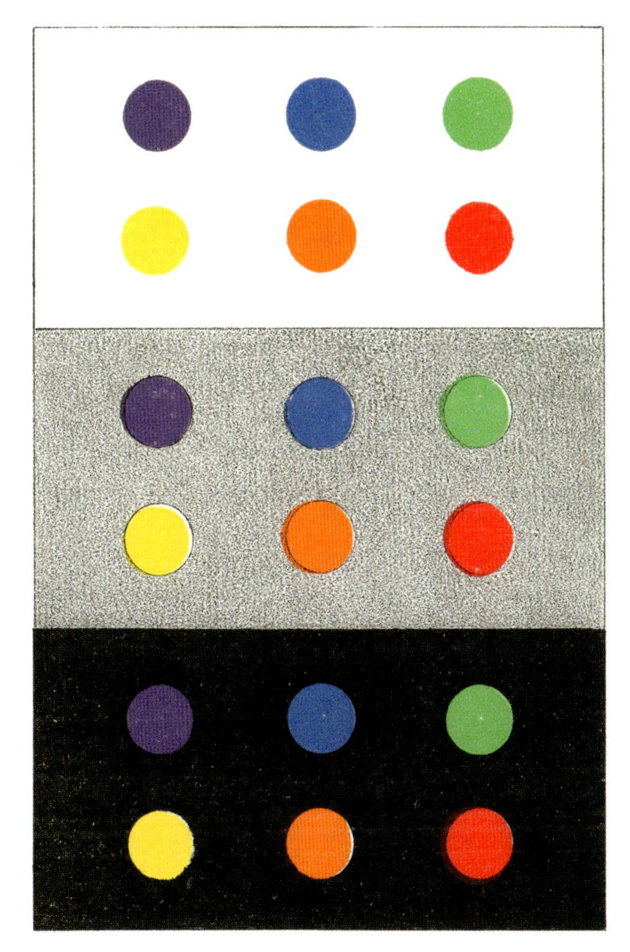

SPECTRAL COLORS
ON BLACK, WHITE AND GRAY

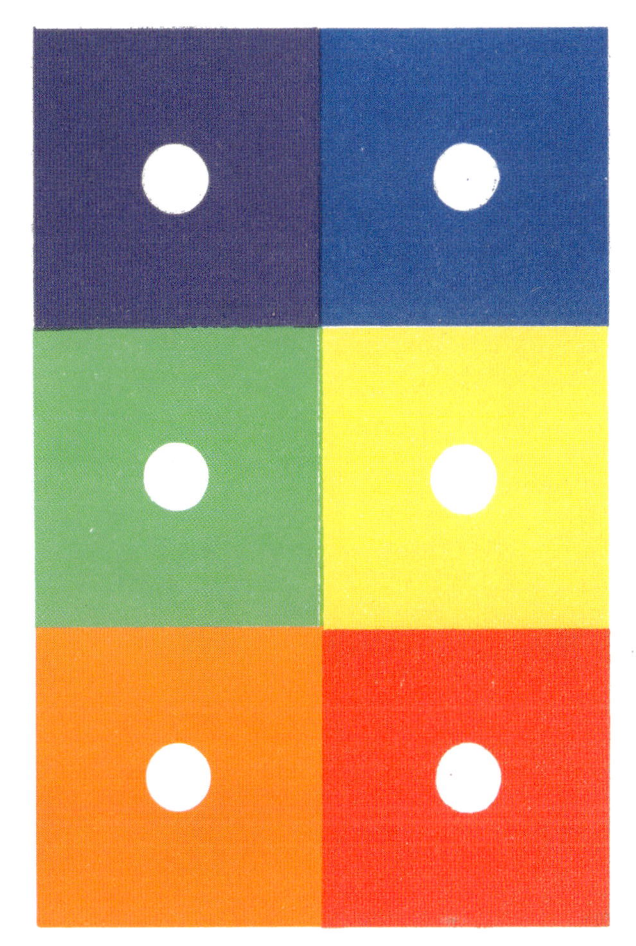

WHITE
ON SPECTRAL COLORS

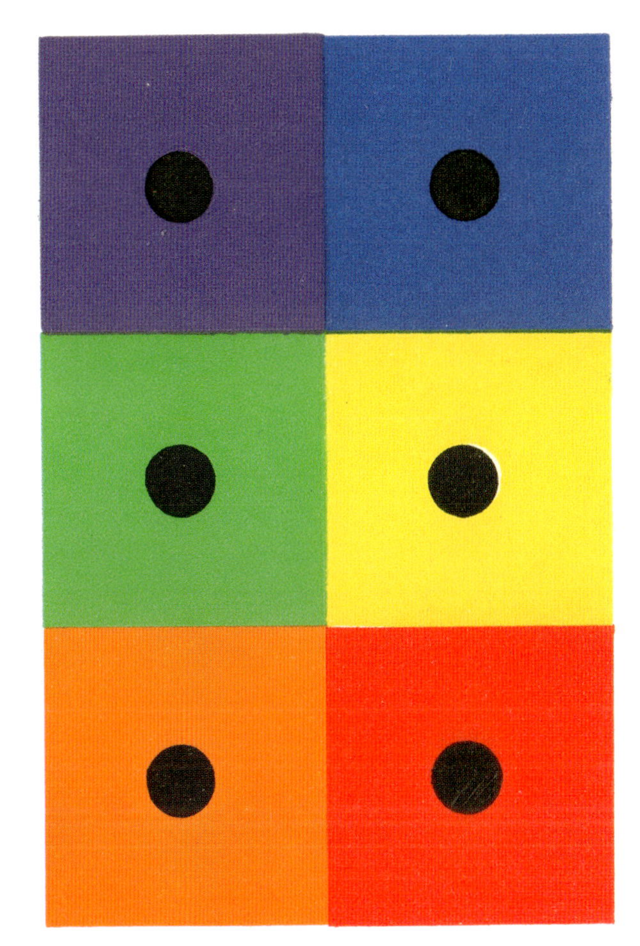

BLACK
ON SPECTRAL COLORS

PLATE XIX

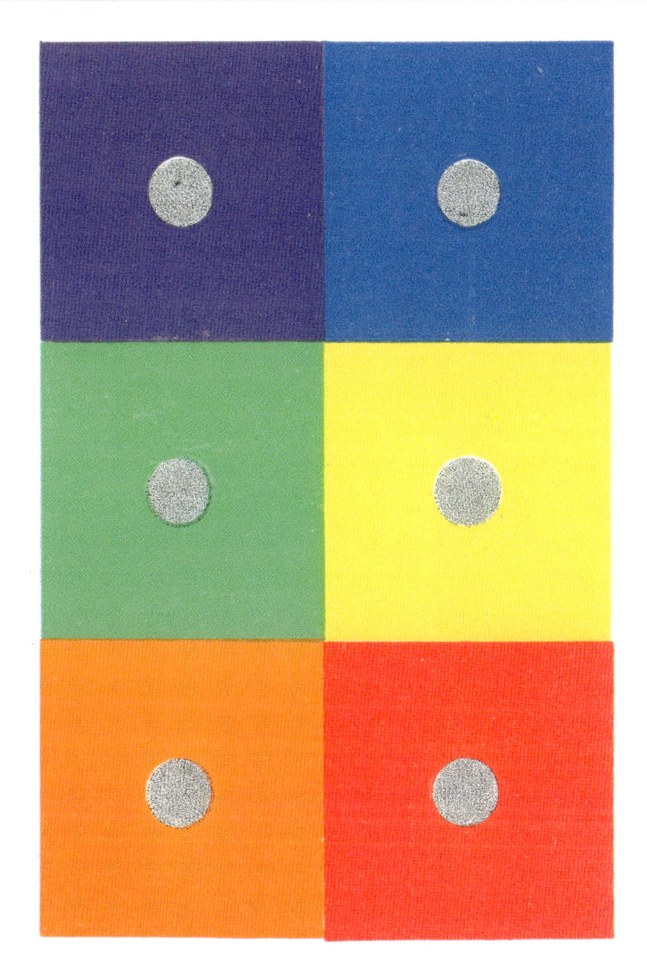

GRAY
ON SPECTRAL COLORS

SPECTRAL RED WITH ITS COMPLEMENT

N. B. The blue-green complementary is here imitated as closely as possible, but when spontaneously called up by the eye it is really brighter than the white paper.

SPECTRAL RED DISK FOR EXPERIMENT IN COMPLEMENTS

Gaze steadily at the red disk for three minutes, cover it quickly with the preceding blank page without removing the eyes and you will see its complementary image.

PLATE XXII

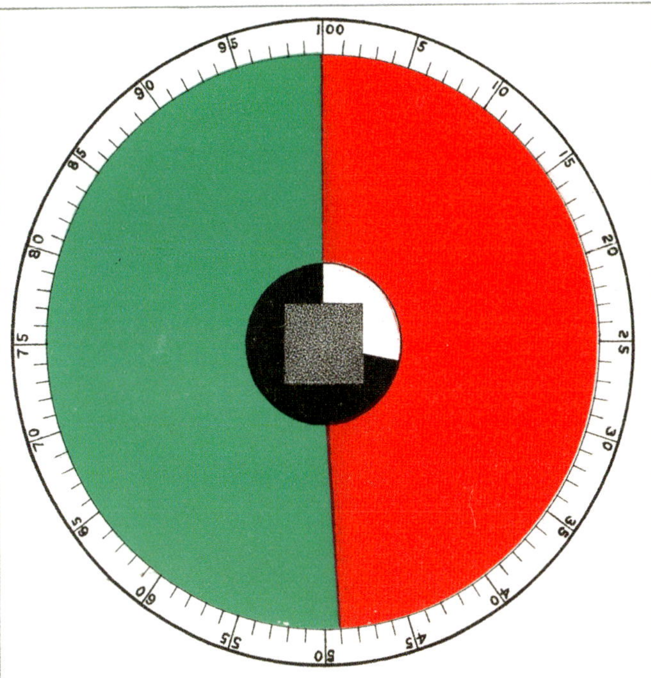


SPECTRAL RED AND ITS COMPLEMENT, BLUE-GREEN, IN THEIR RELATIVE PROPORTIONS

The gray in the centre of this Plate is the gray produced by the above two complements when mixed on a color wheel, and corresponds exactly to the gray produced by the given amounts of black and white.

(N. B. The above proportions were obtained in an average light. They will vary with all variations in the quality and quantity of the illumination. This applies as well to the following four Plates.)

PLATE XXIII

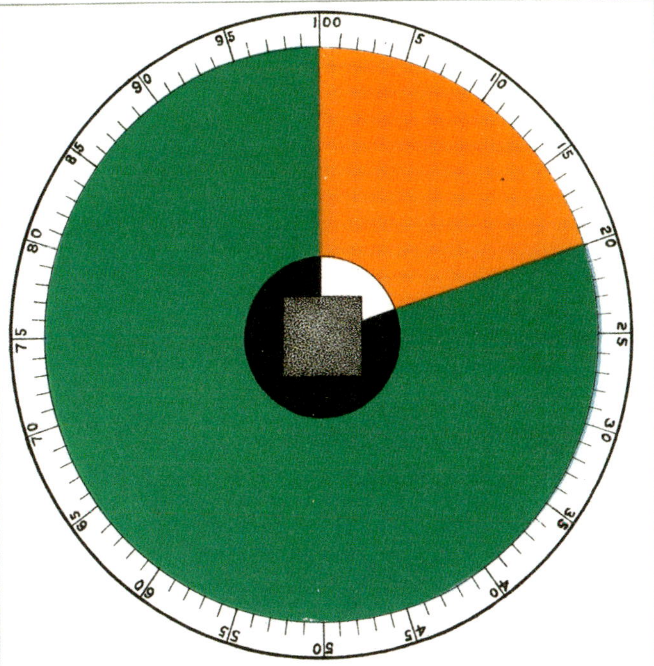


SPECTRAL ORANGE AND ITS COMPLEMENT, GREEN-BLUE, IN THEIR RELATIVE PROPORTIONS

The gray in the centre of this Plate is the gray produced by the above two complements when mixed on a color wheel, and corresponds exactly to the gray produced by the given amounts of black and white.

(N. B. The above proportions were obtained in an average light. They will vary with all variations in the quality and quantity of the illumination.)

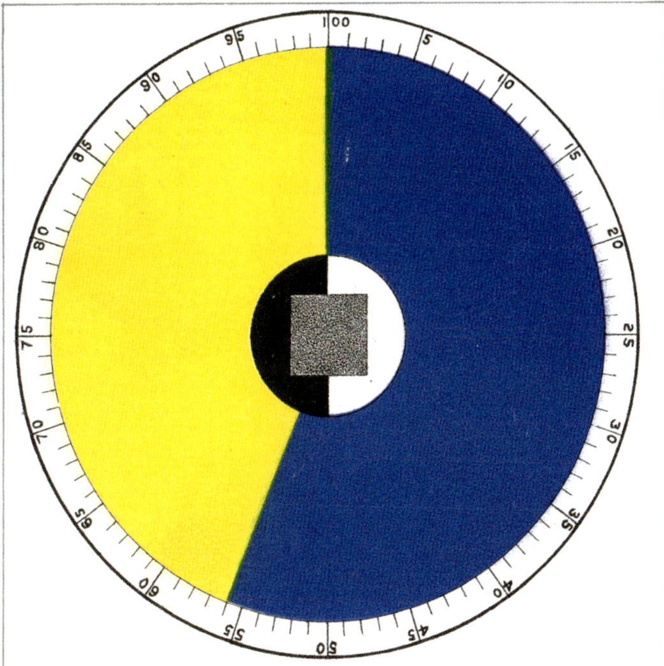


SPECTRAL YELLOW AND ITS COMPLEMENT,
SPECTRAL BLUE,

OR

SPECTRAL BLUE AND ITS COMPLEMENT,
SPECTRAL YELLOW,
IN THEIR RELATIVE PROPORTIONS

The gray in the centre of this Plate is the gray produced by the above two complements when mixed on a color wheel, and corresponds exactly to the gray produced by the given amounts of black and white.

(N. B. The above proportions were obtained in an average light. They will vary with all variations in the quality and quantity of the illumination.)

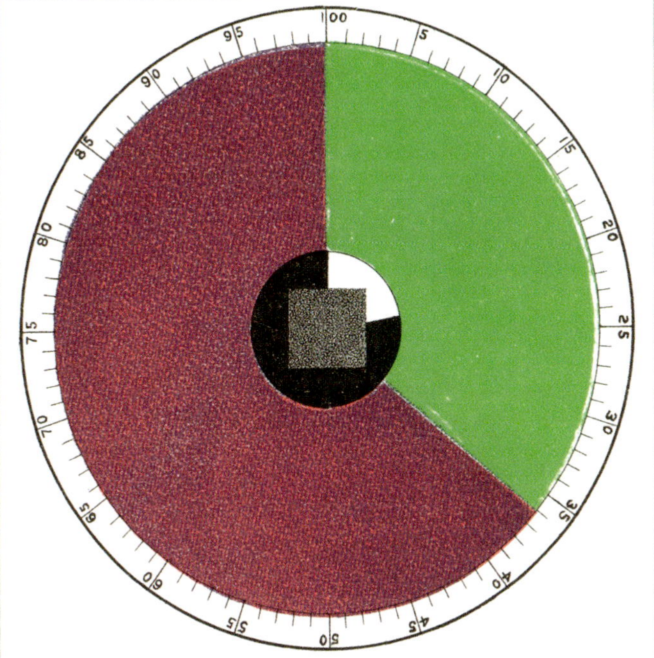


SPECTRAL GREEN AND ITS COMPLEMENT, PURPLE, IN THEIR RELATIVE PROPORTIONS.

The gray in the centre of this plate is the gray produced by the above two complements when mixed on a color wheel, and corresponds exactly to the gray produced by the given amounts of black and white.

(N. B. The above proportions were obtained in an average light. They will vary with all variations in the quality and quantity of the illumination.)

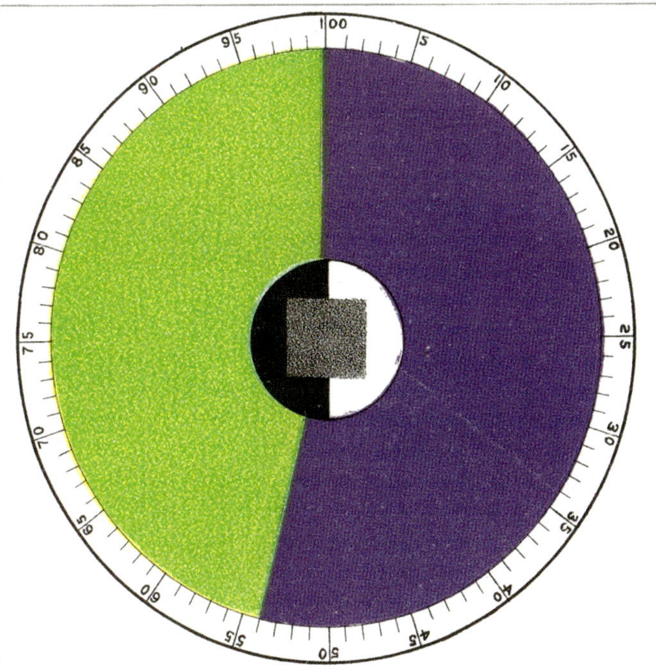


SPECTRAL VIOLET AND ITS COMPLEMENT, YELLOW-GREEN, IN THEIR RELATIVE PROPORTIONS

The gray in the centre of this plate is the gray produced by the above two complements when mixed on a color wheel, and corresponds exactly to the gray produced by the given amounts of black and white.

(N. B. The above proportions were obtained in an average light. They will vary with all variations in the quality and quantity of the illumination.)

PLATE XXVII

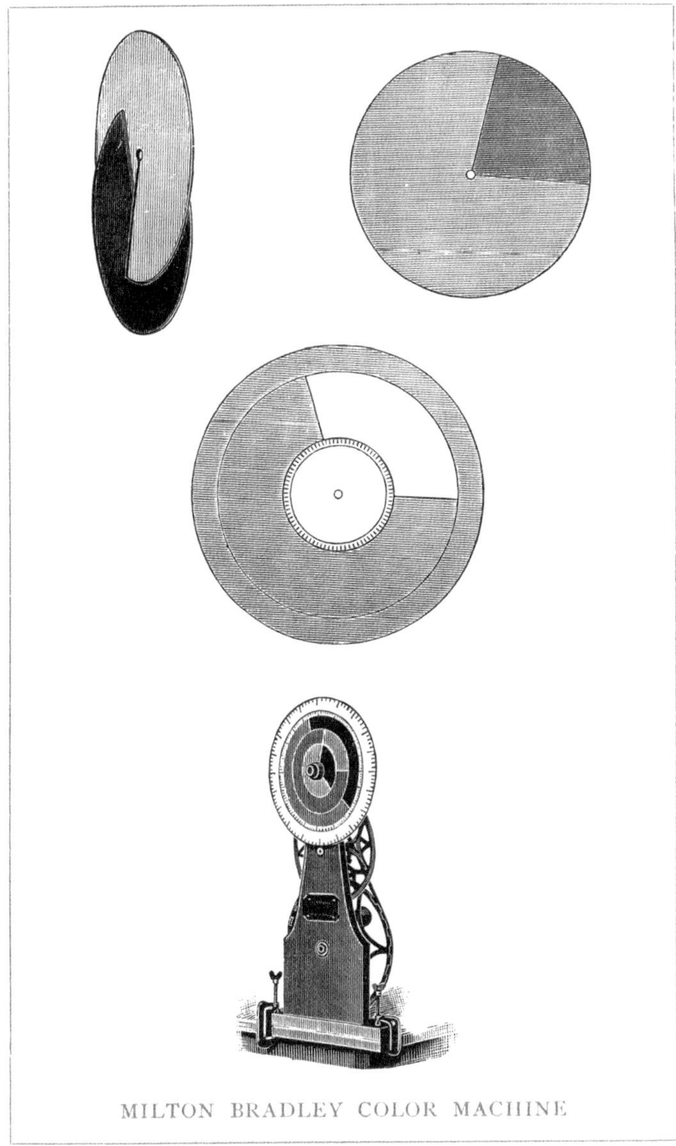

MILTON BRADLEY COLOR MACHINE

PLATE XXVIII

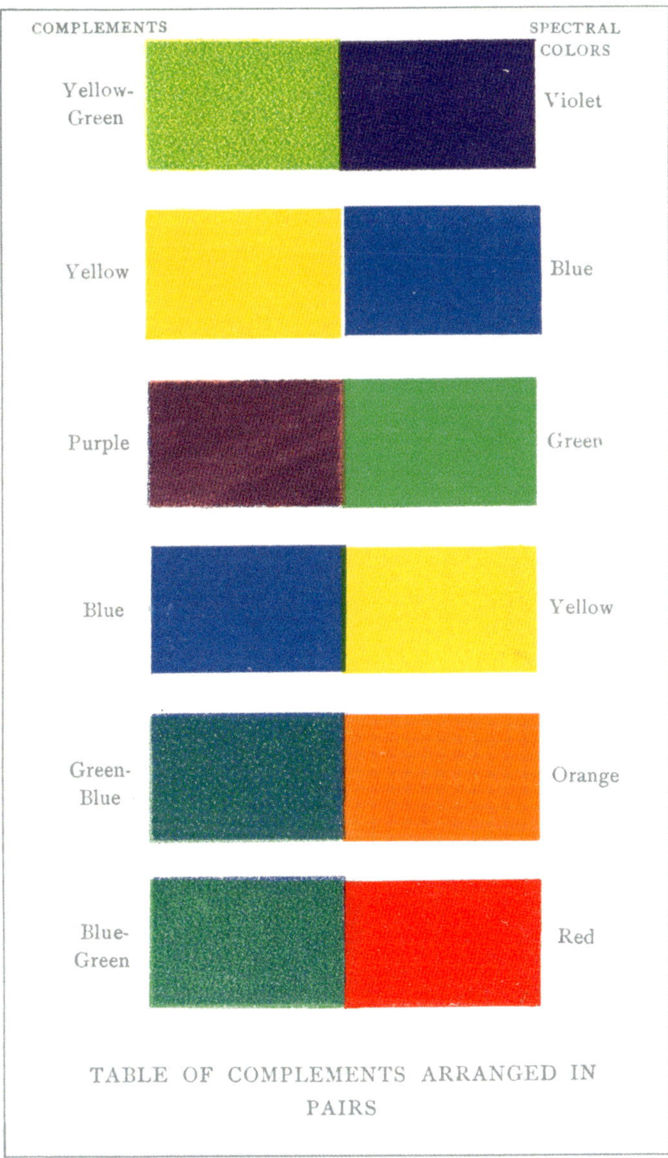


TABLE OF COMPLEMENTS ARRANGED IN PAIRS

PLATE XXIX

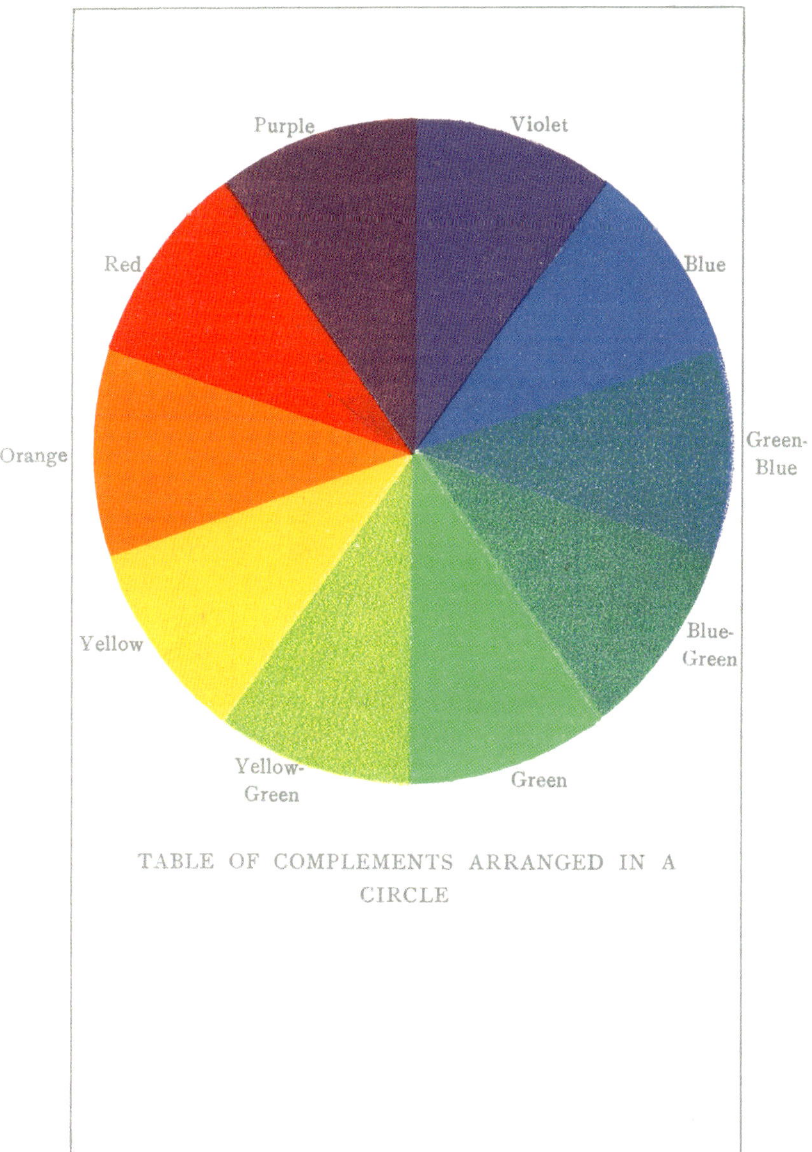


TABLE OF COMPLEMENTS ARRANGED IN A CIRCLE

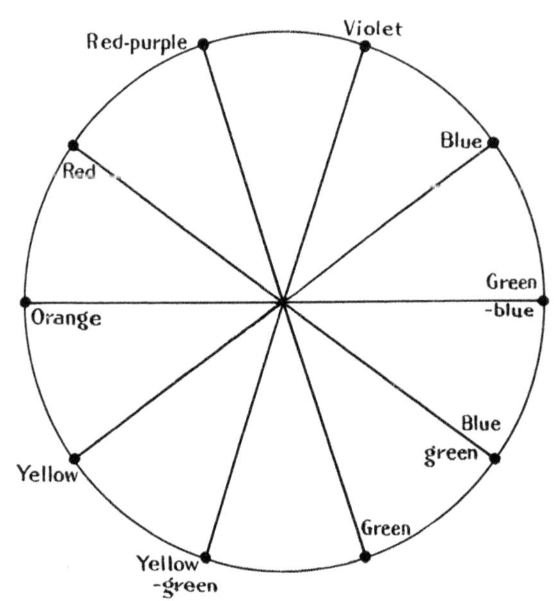


CONTRAST DIAGRAM

See page 58. Transparency accompanying the volume is for use with this plate.

Plate XXXI

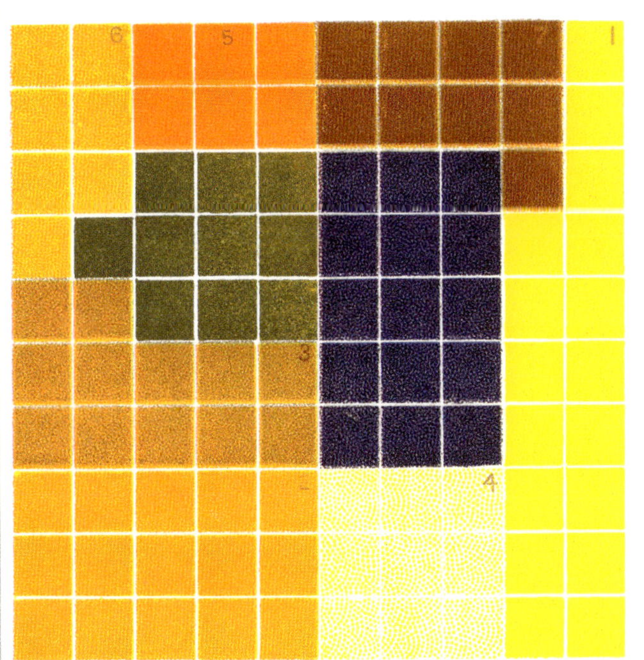


COLOR ANALYSIS FROM A PRIZE DINNER TABLE

A harmony of yellow and blue.

See page 70.

PLATE XXXII

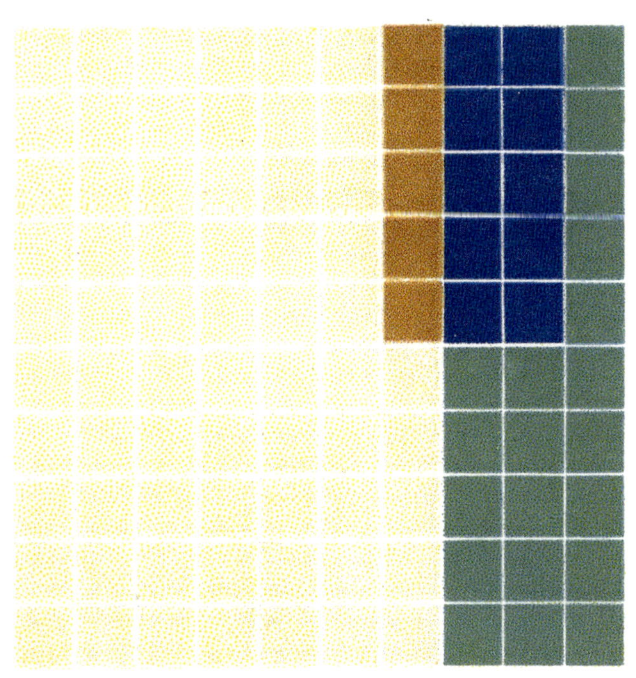

COLOR ANALYSIS FROM TEACUP AND SAUCER

| | |
|---|---|
| Yellow Tint . . . . . . . . . . . . . . . . . | 65 |
| Yellow Shade . . . . . . . . . . . . . . . . | 5 |
| Blue Tint . . . . . . . . . . . . . . . . . | 20 |
| Spectral Blue . . . . . . . . . . . . . . . . | 10 |
| | 100 |

Plate XXXIII

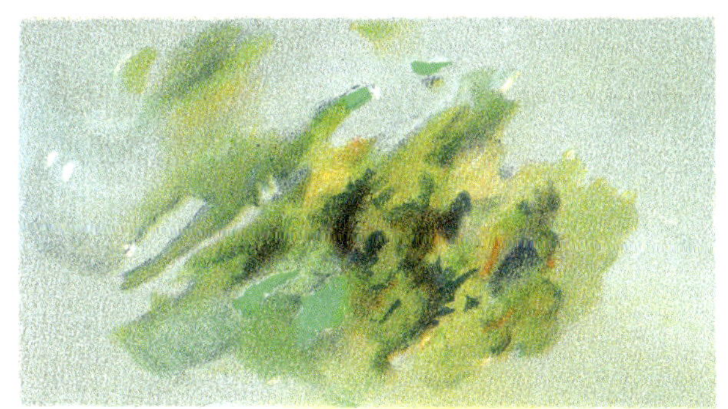

A HARMONY OF ONE COLOR

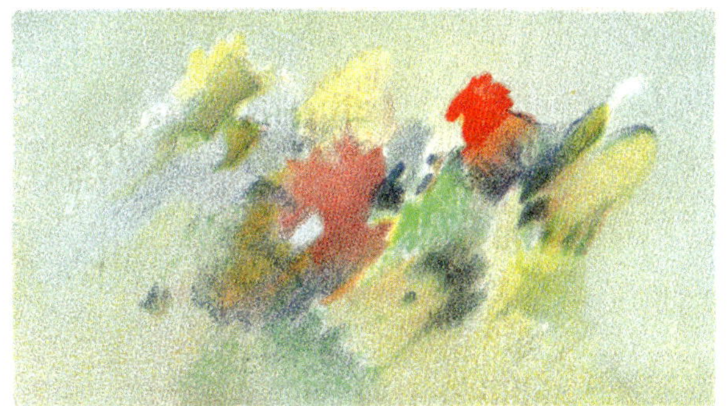

A HARMONY OF CONTRAST

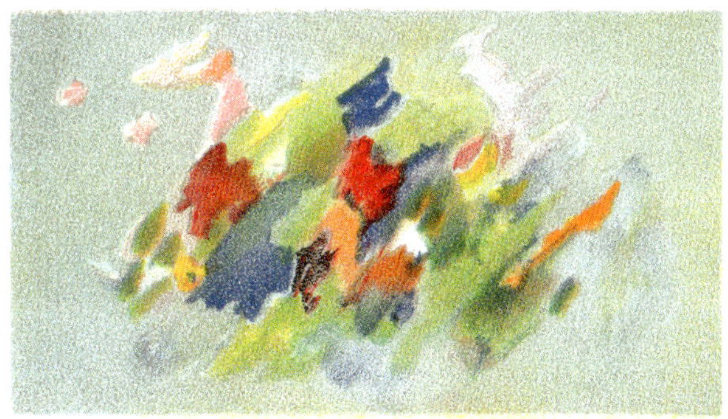

COMPLEX HARMONY

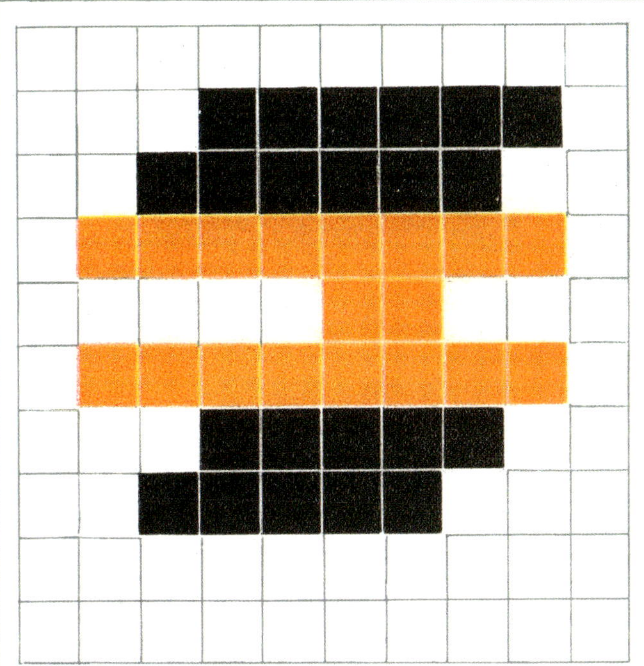

COLOR ANALYSIS OF A BOOK ADVERTISEMENT

| | |
|---|---|
| White | 60 |
| Black | 22 |
| Yellow | 18 |
| | 100 |

Plate XXXV

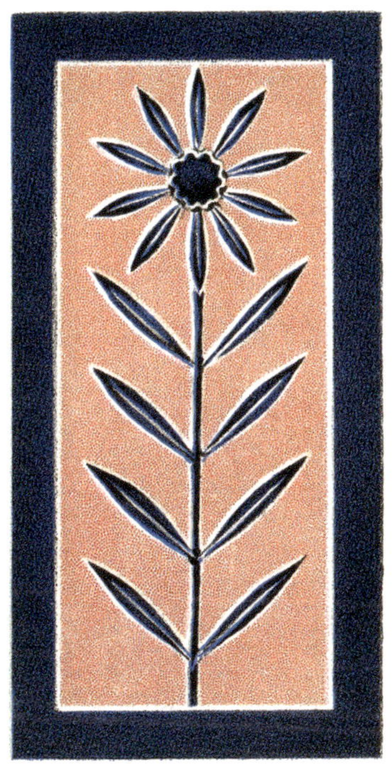

HARMONY HELPED BY OUTLINE

PLATE XXXVI

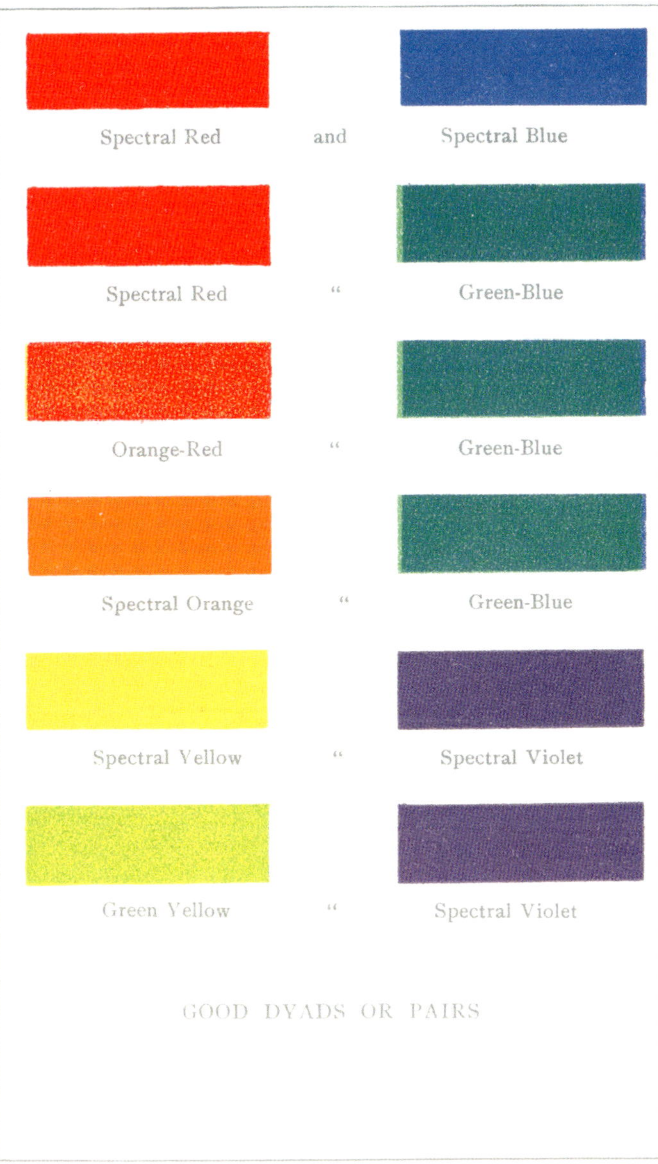


GOOD DYADS OR PAIRS

PLATE XXXVII

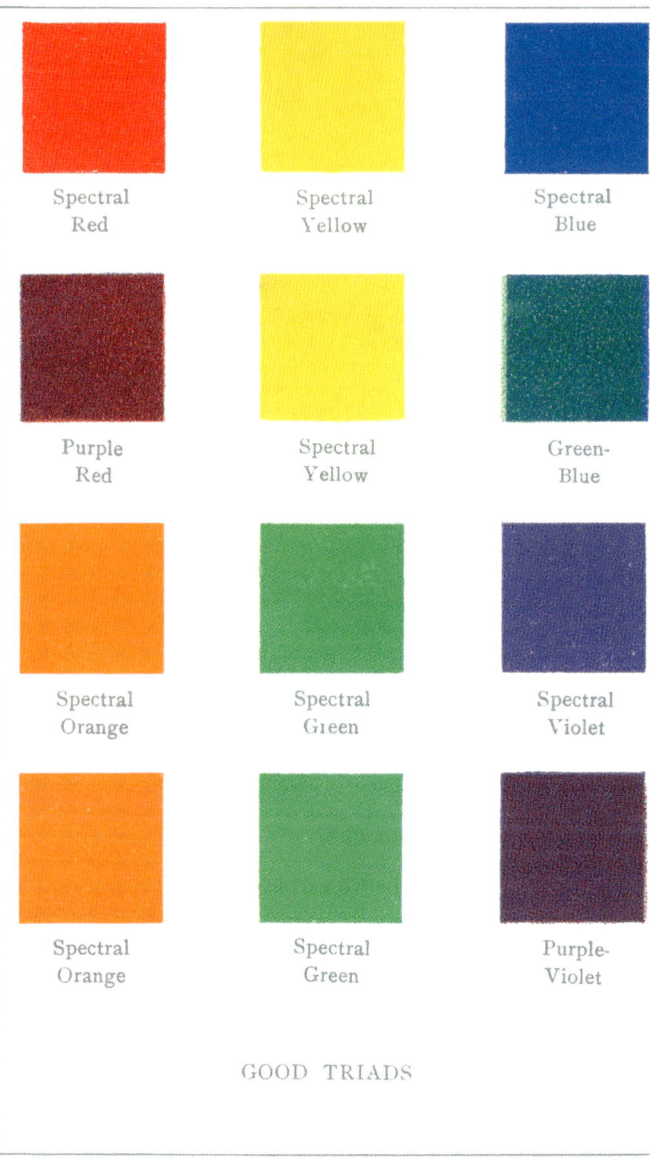


GOOD TRIADS

Plate XXXVIII

HARMONY BY GRADATION

PLATE XXXIX

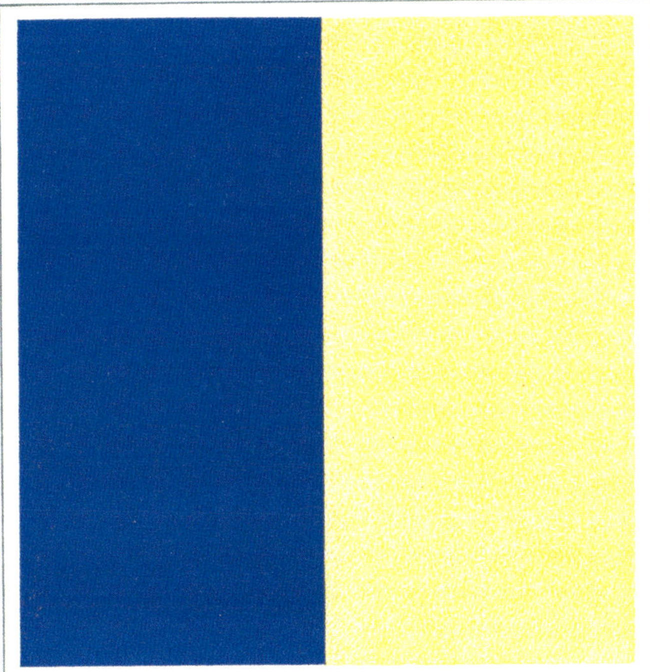

HARMONY BY CHANGE OF QUALITY

(In the yellow.)

PLATE XL

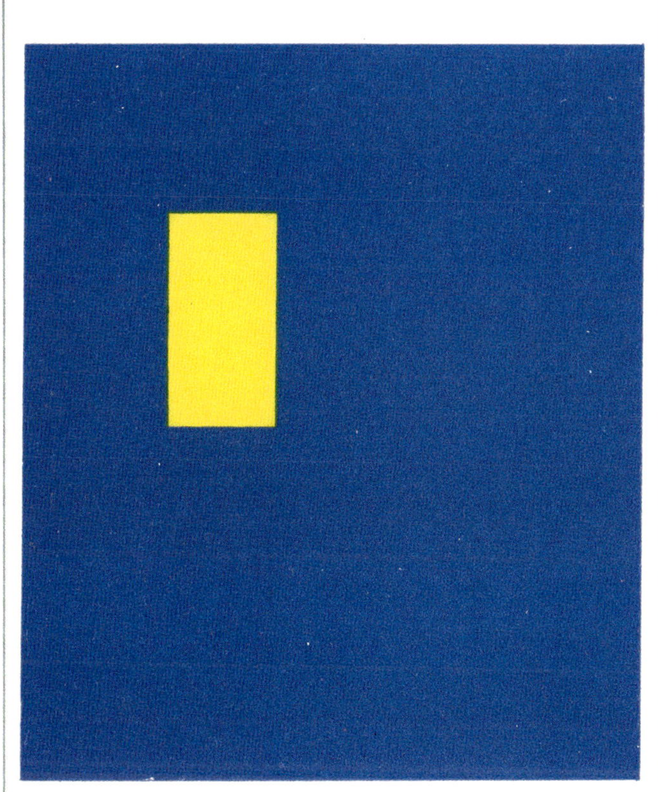

HARMONY BY CHANGE OF QUANTITY

PLATE XLI

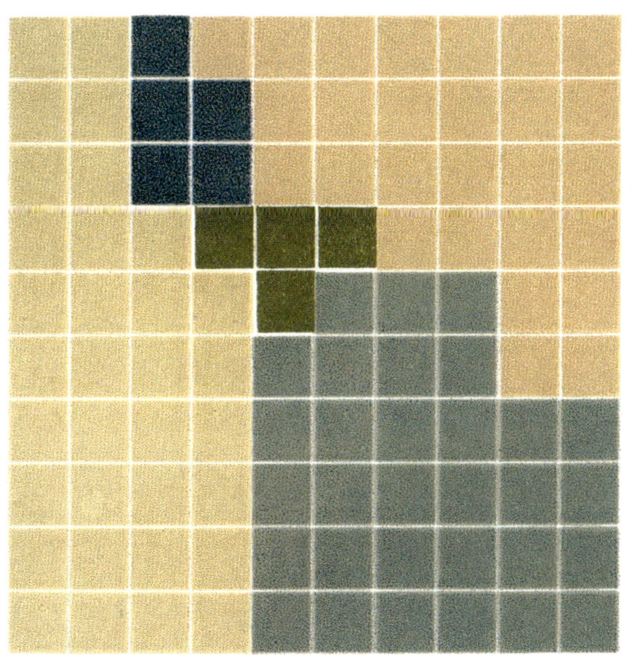

HARMONY BY CHANGE OF BOTH QUANTITY AND QUALITY

Three yellows, two blues.

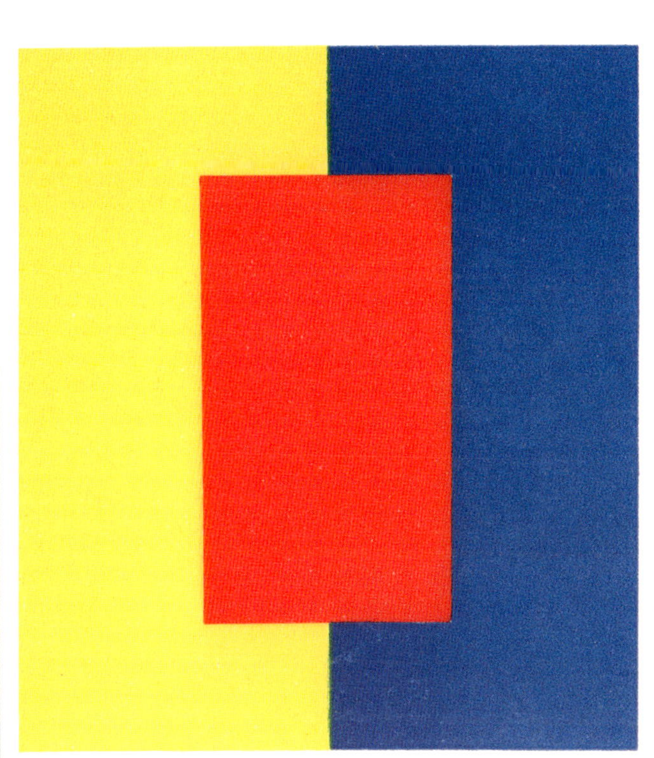

HARMONY BY THE ADDITION OF ANOTHER COLOR

PLATE XLIII

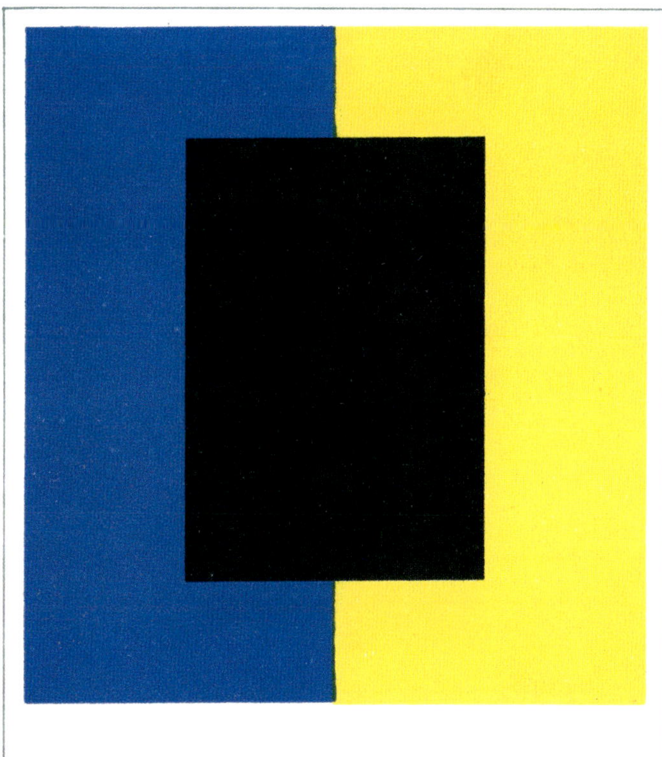

HARMONY BY THE ADDITION OF BLACK

Plate XLIV

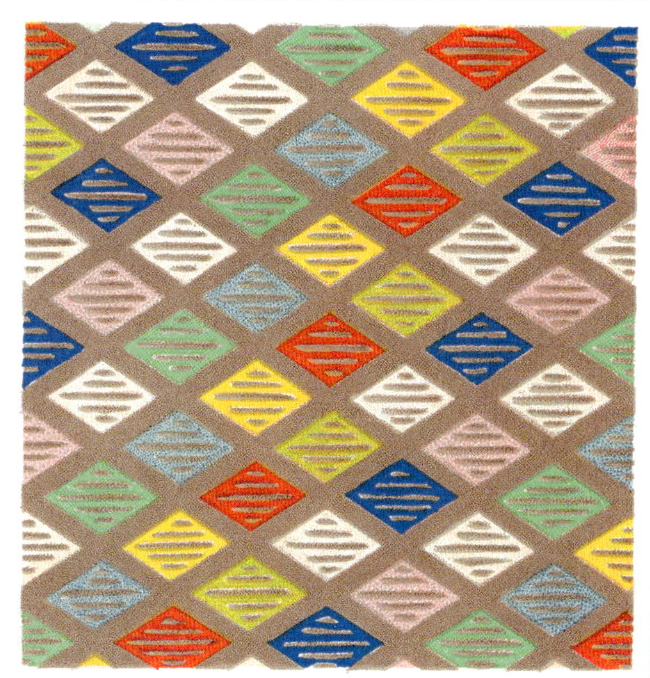

HARMONY FROM A DOMINANT HUE

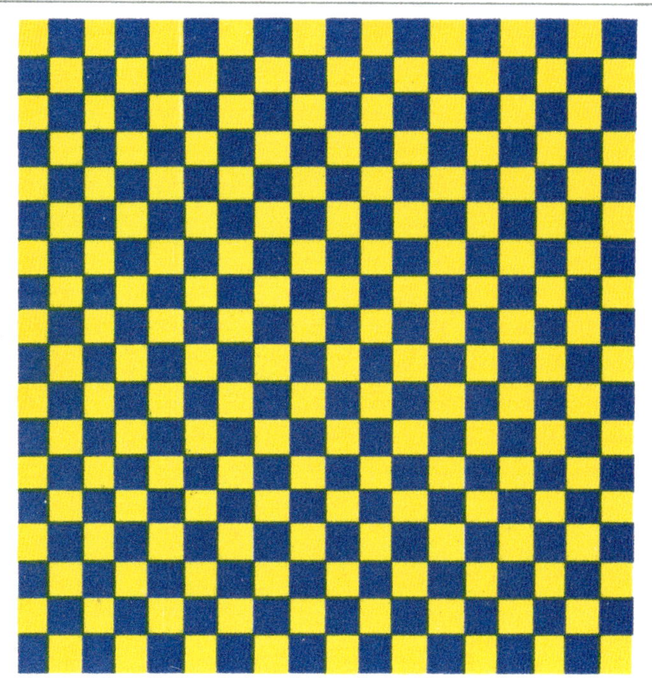

HARMONY BY INTERCHANGE

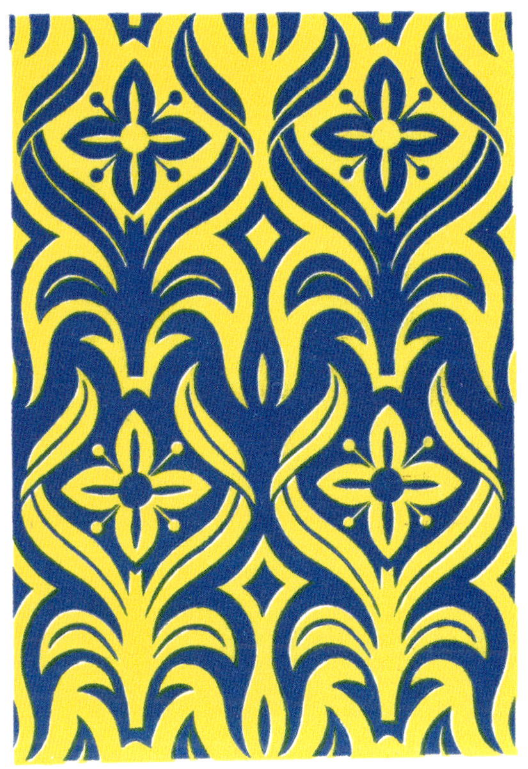

HARMONY BY COUNTERCHANGE

From Orange to Cream-White

From Yellow to Yellow-White

From Green to Green-White

From Blue to Blue-White

THE TRUE CHARACTER OF SOME OF THE SO-CALLED "WHITES"

(which are really pale tints)

From Brown to Yellow

From Green to Yellow

From Pink to Yellow

From Red to Yellow

SOME CHANGES BY GRADATION FROM ONE COLOR TO ANOTHER

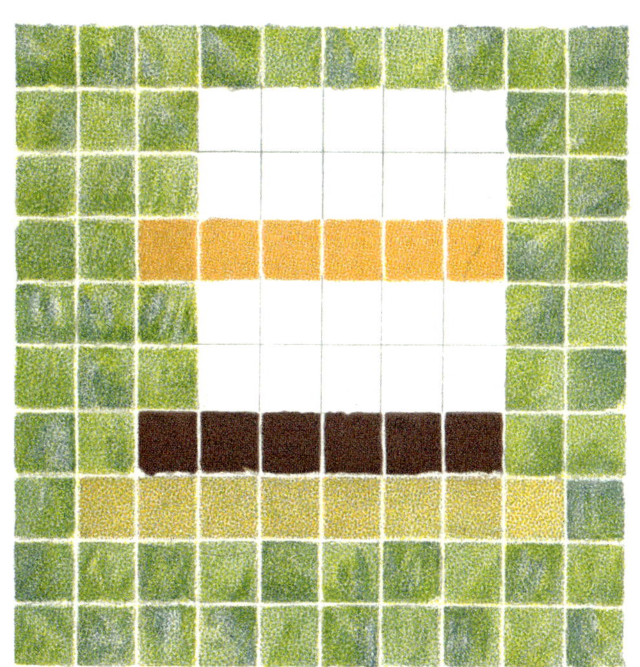

COLOR ANALYSIS FROM ASSYRIAN TILES

| | |
|---|---|
| Blue-Green Ground | 60 |
| Greenish Yellow | 8 |
| Orange | 6 |
| Purple-Brown | 6 |
| White | 20 |
| | 100 |

The variation of color in the blue-green tiles is especially fine.

PLATE L

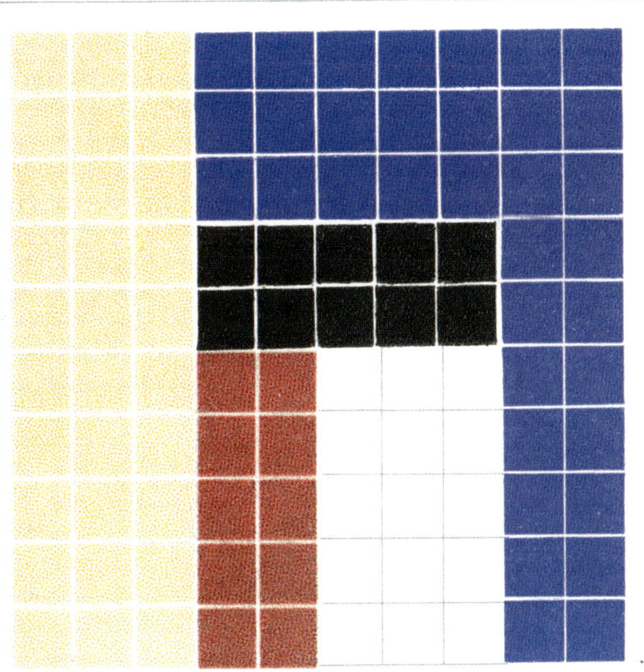

COLOR ANALYSIS FROM ASSYRIAN TILES

| | |
|---|---|
| Blue | 35 |
| Yellow | 30 |
| White | 15 |
| Dull Red | 10 |
| Black | 10 |
| | 100 |

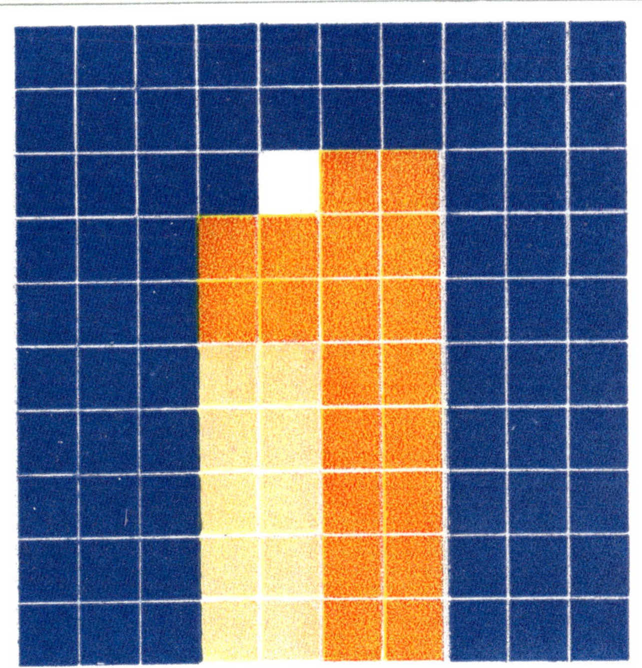

COLOR ANALYSIS FROM ASSYRIAN TILES

| | |
|---|---|
| Blue | 69 |
| Deep Yellow | 20 |
| Light Yellow | 10 |
| White | 1 |
| | 100 |

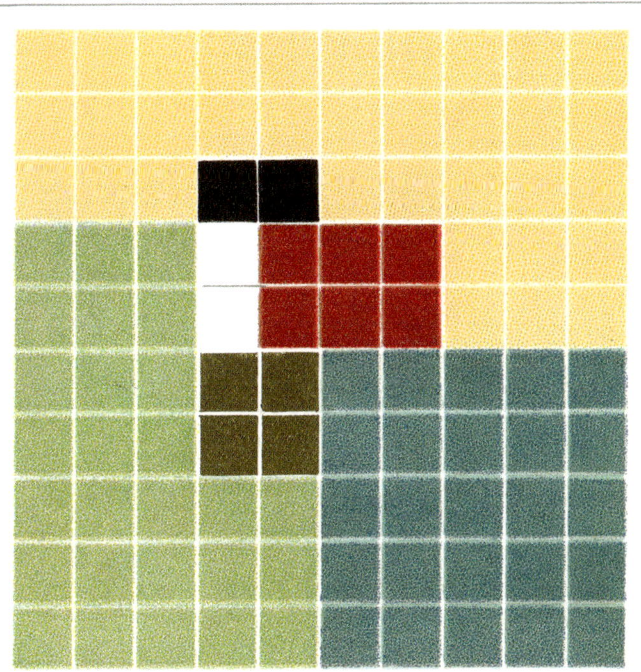

COLOR ANALYSIS FROM A MUMMY COVER

| | |
|---|---|
| Pale Yellow | 34 |
| Green | 27 |
| Blue | 25 |
| Red | 6 |
| Gold | 4 |
| Black | 2 |
| White | 2 |
| | 100 |

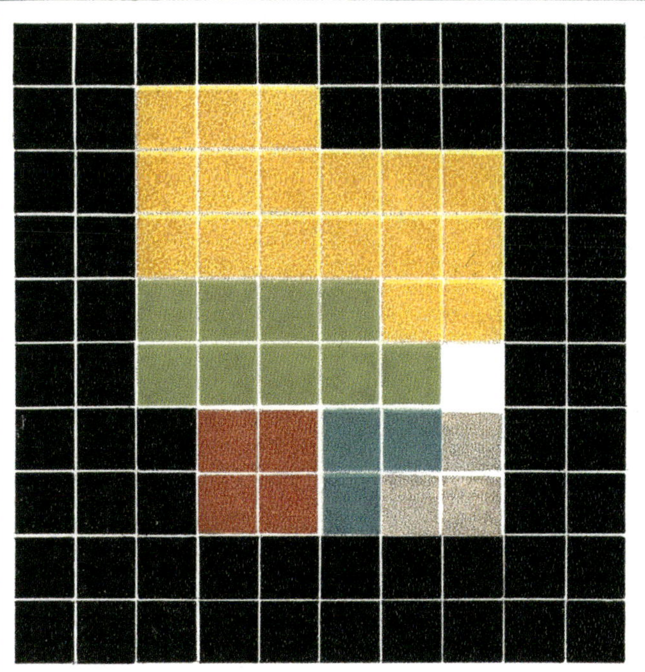

COLOR ANALYSIS FROM AN EGYPTIAN MUMMY CASE

| | |
|---|---|
| Black Ground | 63 |
| Yellow (all through design) | 17 |
| Green | 9 |
| Red | 4 |
| Light Red | 3 |
| Blue | 3 |
| White | 1 |
| | 100 |

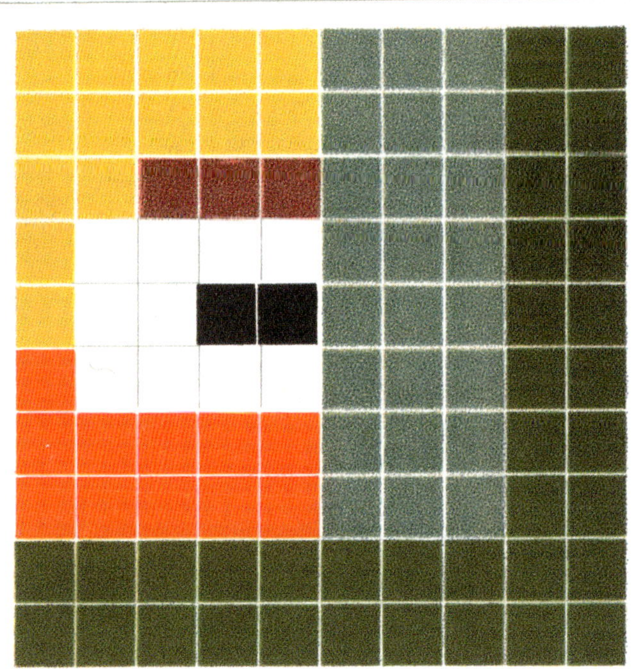

COLOR ANALYSIS FROM A MUMMY CASE

| | |
|---|---|
| Green | 36 |
| Blue-Green | 24 |
| Yellow | 14 |
| Red | 11 |
| White | 10 |
| Dull Red | 3 |
| Black | 2 |
| | 100 |

Much like a parrot's plumage.

PLATE LV

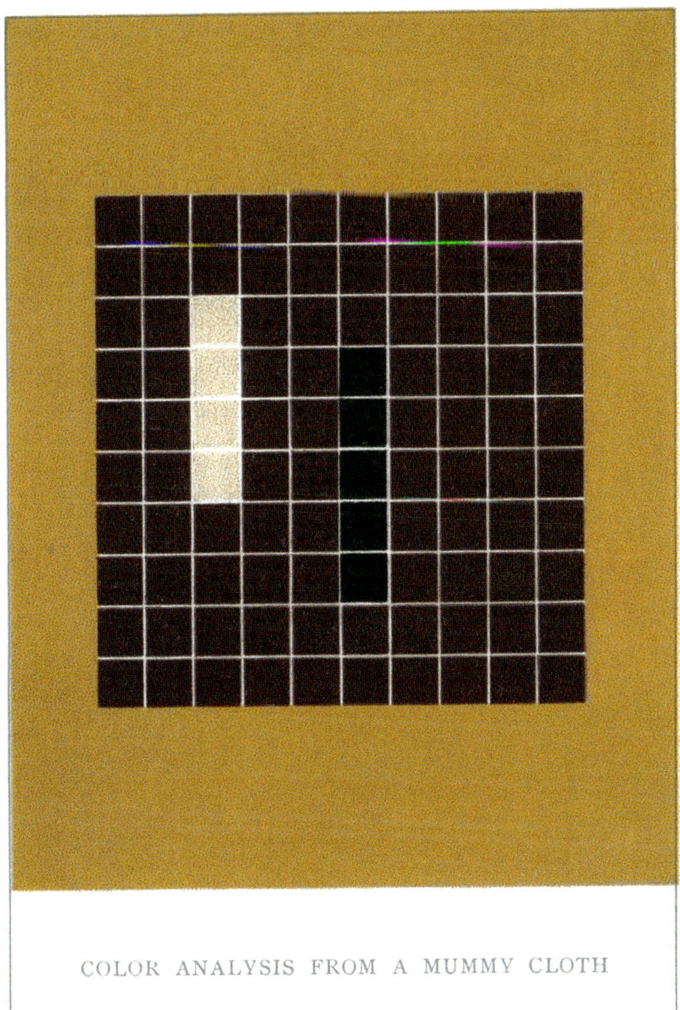

COLOR ANALYSIS FROM A MUMMY CLOTH

| | |
|---|---|
| Purple Red | 91 |
| Black | 5 |
| Pale Gray | 4 |
| | 100 |

Dull yellow ground.

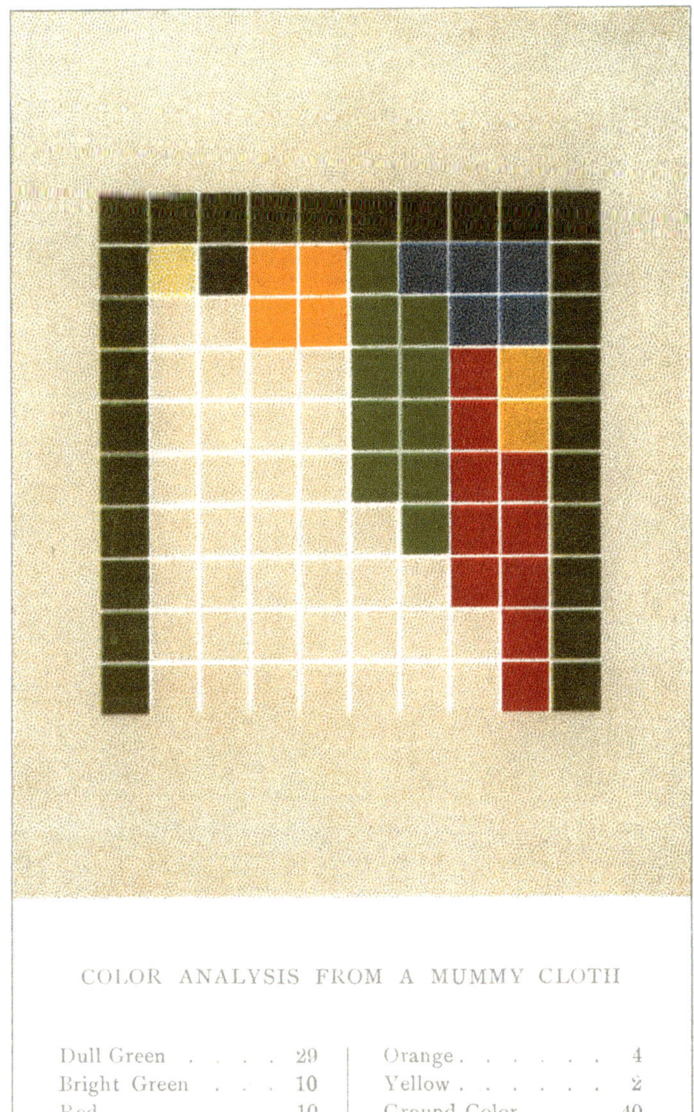

COLOR ANALYSIS FROM A MUMMY CLOTH

| | | | |
|---|---|---|---|
| Dull Green | 29 | Orange | 4 |
| Bright Green | 10 | Yellow | 2 |
| Red | 10 | Ground Color | 40 |
| Blue | 5 | | 100 |

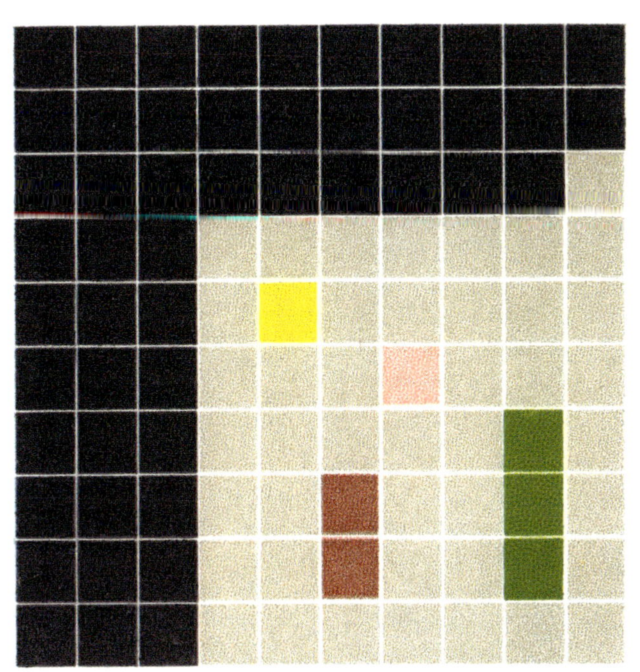

COLOR ANALYSIS FROM A MUMMY CLOTH

| | |
|---|---|
| Deep, Dull Blue | 50 |
| Gray | 43 |
| Green | 3 |
| Dull Red | 2 |
| Pale Red | 1 |
| Yellow | 1 |
| | 100 |

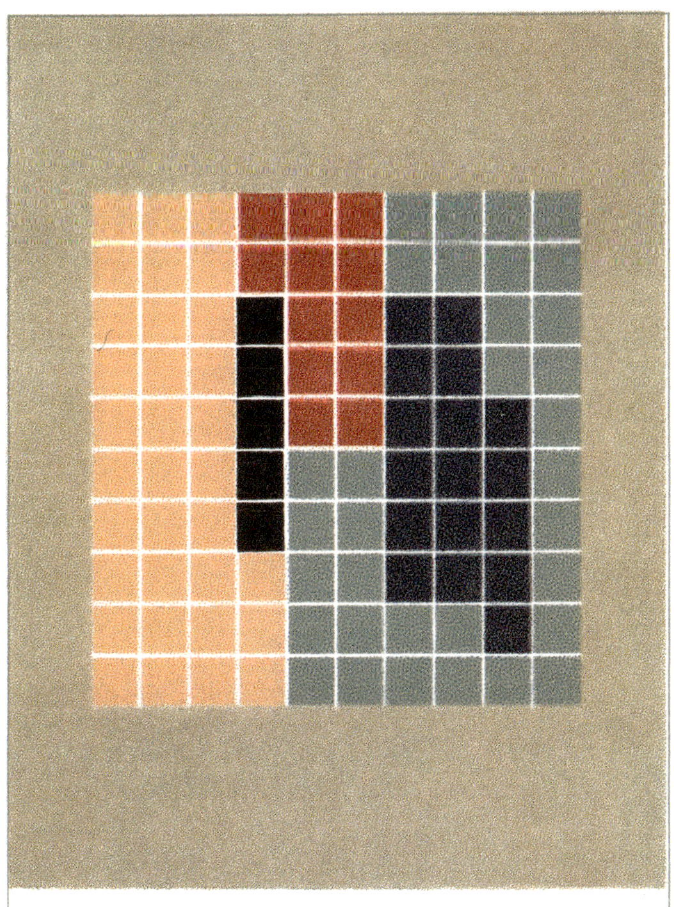

COLOR ANALYSIS FROM A MUMMY CLOTH

| | |
|---|---|
| Light Blue | 32 |
| Dark Blue | 17 |
| Light Red | 33 |
| Dark Red | 12 |
| Black Stems | 5 |
| | 100 |

Gray ground; the ornament a stripe of embroidered leaves and stems.

Plate LIX

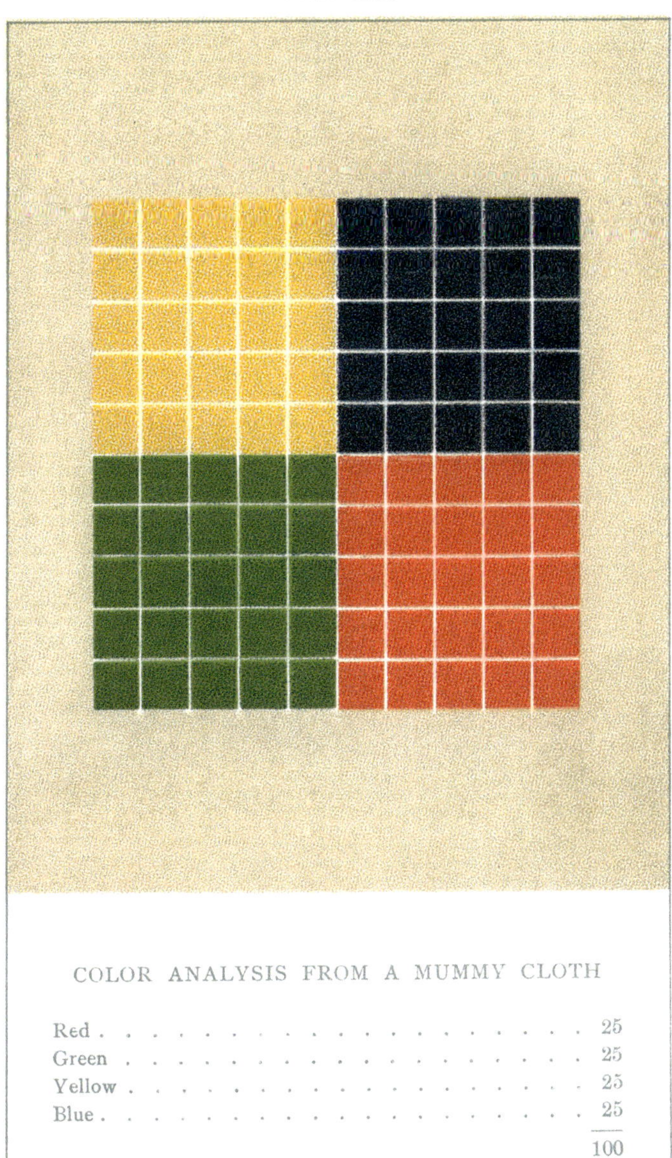

COLOR ANALYSIS FROM A MUMMY CLOTH

| | |
|---|---|
| Red | 25 |
| Green | 25 |
| Yellow | 25 |
| Blue | 25 |
| | 100 |

Gray ground.

PLATE LX

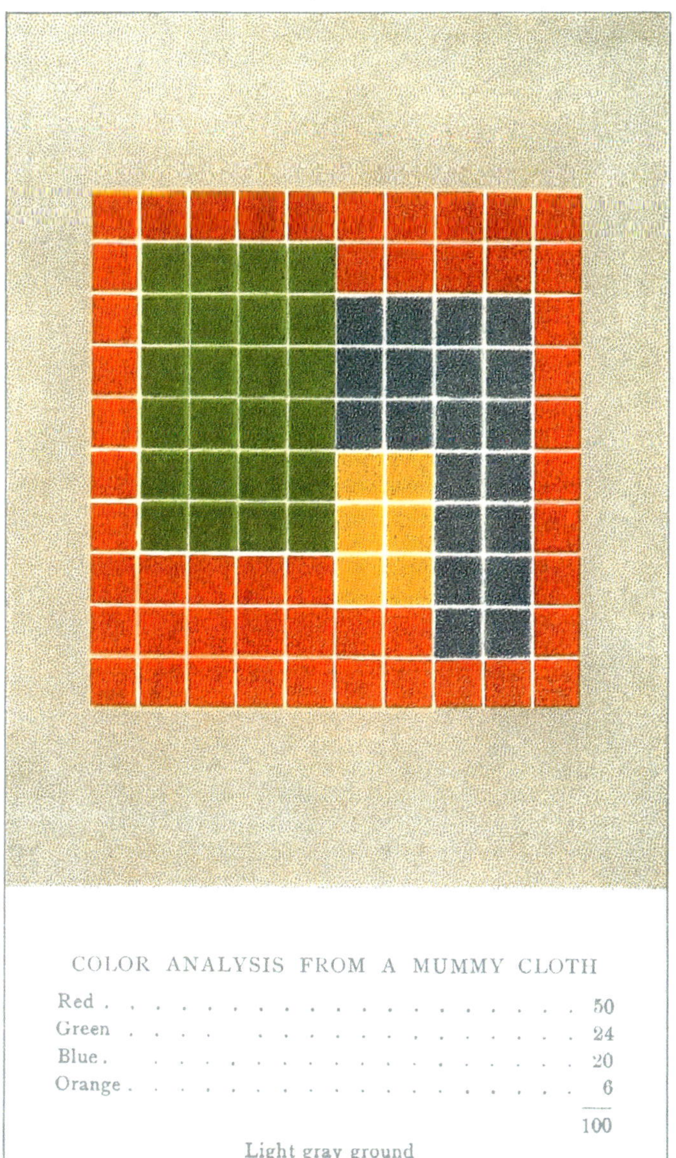

COLOR ANALYSIS FROM A MUMMY CLOTH

| | |
|---|---|
| Red | 50 |
| Green | 24 |
| Blue | 20 |
| Orange | 6 |
| | 100 |

Light gray ground

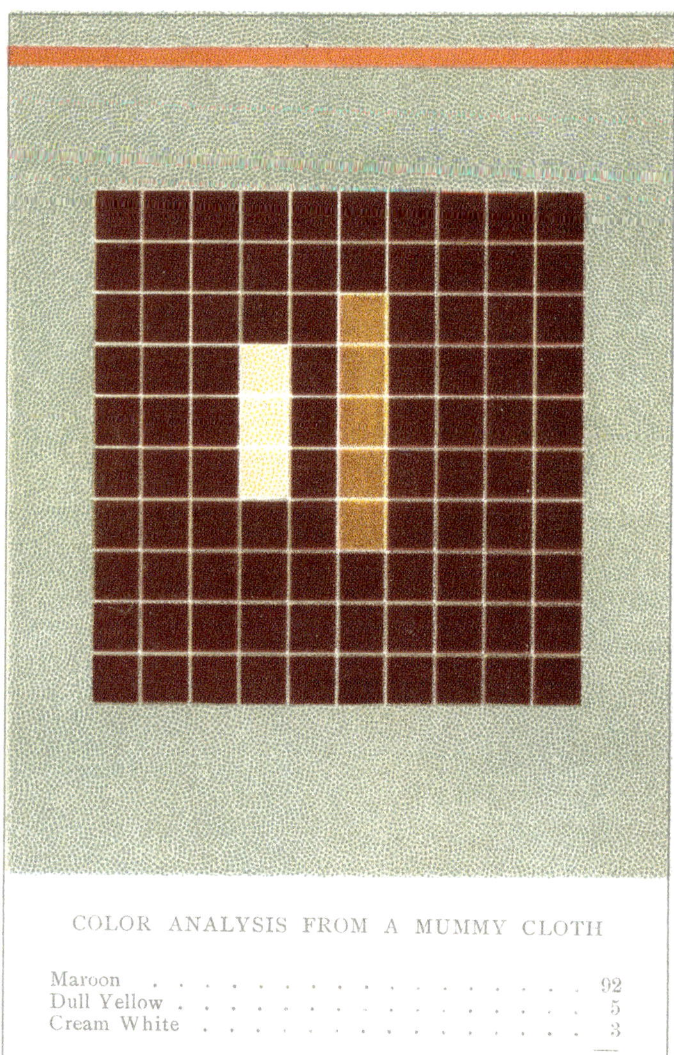

COLOR ANALYSIS FROM A MUMMY CLOTH

| | |
|---|---|
| Maroon | 92 |
| Dull Yellow | 5 |
| Cream White | 3 |
| | 100 |

Green linen ground with red border. Cream and yellow runs through design in small portions.

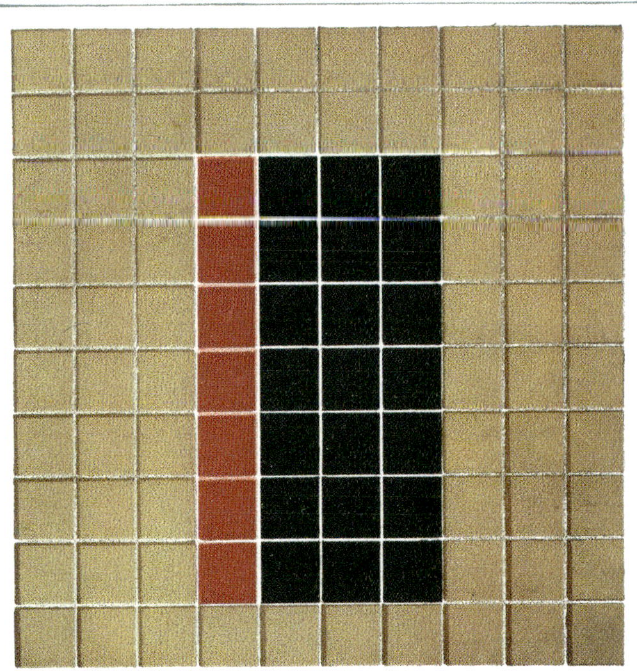

COLOR ANALYSIS FROM AN EARLY GREEK VASE

| | |
|---|---|
| Gray | 72 |
| Black | 21 |
| Dull Red | 7 |
| | 100 |

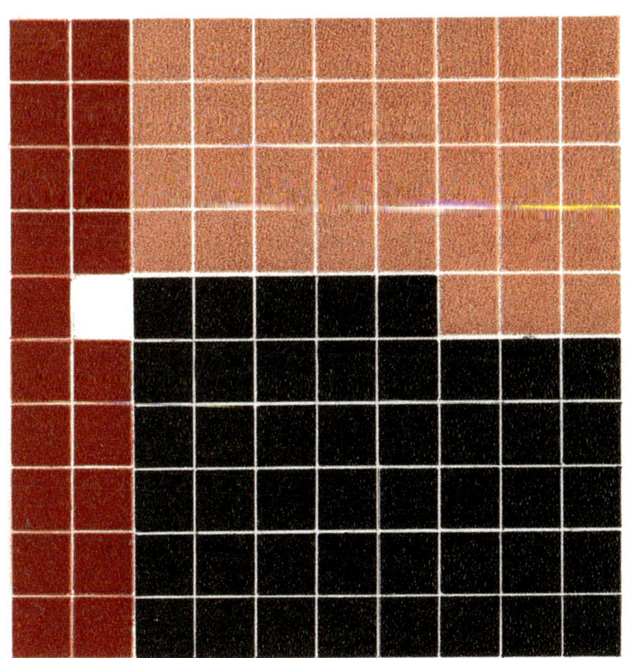

COLOR ANALYSIS FROM A GREEK VASE

| | |
|---|---|
| Light Red | 35 |
| Dark Red | 19 |
| Black | 45 |
| White | 1 |
| | 100 |

The Ground partly red, partly black, white in fine outlines or small dotted outlines.

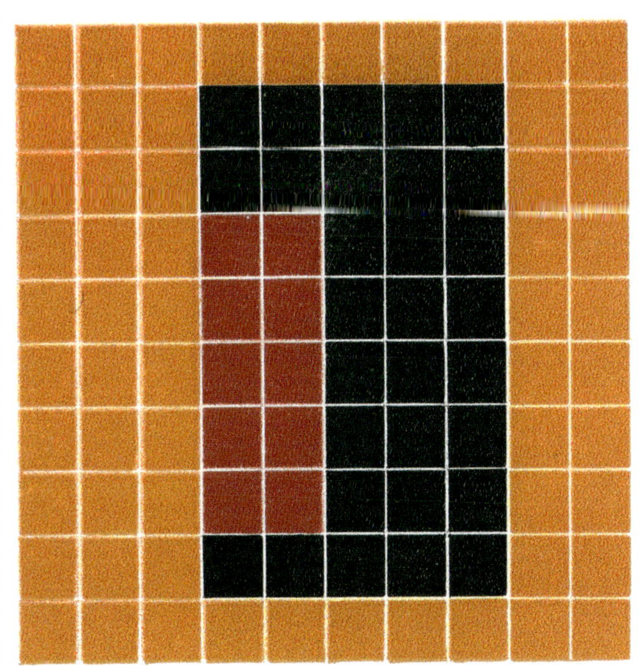

COLOR ANALYSIS FROM A GREEK VASE

| | |
|---|---|
| Dull Orange | 60 |
| Dull Red | 10 |
| Black | 30 |
| | 100 |

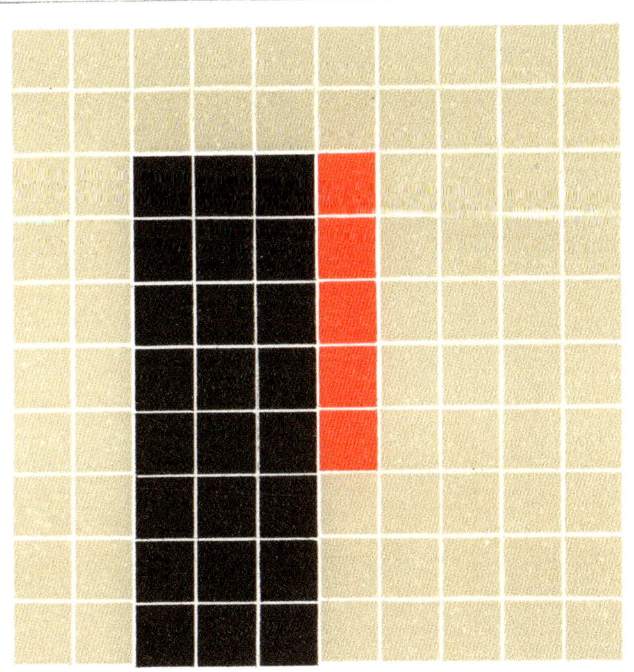

COLOR ANALYSIS FROM A GREEK VASE

| | |
|---|---|
| Gray Ground | 71 |
| Black | 24 |
| Red | 5 |
| | 100 |

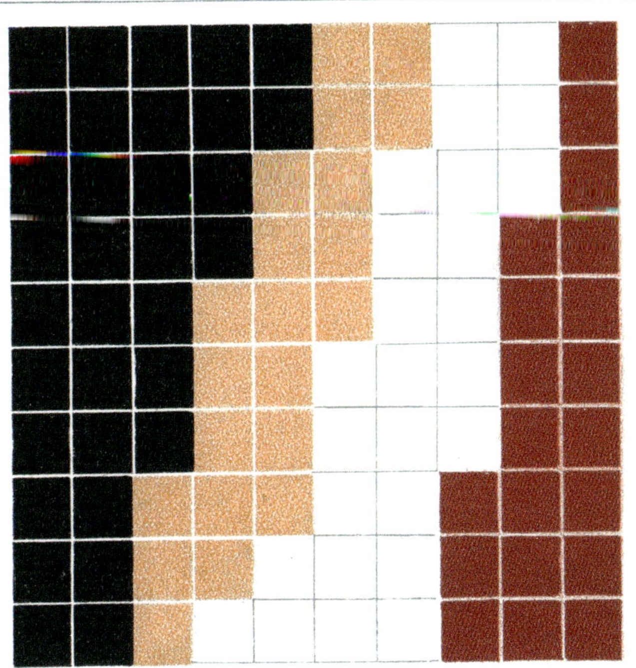

COLOR ANALYSIS FROM ARAB MOSAICS

| | |
|---|---|
| Black | 33 |
| White | 26 |
| Light Red | 21 |
| Dull Red | 20 |
| | 100 |

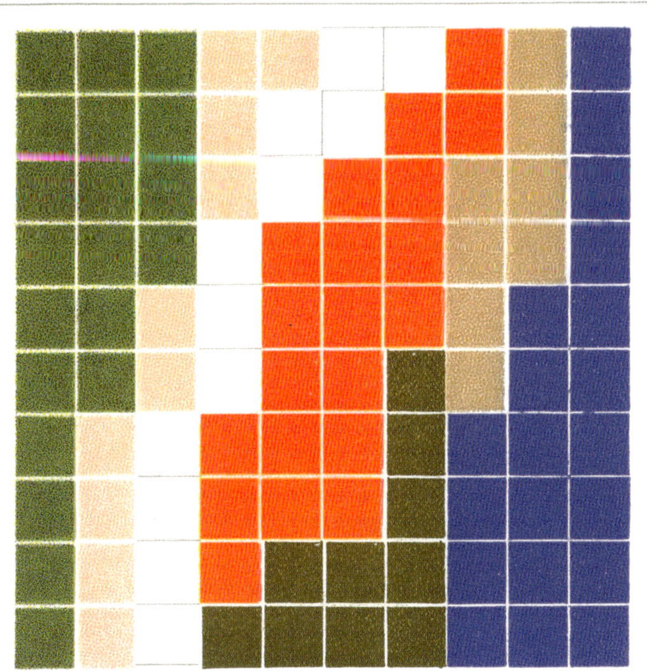

COLOR ANALYSIS FROM ARABIAN ILLUMINATION

| | |
|---|---|
| Blue | 20 |
| Green | 20 |
| Red | 20 |
| Pale Red | 10 |
| Gray | 8 |
| Gold | 10 |
| White | 12 |
| | 100 |

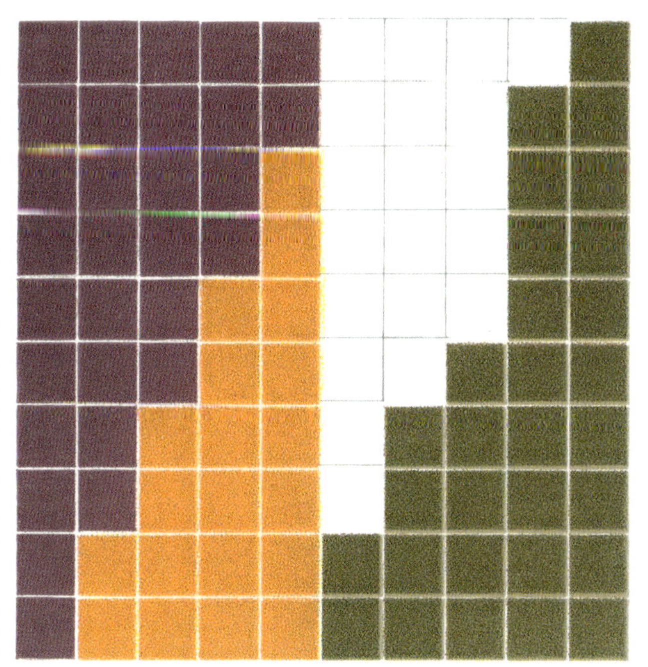

COLOR ANALYSIS FROM MOORISH TILES

| | |
|---|---|
| Olive Green | 30 |
| White | 20 |
| Yellow | 20 |
| Violet | 30 |
| | 100 |

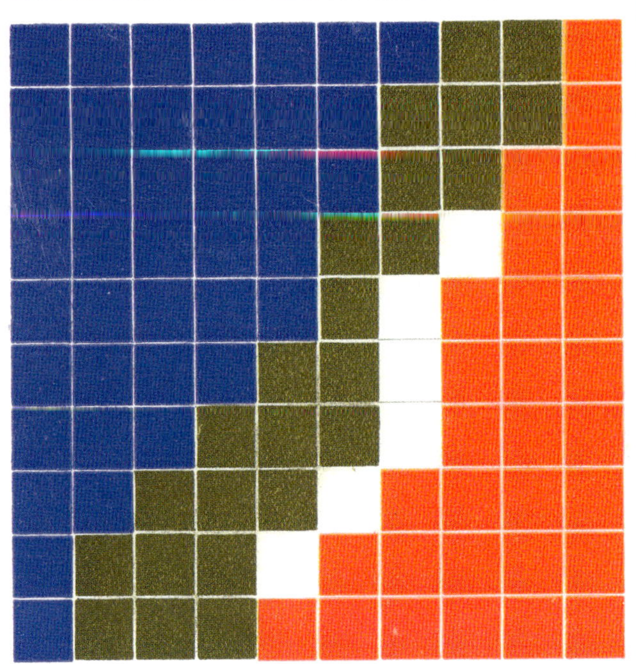

COLOR ANALYSIS FROM A PANEL OF THE ALHAMBRA

| | |
|---|---|
| Blue | 40 |
| Red | 30 |
| Gold | 24 |
| White | 6 |
| | 100 |

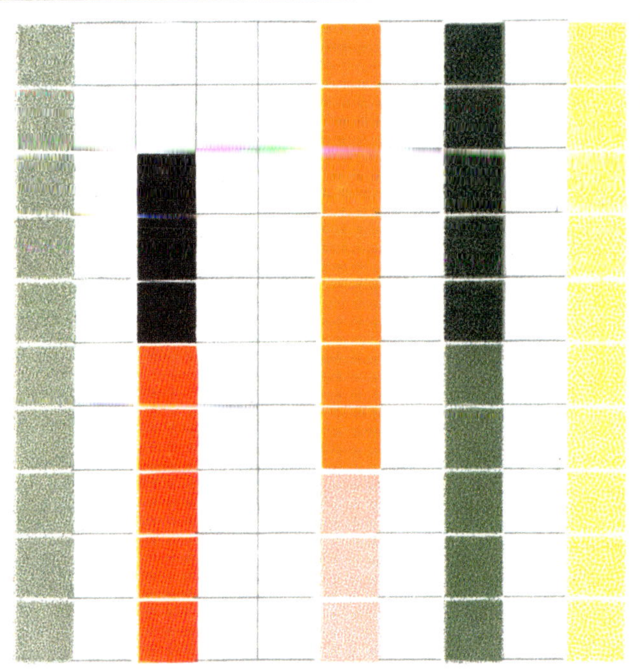

COLOR ANALYSIS FROM A PANEL OF THE TAJ MAHAL, INDIA

| | |
|---|---|
| White Ground | 52 |
| Pale Yellow | 10 |
| Deep Yellow | 7 |
| Red | 5 |
| Pale Green | 10 |
| Medium Green | 5 |
| Dark Green | 5 |
| Black | 3 |
| Pale Pink | 3 |
| | 100 |

Lilies and leaves on white ground.

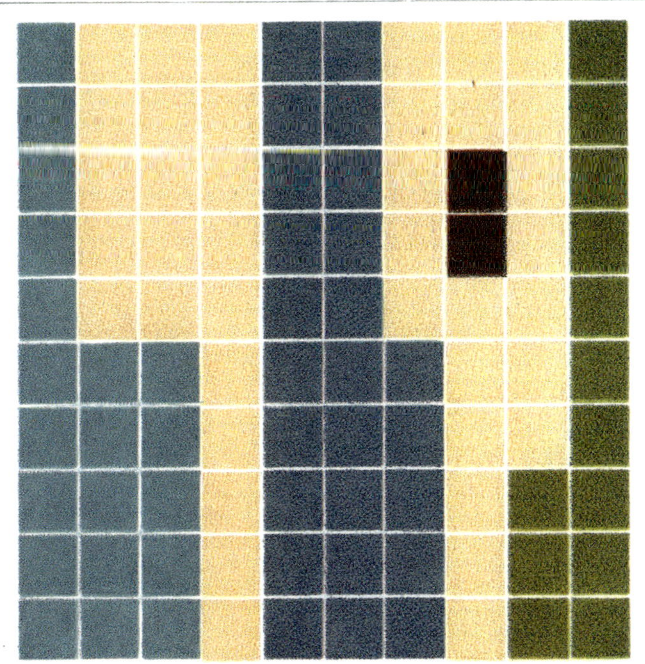

COLOR ANALYSIS FROM DAMASCUS TILES

| | |
|---|---|
| Pale Yellow Ground . . . . . . . . . . . . . . | 40 |
| Deep Cool Blue . . . . . . . . . . . . . . | 25 |
| Light Blue . . . . . . . . . . . . . . . | 20 |
| Green . . . . . . . . . . . . . . . . . | 13 |
| Brown . . . . . . . . . . . . . . . . . | 2 |
| | 100 |

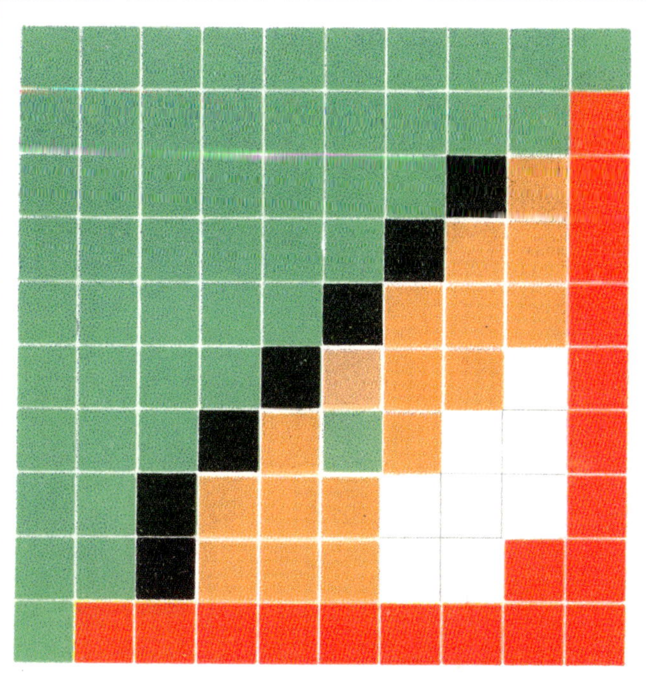

COLOR ANALYSIS FROM CELTIC ORNAMENT

| | |
|---|---|
| Green | 50 |
| Red | 18 |
| Yellow | 17 |
| Black | 7 |
| White | 8 |
| | 100 |

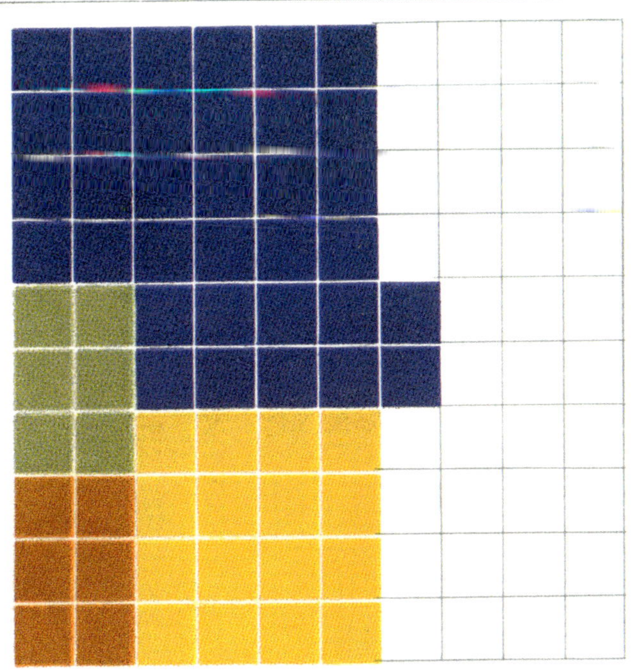

COLOR ANALYSIS FROM ITALIAN MAJOLICA VASE

| | |
|---|---|
| White Ground | 38 |
| Deep Blue | 34 |
| Yellow | 16 |
| Dark Yellow | 6 |
| Green | 6 |
| | 100 |

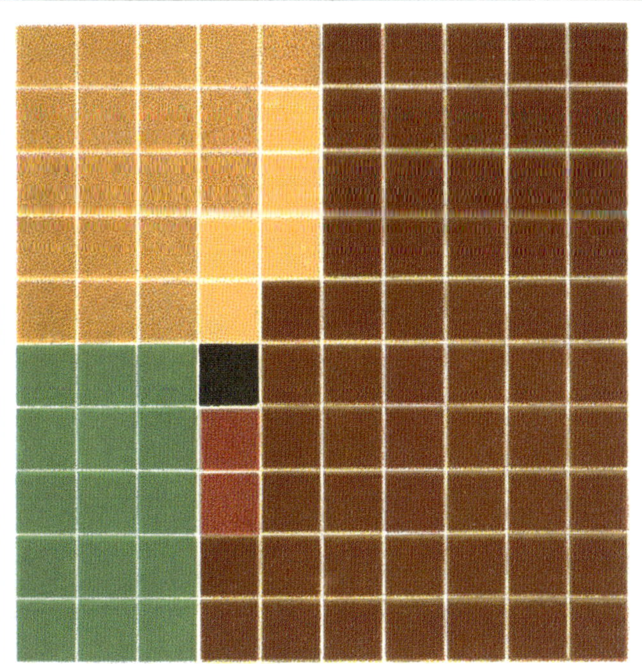

COLOR ANALYSIS FROM PANEL OF DUTCH INLAID CABINET OF THE 15TH CENTURY

| | |
|---|---|
| Brown Wood | 58 |
| Light " | 19 |
| Yellow " | 5 |
| Green " | 15 |
| Dull Red " | 2 |
| Black " | 1 |
| | 100 |

PLATE LXXV

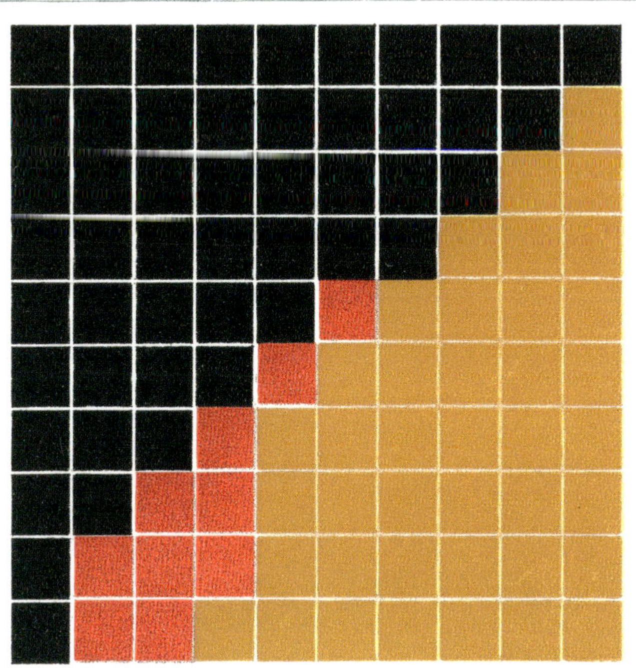

COLOR ANALYSIS FROM SPANISH EMBROIDERY

| | |
|---|---|
| Black Ground . . . . . . . . . . . . . . . . | 50 |
| Yellow Design . . . . . . . . . . . . . . . . | 40 |
| Red in Design . . . . . . . . . . . . . . . . | 10 |
| | 100 |

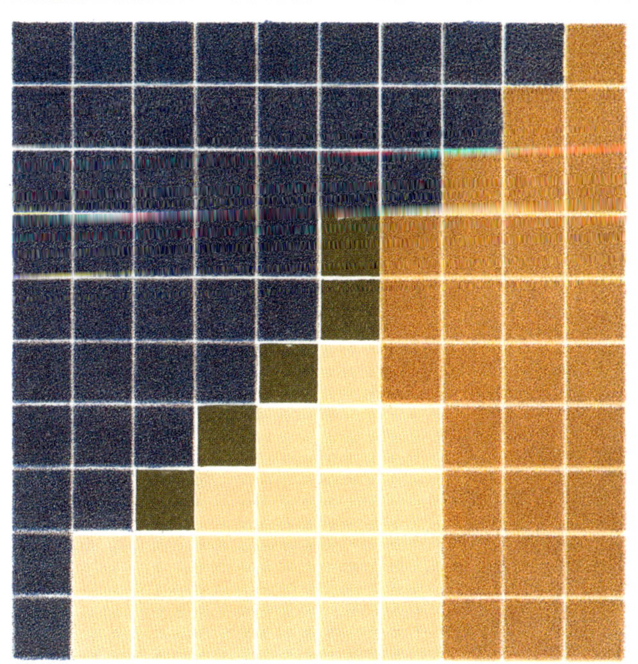

COLOR ANALYSIS FROM SPANISH EMBROIDERY

A harmony of contrast.

| | |
|---|---|
| Blue Ground | 45 |
| Dark Neutral Yellow | 30 |
| Pale Yellow | 20 |
| Gold | 5 |
| | 100 |

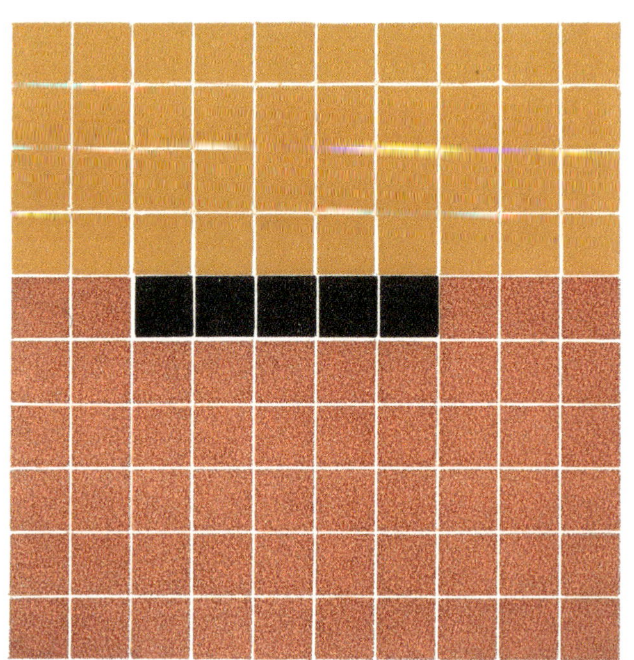

COLOR ANALYSIS FROM AN ANTIQUE PERSIAN RUG

| | |
|---|---|
| Old Rose | 55 |
| Old Yellow | 40 |
| Black | 5 |
| | 100 |

The black was used in fine outlines between the rose and yellow to harmonize them.

The following eight examples have had their harmony greatly increased by time which has toned their colors.

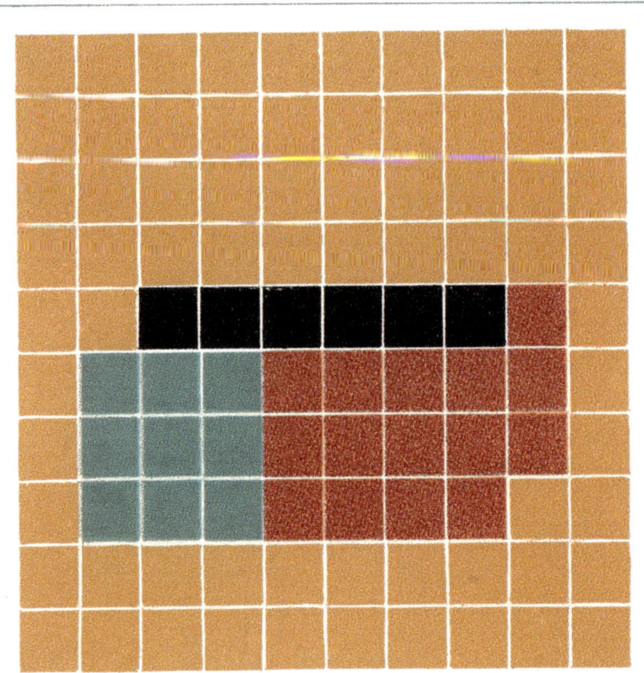

ANALYSIS FROM AN ANTIQUE RUG

| | |
|---|---|
| Old Yellow | 70 |
| Old Rose | 15 |
| Green-Blue | 9 |
| Black | 6 |
| | 100 |

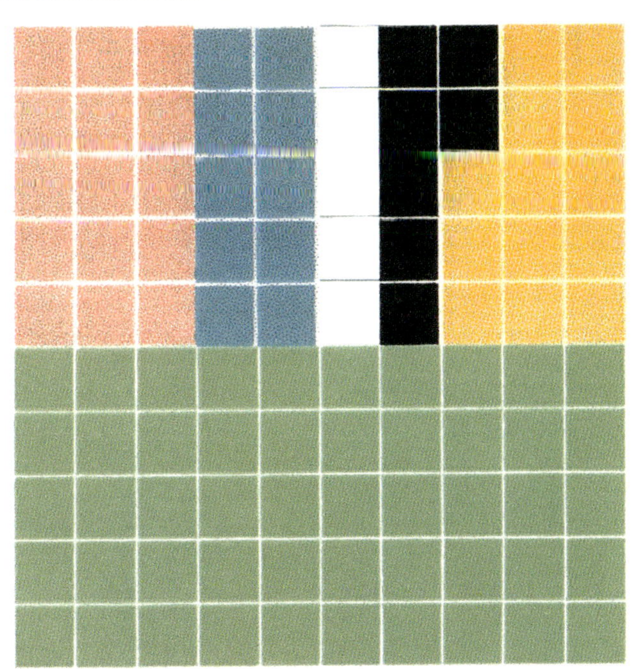

COLOR ANALYSIS FROM AN ANTIQUE RUG

| | |
|---|---|
| Pale Green Tint Ground | 50 |
| Yellow-Pink | 15 |
| Yellow | 13 |
| Blue | 10 |
| Black | 7 |
| White | 5 |
| | 100 |

Black used in fine lines.

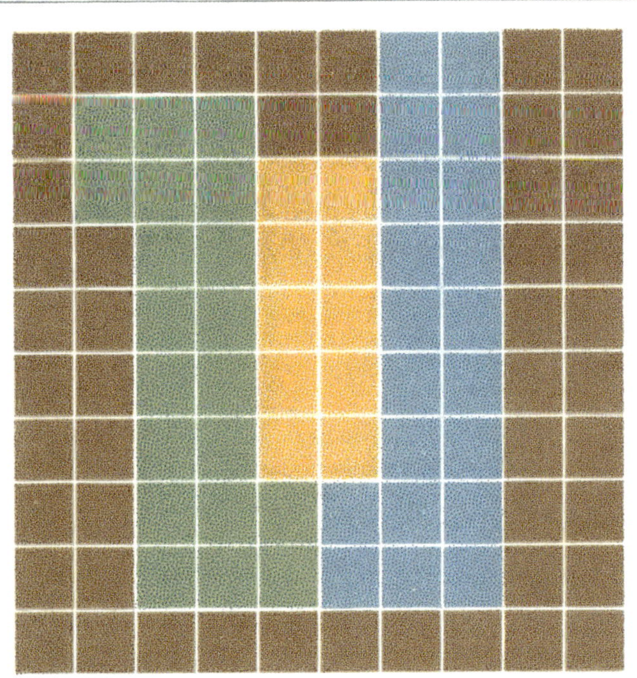

COLOR ANALYSIS FROM AN ANTIQUE RUG

| | |
|---|---|
| Camel's-Hair Gray | 50 |
| Cool Blue Tint | 20 |
| Green | 20 |
| Yellow | 10 |
| | 100 |

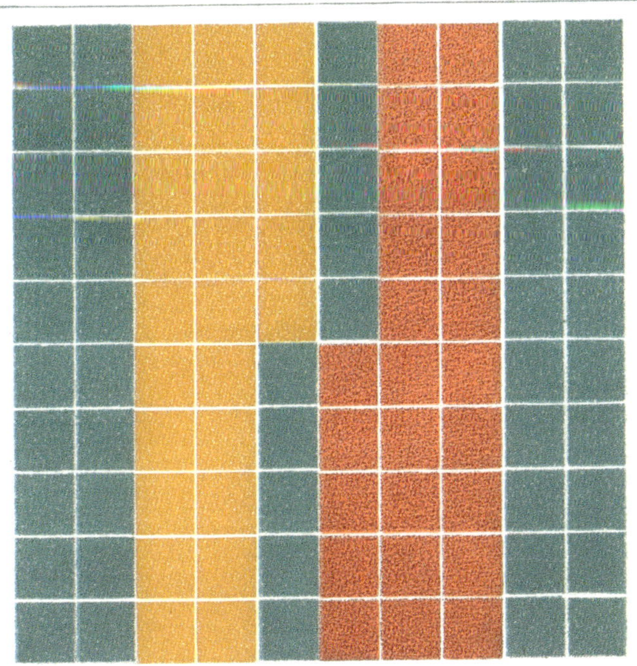

COLOR ANALYSIS FROM AN ANTIQUE RUG

| | |
|---|---|
| Green-Blue Ground | 50 |
| Red Tint | 25 |
| Yellow | 25 |
| | 100 |

Plate LXXXII

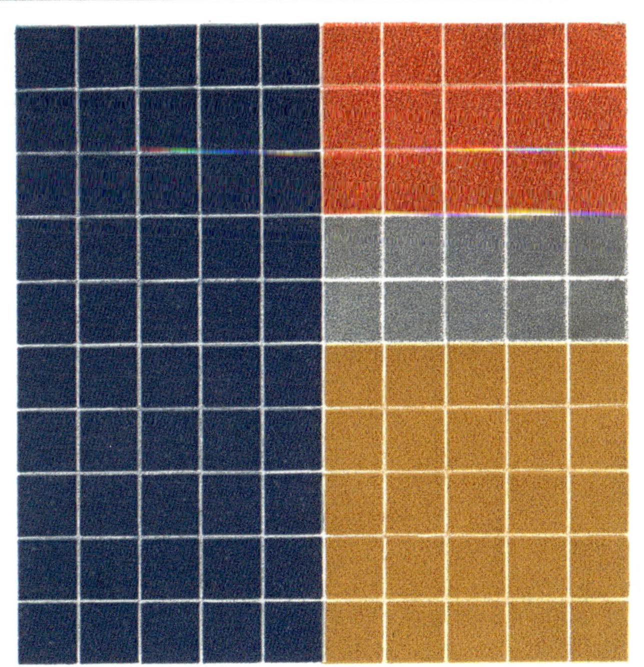

COLOR ANALYSIS FROM AN ANTIQUE RUG

| | |
|---|---|
| Blue Shade | 50 |
| Yellow Shade | 25 |
| Red | 15 |
| Light Blue Tint | 10 |
| | 100 |

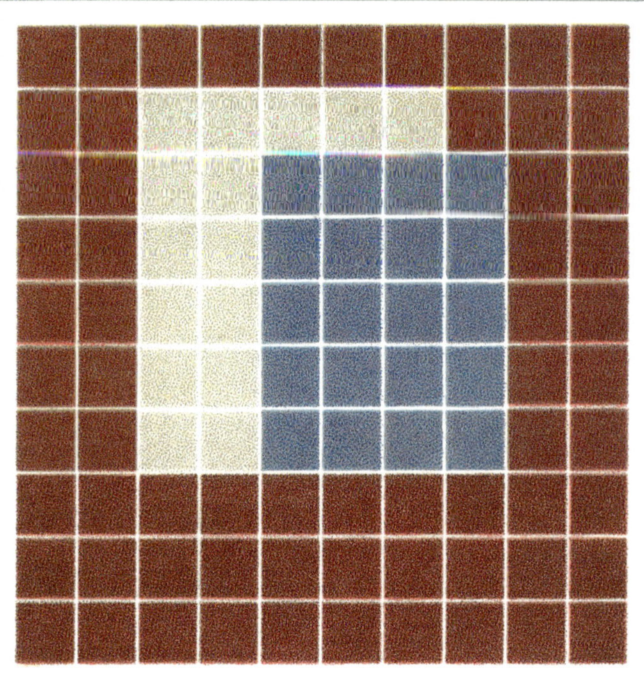

COLOR ANALYSIS FROM AN ANTIQUE RUG

| | |
|---|---|
| Neutral Red | 65 |
| Cold Blue | 20 |
| Silver | 15 |
| | 100 |

PLATE LXXXIV

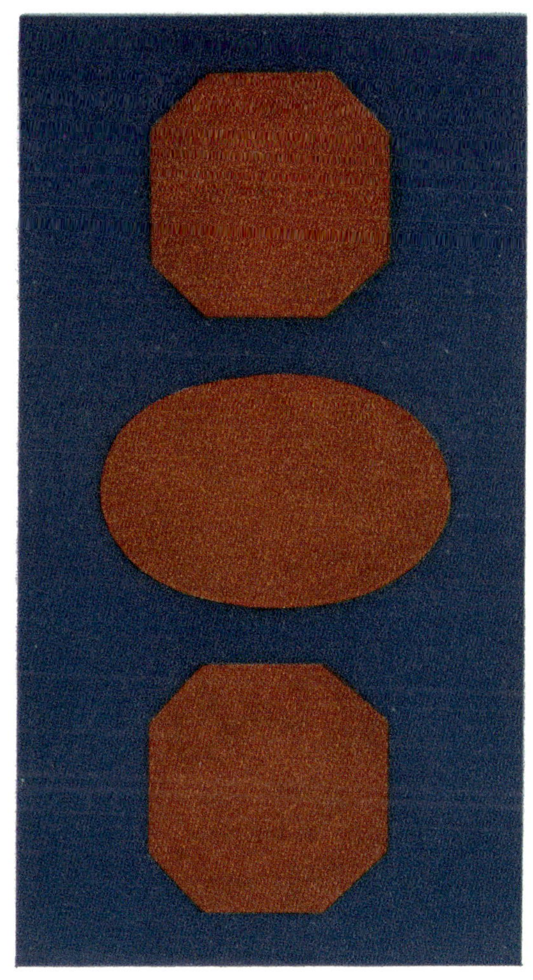

THE COLOR SCHEME OF AN ANTIQUE RUG FROM WHICH PLATE LXXXV IS AN ANALYSIS

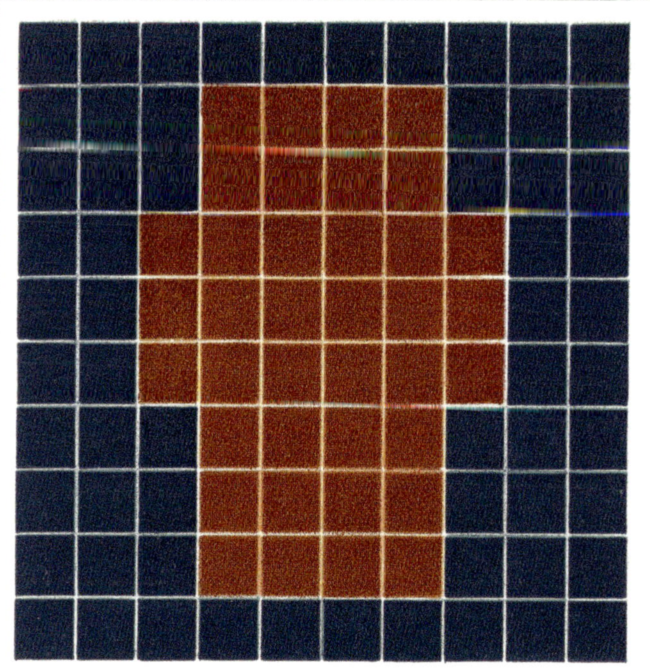

ANALYSIS OF AN ANTIQUE RUG

(See Plate LXXXIV)

| | |
|---|---|
| Dull Blue Shade | 62 |
| Dull Yellow Shade | 38 |
| | 100 |

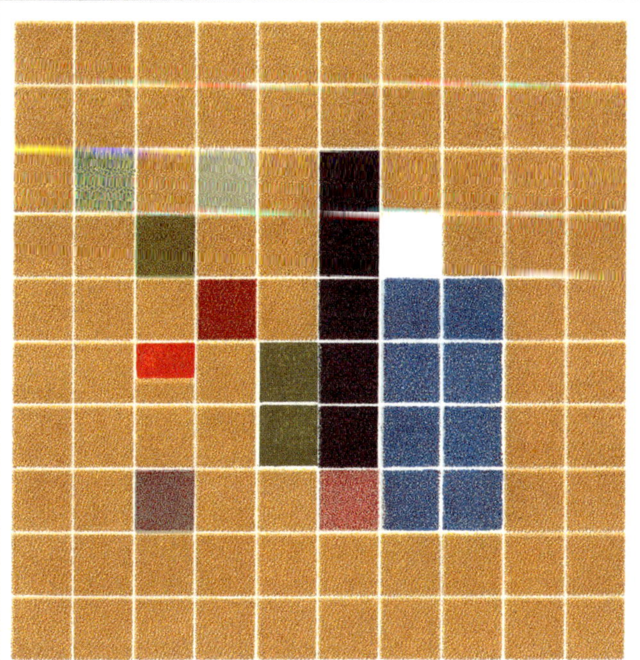

COLOR ANALYSIS FROM JAPANESE SILK TAPESTRY

| | | | |
|---|---|---|---|
| Old Gold Ground | 77.5 | Light Green | 1 |
| Blue | 8 | Gray-Green | 1 |
| Brown | 5 | Dull Red | 1 |
| Light Brown | 1 | Light Red | .5 |
| Gray | 1 | Gold | 2 |
| Dark Green | 1 | White | 1 |
| | | | 100 |

Plate LXXXVII

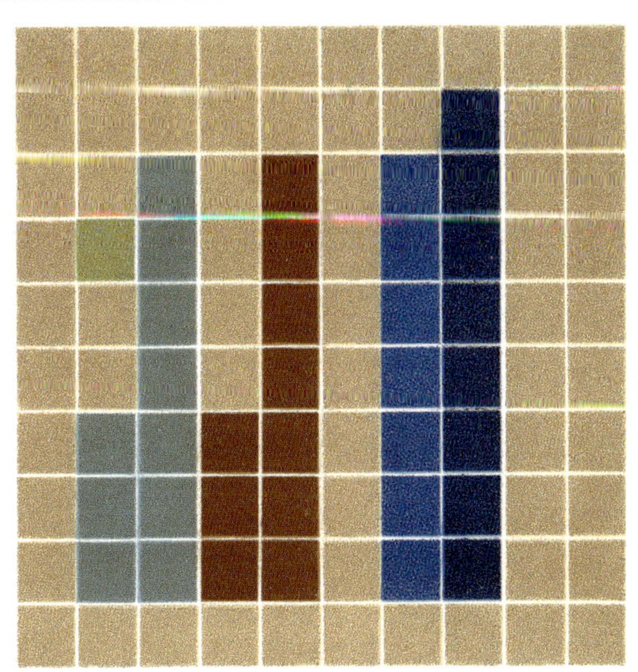

COLOR ANALYSIS FROM JAPANESE SILK TAPESTRY

| | |
|---|---|
| Gray Ground | 64 |
| Dark Blue | 8 |
| Light Blue | 7 |
| Gray-Blue | 10 |
| Brown | 10 |
| Green | 1 |
| | 100 |

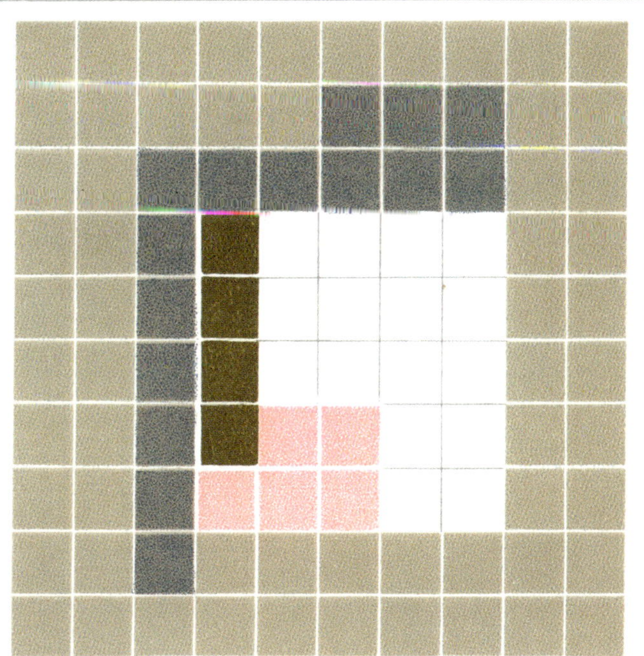

COLOR ANALYSIS FROM JAPANESE SILK BROCADE

| | |
|---|---|
| Yellow-Gray Ground . . . . . . . . . . . . . . . | 60 |
| Blue-Gray Leaves . . . . . . . . . . . . . . . | 15 |
| White Daisies . . . . . . . . . . . . . . . . | 16 |
| Pink Tips to Daisies . . . . . . . . . . . . . | 5 |
| Gold Veins to Leaves and Centres to Daisies . . . . | 4 |
| | 100 |

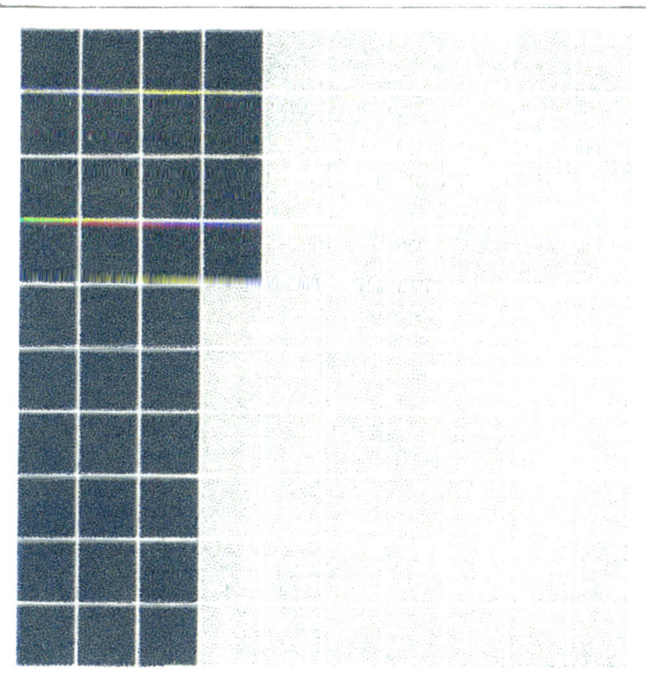

COLOR ANALYSIS FROM BORDER OF JAPANESE CLOISONNÉ VASE, Pl. XC

| | |
|---|---|
| Greenish White . . . . . . . . . . . . . . . . | 66 |
| Blue . . . . . . . . . . . . . . . . . . . . | 34 |
| | 100 |

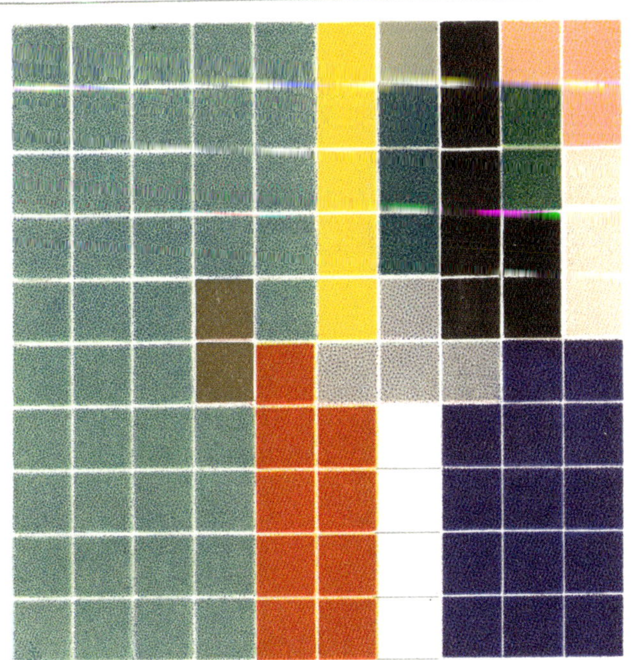

COLOR ANALYSIS FROM JAPANESE CLOISONNÉ VASE

| | | | |
|---|---|---|---|
| Green-Blue Ground | 43 | Light Red | 3 |
| Dark Blue | 14 | Lightest Red | 3 |
| Black | 7 | Greenish Blue | 3 |
| Red | 9 | Green | 2 |
| Yellow | 5 | Gray | 1 |
| Violet | 4 | Brass | 2 |
| White | 4 | | 100 |

The fine brass outlines add much to the harmony.

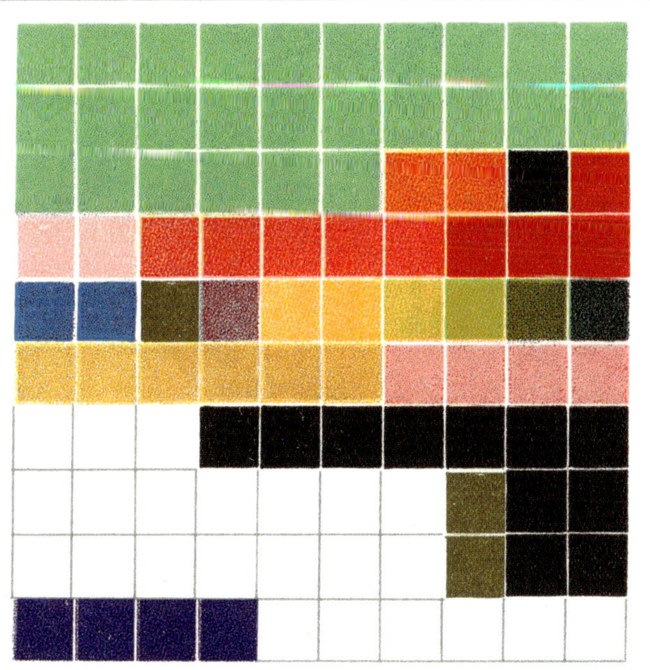

COLOR ANALYSIS FROM A JAPANESE SKIRT PANEL

| BORDER | |
|---|---|
| White Ground . . | 23 |
| Black . . . . . . . | 11 |
| Gold Edge . . . . | 2 |
| Purple-Blue . . . . | 4 |
| Dull Gold . . . . . | 6 |
| Dull Pink . . . . . | 4 |

| CENTRE | |
|---|---|
| Green Ground . . . | 26 |
| Shades of Red . . . | 11 |
| Yellow . . . . . . . | 2 |
| Blue . . . . . . . | 2 |
| Greens . . . . . . . | 4 |
| Lavender . . . . . | 1 |
| Gold Edge . . . . | 1 |
| Black . . . . . . . | 1 |
| Orange . . . . . . | 2 |
| | 100 |

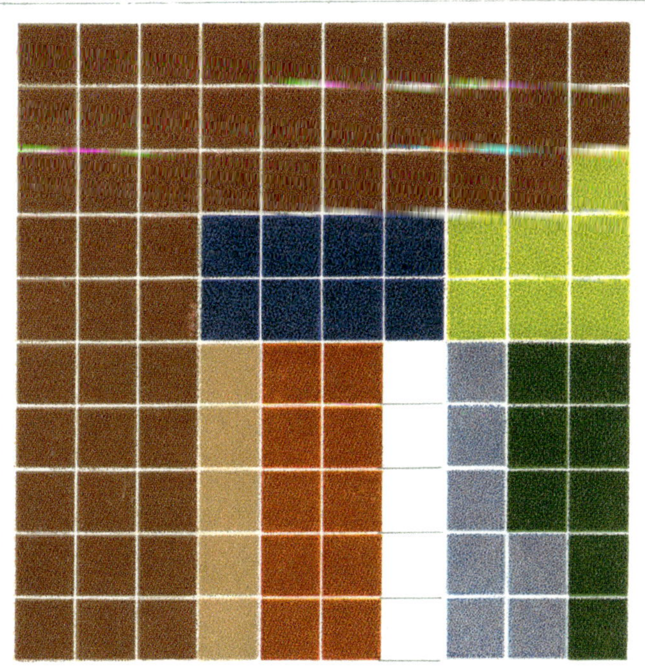

COLOR ANALYSIS FROM JAPANESE BROCADE

| | |
|---|---|
| Brown | 50 |
| Red | 10 |
| Dark Blue | 8 |
| Dark Green | 8 |
| Light Blue | 7 |
| Light Green | 7 |
| Light Brown | 5 |
| White | 5 |
| | 100 |

Fine example of a harmony of a dominant hue.

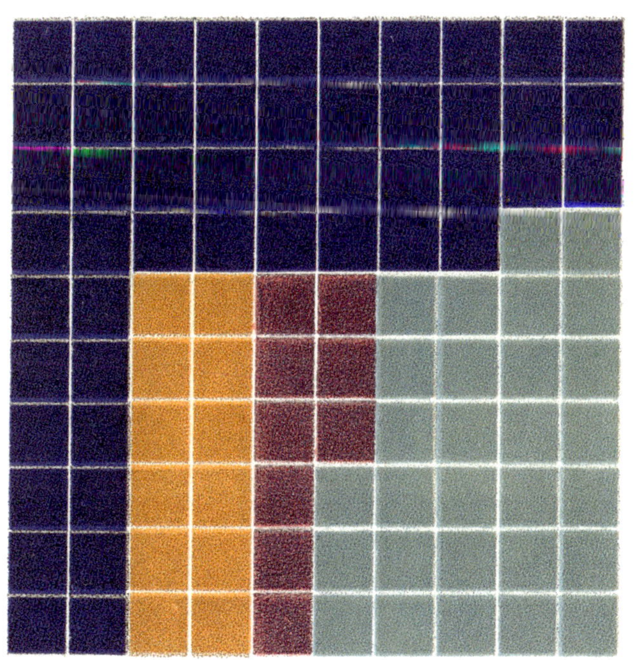

COLOR ANALYSIS FROM CHINESE PORCELAIN

| | |
|---|---|
| Deep Lapis Lazuli Blue Ground | 50 |
| Turquoise Blue | 29 |
| Ochre Yellow | 12 |
| Violet | 9 |
| | 100 |

Plates XCIII to XCVII inclusive are from Chinese porcelain, the colors having remained brilliant.

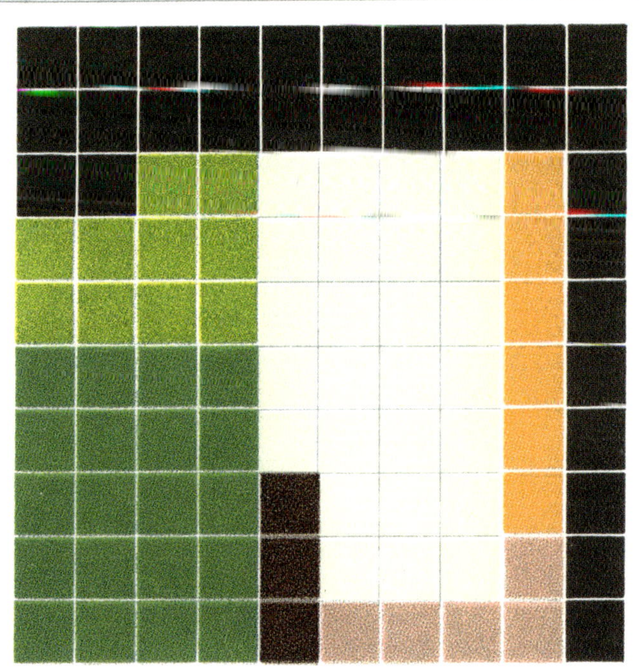

COLOR ANALYSIS FROM A "BLACK HAWTHORN VASE"

| | |
|---|---|
| Black Ground | 30 |
| Green-White Flowers | 26 |
| Green Leaves | 20 |
| Yellow-Green Leaves | 10 |
| Brown Stems | 3 |
| Pale Red Flowers | 5 |
| Yellow " | 6 |
| | 100 |

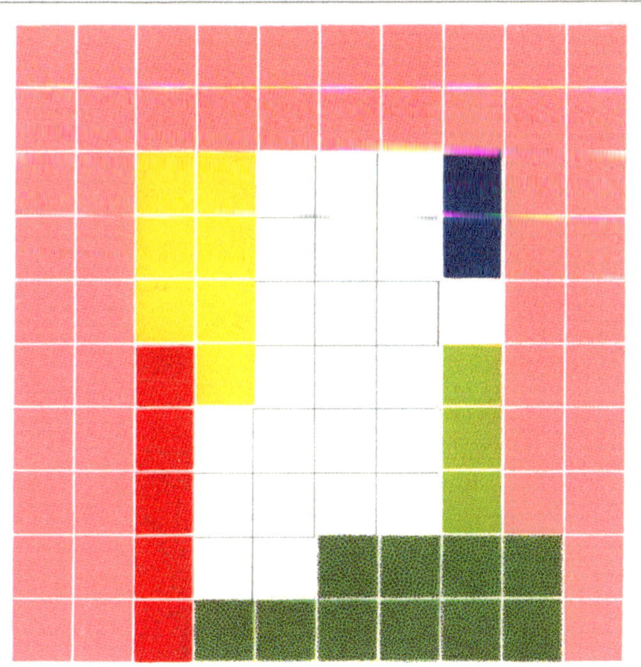

COLOR ANALYSIS FROM A ROSE-COLORED VASE

| | |
|---|---|
| Rose Ground | 50 |
| White Panel | 23 |
| Blue-Green | 10 |
| Yellow-Green | 3 |
| Yellow | 7 |
| Deep Pink | 5 |
| Blue | 2 |
| | 100 |

PLATE XCVI

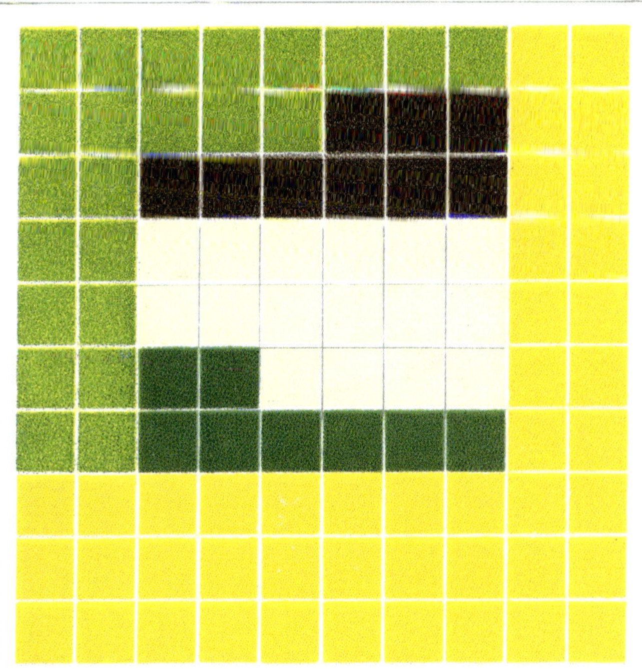

COLOR ANALYSIS FROM YELLOW CHINESE PORCELAIN VASE

| | |
|---|---|
| Yellow Ground | 44 |
| Light Green Leaves | 23 |
| Dark Green " | 8 |
| Cream White Flowers | 16 |
| Brown Stems | 9 |
| | 100 |

PLATE XCVII

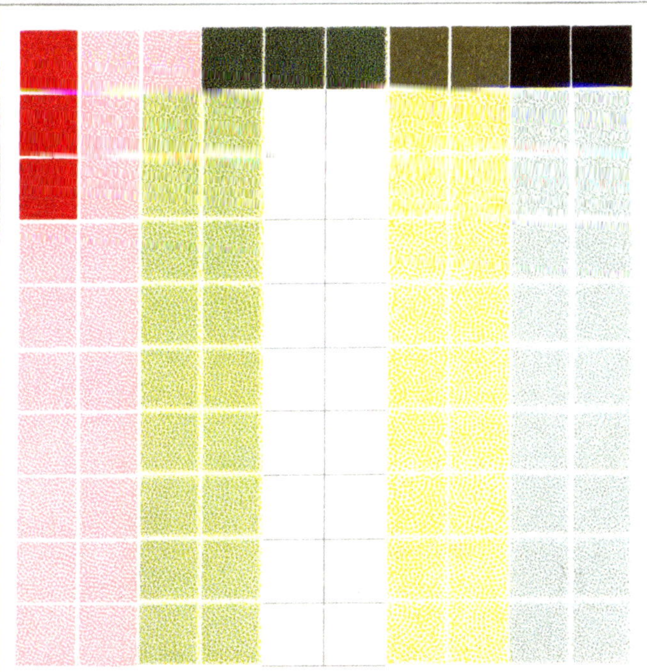

COLOR ANALYSIS FROM A CHINESE "EGG-SHELL" PLATE

| | |
|---|---|
| Blue | 18 |
| Yellow | 18 |
| White | 18 |
| Green | 18 |
| Pink | 18 |
| Dark Pink | 3 |
| Dark Green | 3 |
| Black | 2 |
| Gold | 2 |
| | 100 |

Pale tints with delicate decoration in strong tones.

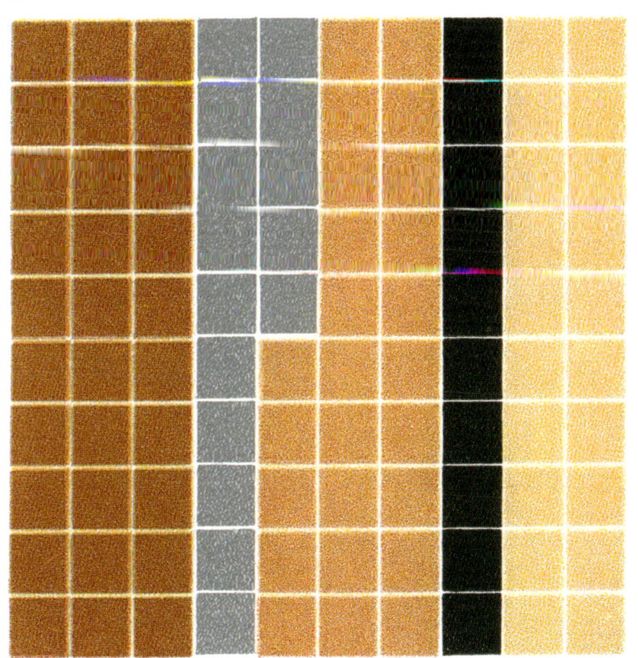

COLOR ANALYSIS FROM A BUTTERFLY

| | |
|---|---|
| Dark Yellow Shade | 30 |
| Medium Yellow | 25 |
| Light Yellow | 20 |
| Silver | 15 |
| Black | 10 |
| | 100 |

The black was well placed to contrast with the light tones, the silver to contrast with the dark tone.

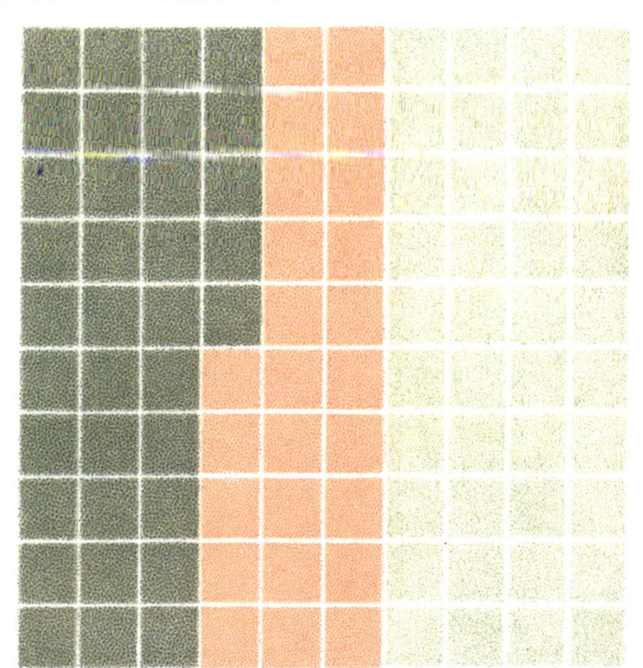

COLOR ANALYSIS FROM A STONE

| | |
|---|---|
| Pale Gray-Green | 40 |
| Gray-Green | 35 |
| Pale Red | 25 |
| | 100 |

Ground, pale green.

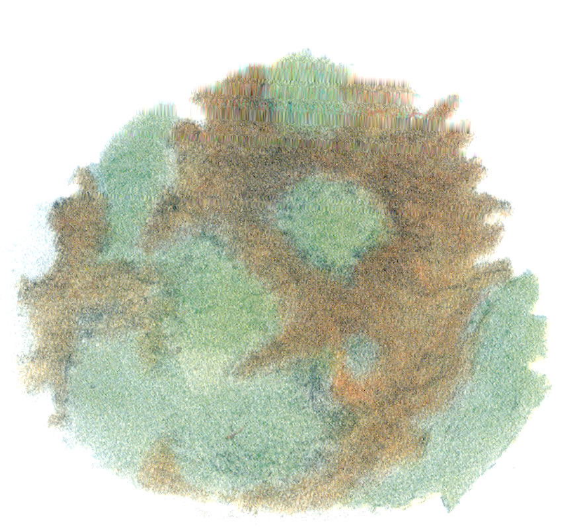

COLOR NOTE FROM AN OLD AND PARTLY DISCOLORED PROPELLER FLANGE

COLOR NOTE FROM LEAVES ON A TREE

The sun glancing across the smooth leaves makes a cool gray, and shining through them makes a warm green.

The shaded leaves are a deep green.

COLOR NOTE FROM A SUNSET SKY

Plate CIII

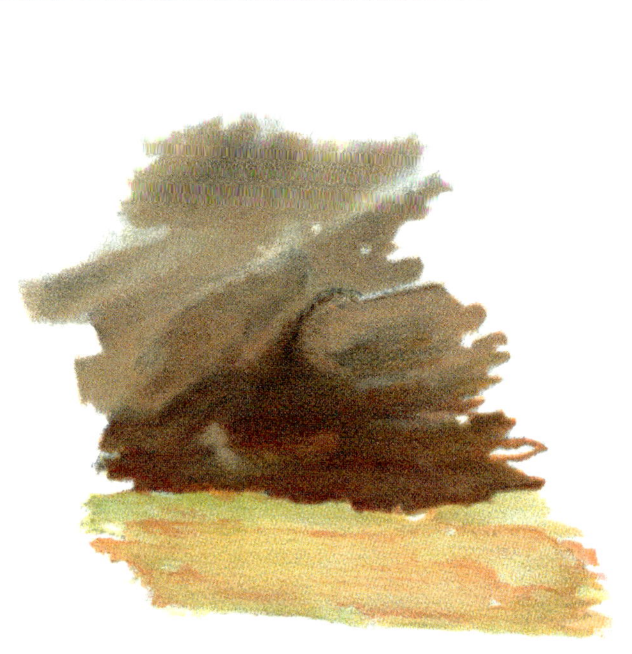

COLOR NOTE FROM BARE WOODS ON THE EDGE OF A MEADOW

Plate CIV

COLOR NOTE FROM EVERGREENS AGAINST A GRAY-BLUE RAIN CLOUD

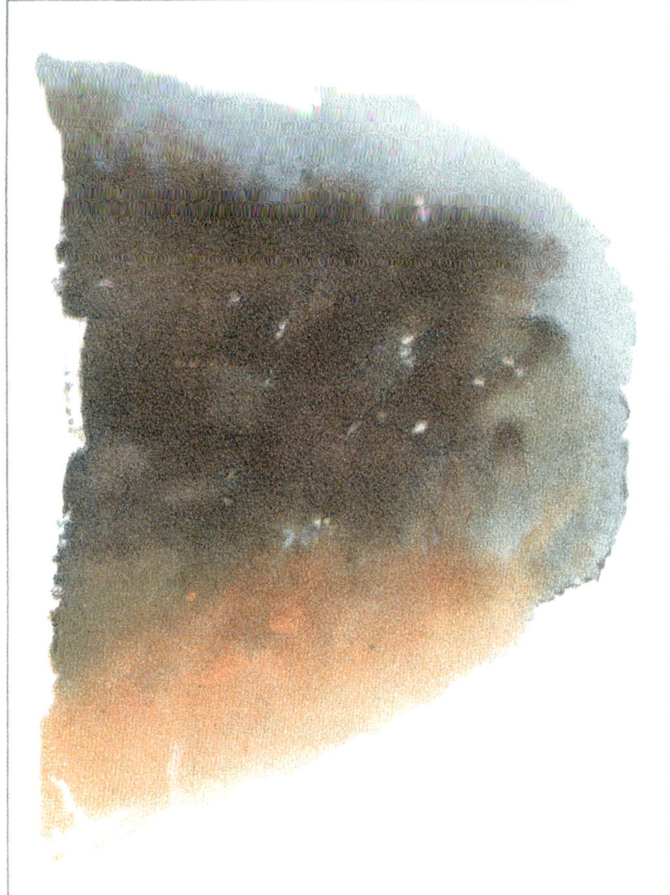

COLOR NOTE FROM A SHADOW ON WHITE GROUND

Plate CVI

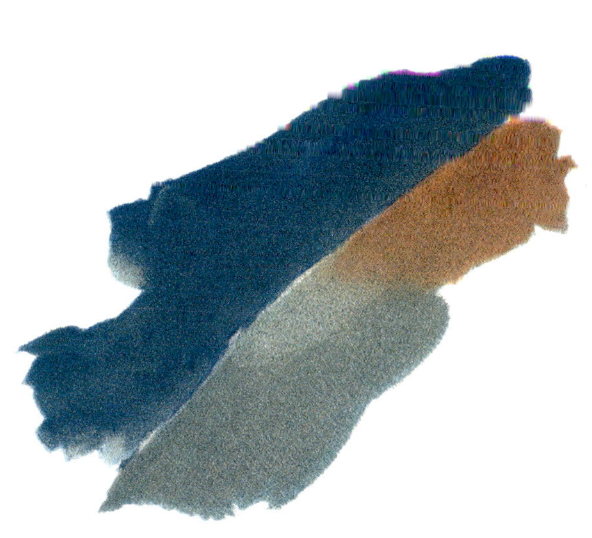

COLOR NOTE FROM A BLUEBIRD

A harmony of cobalt and light red.

Plate CVII

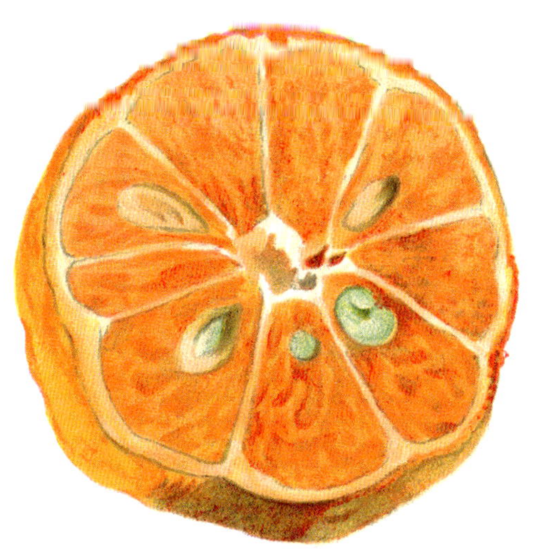

COLOR NOTE FROM A SLICE OF AN ORANGE

Plate CVIII

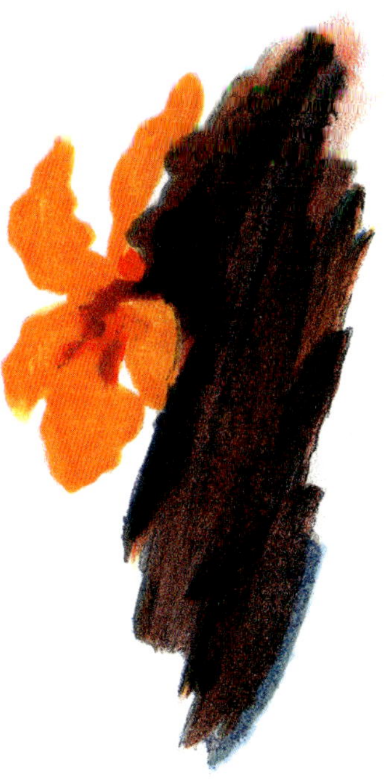

COLOR NOTE FROM ORANGE CANNA BLOSSOM

with part of leaf

Plate CIX

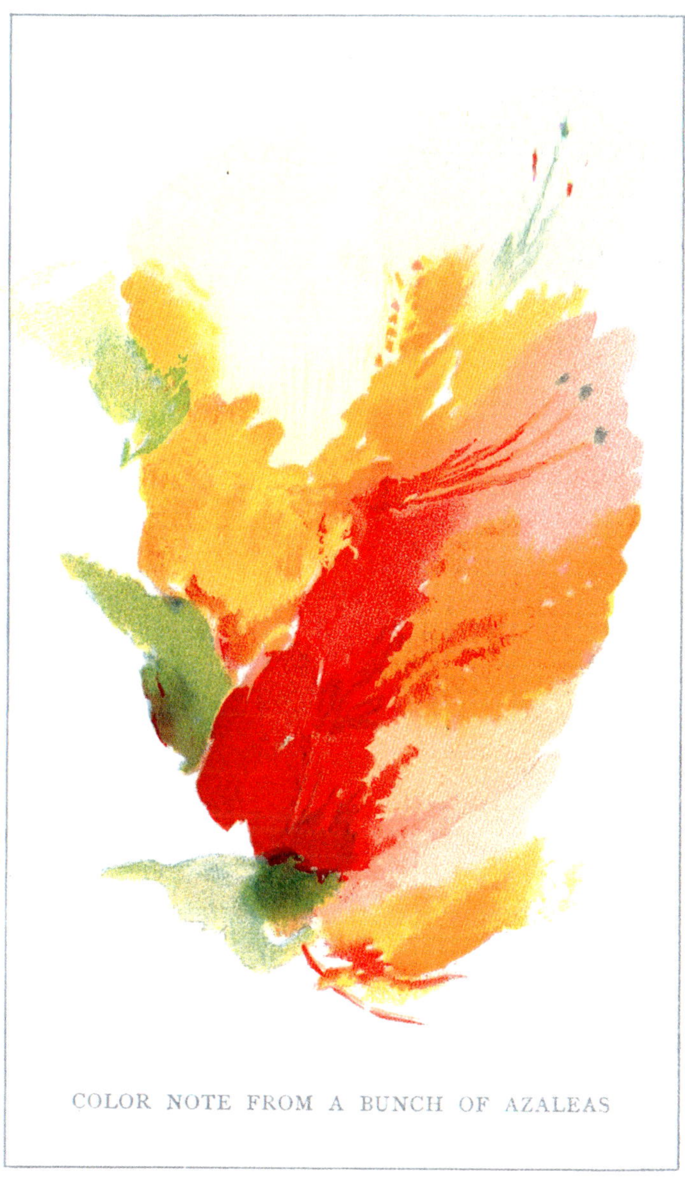

COLOR NOTE FROM A BUNCH OF AZALEAS

PLATE CX

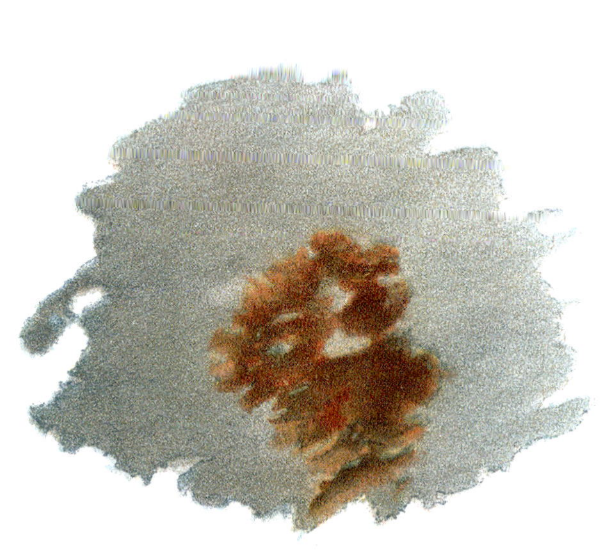

COLOR NOTE FROM OAK LEAVES AGAINST A DISTANT HILLSIDE

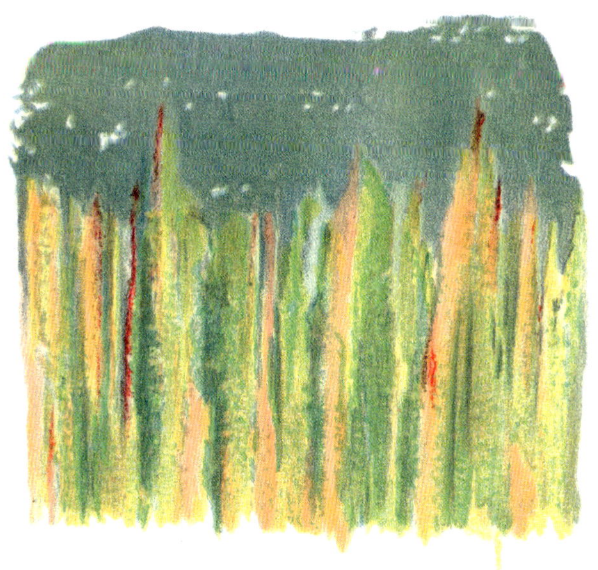

COLOR NOTE FROM OATS SEEN FROM THE EDGE OF THE FIELD

So the top was a mass of soft blue-gray-green, while the stalks were highly colored.

Plate CXII

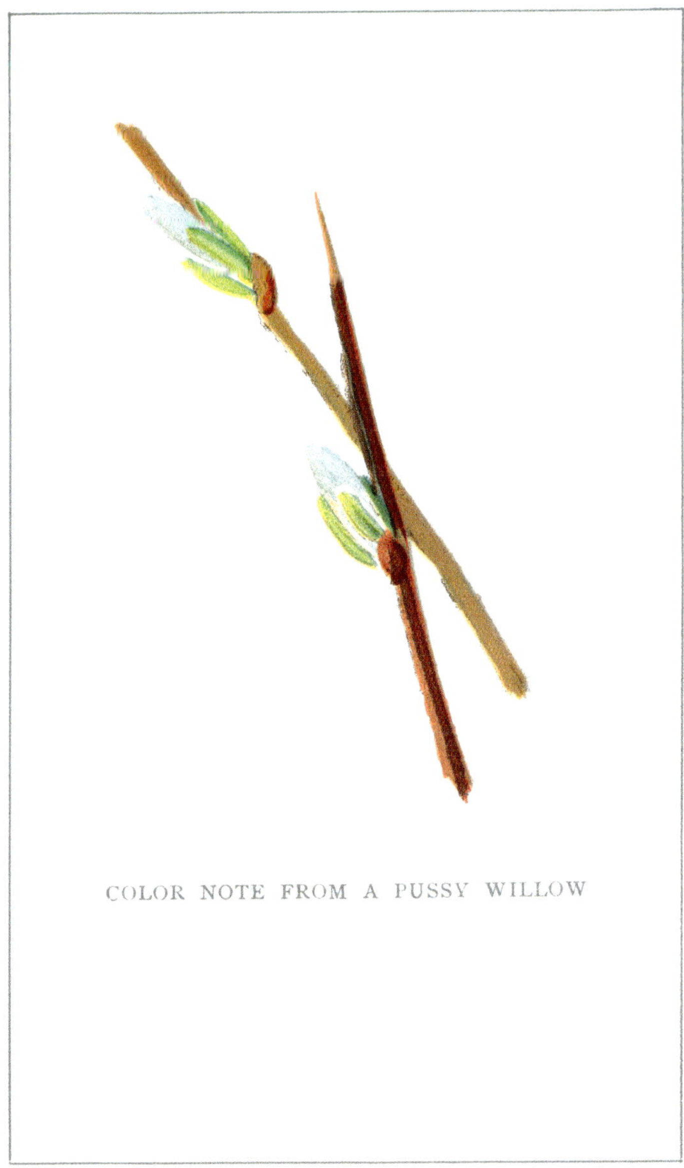

COLOR NOTE FROM A PUSSY WILLOW

Plate CXIII

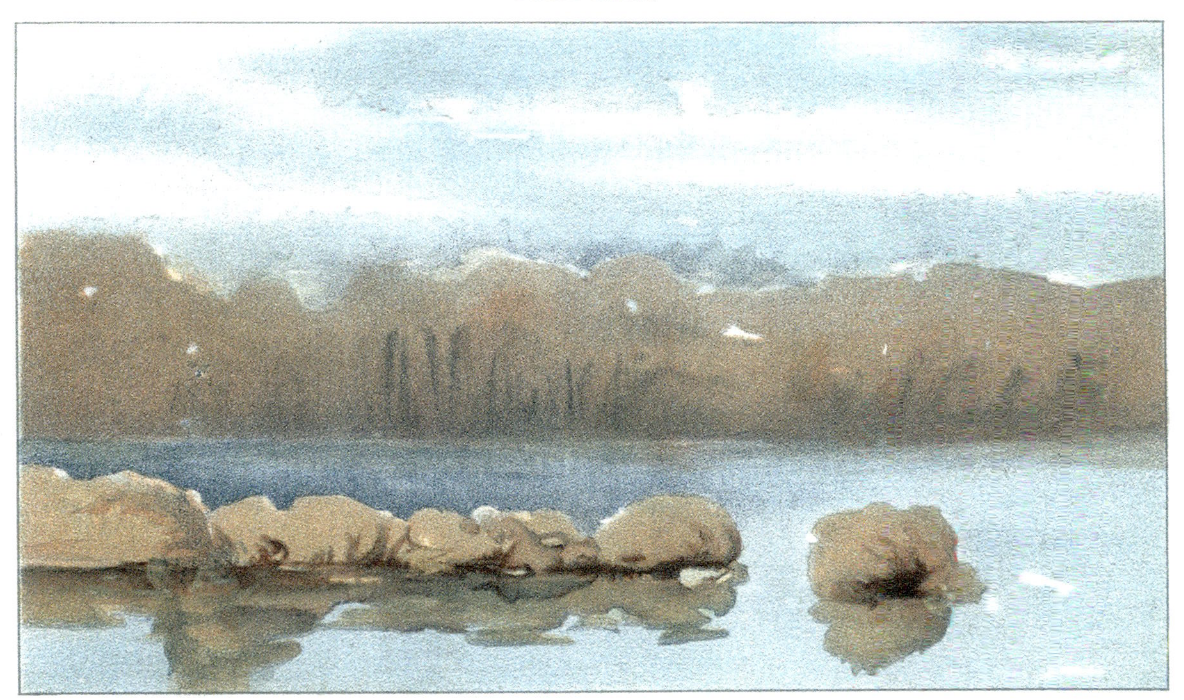

COLOR NOTE FROM A TROUT POND

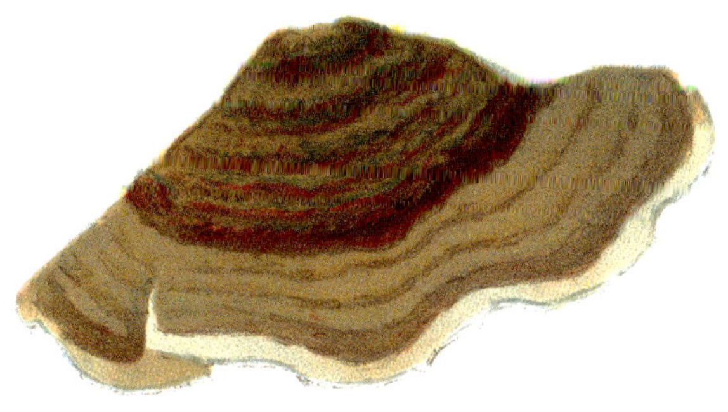

COLOR NOTE FROM A TREE FUNGUS

Texture like velvet.

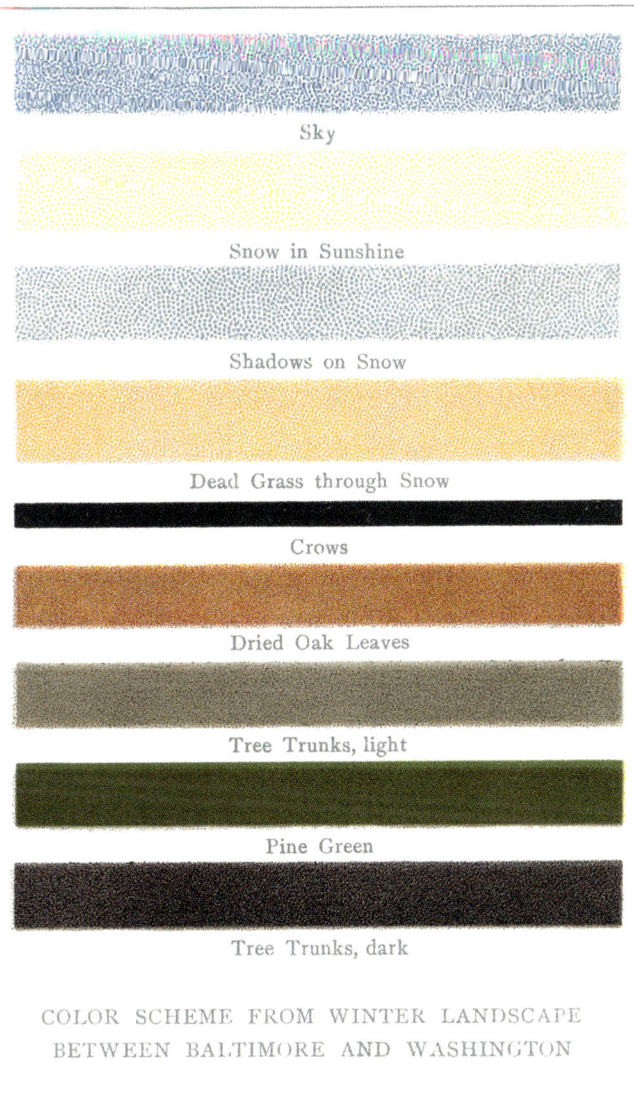


COLOR SCHEME FROM WINTER LANDSCAPE BETWEEN BALTIMORE AND WASHINGTON

SPECTRAL RED
NEUTRALIZED BY BLACK AND WHITE

SPECTRAL YELLOW
NEUTRALIZED BY BLACK AND WHITE